Barbara Wright: Translation as Art

John Calder's poem "For Barbara Wright," page 26, was first published in his collection *Being—Seeing—Feeling—Healing—Meaning*, London: Herla Publishing, Alma Books Ltd., 2011.

First edition, 2013
Second printing, 2013

Library of Congress Cataloging-in-Publication Data

Barbara Wright : translation as art / edited by Madeleine Renouard and Debra Kelly. -- First edition.
pages cm
Includes bibliographical references.
ISBN 978-1-56478-886-3 (pbk. : acid-free paper)
1. Wright, Barbara, 1915-2009. 2. French language--Translating.
3. Translating and interpreting. 4. Translators--Great Britain--Biography. I. Renouard, Madeleine. II. Kelly, Debra.
P306.92.W75B37 2013
418'.02092--dc23
2013007424

Partially funded by a grant from the Illinois Arts Council,
a state agency

www.dalkeyarchive.com

Cover: design and composition by Mikhail Iliatov

Printed on permanent/durable acid-free paper

Barbara Wright: Translation as Art

Edited by
Madeleine Renouard
and Debra Kelly

DALKEY ARCHIVE PRESS
CHAMPAIGN / LONDON / DUBLIN

Contents

Acknowledgments

The Editors would like to thank: Arlette Albert-Birot; Roger Allen; Christian Anglade; Jamie Andrews; Laurence Auer; the Cultural Service of the French Embassy in London; the Department of Applied Linguistics, Birkbeck University of London; the Department of Modern and Applied Languages, University of Westminster, London; Jean-Marc Dewaele; Philippe Lane; Emma Mackie; Jim Mackie; Philippe Miquel; Michel Mousseau; John Phillips; Jacques Pinget; Lucciola Pinget; Jasia Reichardt; the University of London; Alistair Whyte; Zoe Wilcox; Juliet Wilson-Bareau; Victoria Wright; Tom Wright; with special thanks to Helena Scott.

Introduction

Barbara Wright: Translation as Art
Madeleine Renouard and Debra Kelly

Barbara Wright could have become a brilliant pianist. She did not, but became, instead, a brilliant translator and made an exceptional contribution to literature. This book is a homage to her.

Barbara Wright introduced to an English-speaking readership and audience some of the most innovative French literary texts of the twentieth century. For over fifty years, she made sometimes difficult avant-garde texts available in English.

Barbara Wright did not train as a translator, nor did she study literature as an academic subject. She was a musician, played the piano, and studied in Paris under Alfred Cortot. She not only thought that her debut as an "accompanist" was an excellent preparation for her work as a translator but she equated translation with accompaniment. This attention to rhythm and tone makes Barbara Wright's approach to translation quite original although close to what another *grande dame* of translation, Svetlana Geier, perceives as a crucial moment in the process of translating, which is when she "finally hears the melody of the text"; but what makes Barbara Wright's approach very specific is what can be defined as "pairing" with the author.[1] To hear (in the sense of being very attentive to but also letting all echoes and nuances manifest themselves) the writer's voice and to find an equivalent in English was what she saw to be the main challenge in her work which she approaches as a composer. She saw the work of the translator as: "to try to reproduce the rhythm, the assonance, the pace, the harmonics, the allusions, of the original."[2]

Translating was a very long process: she immersed herself in the text to be translated, be it a poem, a play or a novel, read other texts by the same writer (to establish their common rhythmical features in particular) and also established close contact with the writer

---

[1] One critic, Peter Broome, reviewing Barbara Wright's translation of Robert Pinget's *The Enemy* went as far as to say that she was "Pinget's virtual twin". See p. 321 below ("Appraisals, Reviews").

[2] *Review of Contemporary Fiction* 3: 2, 1983, p. 114.

(corresponding, telephoning, meeting him or her). Working with living authors was an experience she enjoyed, and being familiar with the real, physical voice of the writer was a very important aspect of her work. She even gave public readings with authors like Nathalie Sarraute or Robert Pinget in New York and London.

The archival material deposited in public institutions (Lilly Library, Indiana, US; IMEC, France; British Library, UK) gives an invaluable insight into Barbara Wright's working methods. Although she was a highly competent typist, she remained faithful to traditional tools: pen, paper and notebooks which she covered with her elegant handwriting, using pens of different colours to underline or highlight passages she wanted to revise, or to rewrite passages on the left-hand page, left blank for that purpose in her notebooks. She was very methodical, precise and well organized. She always carried a notebook wherever she went and she would frequently ask French speakers at parties to enlighten her on French idiomatic expressions. Translating was a way of life.

Referring to her work on Pinget and trying to find an equivalent to what she calls the "hypnotic mystery implicit in his frequent repetions of the same word or phrase", she notes that "this calls for especial vigilance on the part of his translator: a moment's inattention and he has woefully betrayed his author." She goes on,

> by trial and error I have found a way to guard against such betrayals. In addition to the separate exercise book that I always keep for every translation, in which I note any particular problems or nuances on which it is advisable to consult French friends, or, *in extremis*, the author—though one is reluctant to bother him unnecessarily—I now keep an alphabetical, cross-referenced index for each Pinget book. "Le calme. Le gris." (*Passacaille*), 10 repetitions. "Le fruit de vos entrailles" (*Fable*), 5 repetitions. "Manque un raccord" (*Cette Voix*), 17 repetitions. This may sound a horribly cold-blooded, pedestrian, pedantic way to approach a poetic translation, but I assure you that without such a basic analysis one cannot possibly achieve the subtle aims that I have mentioned. Let alone get anywhere near the reproduction of what

is always present between the lines in Pinget—the inexpressible.[3]

Barbara Wright was both meticulous (in her work) and adventurous (in her choice of texts and authors). In 1947 she was introduced to an unconventional way of looking at the world by the Polish artists, writers and thinkers Franciszka and Stefan Themerson, the founders of Gaberbocchus Press. She first translated, with Stefan Themerson, a Polish children's book, although she did not read or speak Polish. She then, in 1951, moved on to translating Alfred Jarry's play *Ubu Roi*, still regarded to this day as a landmark in avant-garde literature. The book was a "*livre d'artiste*": handwritten by Barbara, and profusely illustrated by Franciszka Themerson.

This first translation established Barbara as an eminent figure in the world of 'Pataphysicians, whose main aims are to explore imaginary solutions and to gather useless knowledge. She became one of the dignitaries of this group together with Fernando Arrabal, Umberto Eco, Dario Fo and Jean Baudrillard. This was to have a major influence on her taste and choices. She would disregard texts and projects (and people) she felt were pretentious and pompous. She wrote book reviews (for the *TLS* in particular) and art criticism in a direct manner answering straightforward questions (like "why do I like this text or painting?"). She was open to new ideas and was keen on meeting artists with an unconventional approach to their work. Not all her translations were published, as some were trials or experiments with artists, or radio scripts for the BBC.

From Jarry, Barbara Wright went on to one of the most difficult and challenging French writers to translate: Raymond Queneau, who can also be seen as a pivotal figure in Barbara Wright's career. Two major editorial and friendly ventures both involved the work of Raymond Queneau: the first one was with the Themersons, the second one with John Calder, who published English translations of the French avant-garde of the day, the *Nouveau Roman* in particular. Barbara Wright was to become the translator of most of the new novelists on Calder's list. She also supported until the end the

---

[3] "The 'Trials' of Translating Pinget", *Review of Contemporary Fiction* 3: 2, 1983 p. 114.

publisher's numerous efforts to promote experimental literature and challenging texts.

Although Queneau's subject matter includes mathematics, madness, history, philosophy and knowledge, his texts are often seen as light because they are witty, playful and ingenious. Queneau was also very concerned with issues of form and content. Barbara Wright was entrusted by Queneau himself with the task of translating his *Exercises in Style*. Her English version was an extraordinary success. It became the source of many translations of the work in other languages; she "invented" (created for an English-speaking readership) some untranslatable exercises. Queneau himself was most impressed by her work. After the writer's death, she regularly attended seminars and conferences of the Queneau Society in Paris and became a highly respected contributor to their debates.

With her work on Queneau's texts, Barbara Wright gained the reputation of a translator of exceptional talent and versatility, and was very much in demand. By 1970, in addition to Jarry and Queneau she had published major writers like Fernando Arrabal, Alain Robbe-Grillet, Marguerite Duras, and Roland Dubillard. Her long and close collaboration with Robert Pinget (novelist and playwright) started with the publication of a poetic novel, *The Libera Me Domine* in 1972, and ended at the author's death in 1997. Barbara Wright was once called "Pinget's voice in English" as she translated his work from 1972 onwards; they played music together, she playing the piano and he the 'cello.

Barbara Wright went on working for decades; in 2003, when her translation of Pierre Albert-Birot's *31 Pocket Poems* was published, she felt that she had succeeded in giving voice to a great artist largely ignored in Great Britain. That was the final episode of a story which started in 1964 when Barbara Wright was asked by the *TLS* to write a review of *Grabinoulor* (a modern saga, written with no punctuation). She met the painter, sculptor, avant-garde writer Pierre Albert-Birot and his wife Arlette Albert-Birot. They became friends and Barbara was introduced to a wealth of artists and poets in France.

Barbara Wright was passionate about literature both in French and in English; she was keen on discovering new talents and was prepared to translate controversial texts like Sylvia Bourdon's *Love is a Feast* for example. She was also prepared to work on texts whose meaning was very elusive. Her collaboration with Nathalie Sarraute is, in that respect, exemplary in that Barbara Wright remained faithful to the writer even when Sarraute's later texts became more obscure.

Although all texts can be retranslated, Barbara Wright's translations of Tzara, Topor, Ionesco, Genet, Beckett and many others[4] will remain landmarks on the European literary scene. The philosopher and feminist Elisabeth Badinter whose book *The Unopposite Sex* was translated by Barbara Wright acknowledged the excellence of the text in English which she felt was even better than hers. Barbara Wright's approach was both artistic and based on an exhaustive exploration of all the dimensions of the text she was translating. She confidently maintained that a good translator knew the text and the author better than any reader or even critic—"Just think," she wrote, "of all that analysis, pedestrian or otherwise, which he has to undertake before he even begins his translation."

In this collection, we have chosen to take up the challenge issued in such trenchant terms. What follows, then, is a book about Barbara's work as a translator in creative response to some of the authors with whom she chose to work. It is also, therefore, a book about some of the major concerns of French literature in the twentieth century, concerns that are linguistic, formal, philosophical, social, and political. References to the importance of Barbara's musicality in her creative response to the rhythms of the French texts and their rendition in English recur, but she is alert also to the material of the text, to the multiple textures of these works, to the fabric, to the very *stuff* of a literature that is itself a response to being human in a time described by Nathalie Sarraute as the "age of suspicion".[5]

This collection of texts and essays attempts to capture the translator at work, caught in the processes of languages and always open to its possibilities. It opens with a series of portraits by some of those who knew Barbara well, and had the privilege of working with her,

---

[4] See "Barbara Wright's principal translations", p. 300 below.

[5] Nathalie Sarraute, *L'Ère du soupçon*, Paris: Gallimard 1956; *The Age of Suspicion. Essays on the Novel*, New York: George Braziller, 1963, 1990; translated by Maria Jolas.

and of sharing her life, in many and varied ways: Nick Wadley, artist and friend; Madeleine Renouard, academic and friend; John Calder, publisher and friend. The scholarly essays presented here treat wide-ranging and diverse aspects of Barbara's translations, and of some of the texts on which she worked, although recurring themes of erudition, pleasure, playfulness, inventiveness, skill and wit are not hard to detect. All of this is underpinned by the conviction, held not with any hint of arrogance but with a delight and a belief in the languages in which she worked, that nothing was (finally, at any rate) "untranslatable". As one critic put it: "For a translator, untranslatability can be as much a lure as a deterrent".[6] The first essay, by Nathalie Piégay-Gros, "Writing Erudite Delirium", takes the concept of erudition, apparent both in several of the authors with whom Barbara worked and in her own knowledge, on which she drew in order to translate them with such success. Piégay-Gros analyzes the ways in which such erudition functions in certain types of literature, constituting what she terms the "erudite delirium" of the chapter title, and demonstrates how erudition, which "is at first sight poles apart from delirium" can in literature, in its methods and processes, render a person "struck down or at least threatened by madness", brought on by their passion for studying. She firstly takes Flaubert as a most extreme example (and later Perec, who also could be considered as such), relentless in his pursuit of every branch of learning. She then moves on to the ways in which erudition sends people mad, "driving them beyond any normal plan of reading (by excess)" and taking them outside the traditional range of books, into what she terms the "margin of tradition". It is here that we meet Barbara and her authors, "whose vocabulary is both rare and difficult" such as Jarry, both "bizarre and precise" such as Queneau, and those who are "fascinated by a particular type of marginality" such as Pinget and Quignard. The translator of such erudite delirium must be prepared to plunge into a world of learned, rare words in which translation is "an uncomfortable but exhilarating task". Accumulation, precision, disorder, arbitrariness and incongruity are all suggested as possible characteristics of the passion for erudition; and the suggestive

---

[6] Alastair Reid, *The New Yorker*, November 8, 1976, writing on the works of Raymond Queneau and with a reference to Barbara Wright's work.

conclusion is that these novelists show how the desire for "scrupulous precision is surrounded on all sides by the shapelessness that is explored and defied by the writing of fiction". This is not unconnected, of course, to the literary translator's art, and Barbara is finally described as "on the alert for this enchantment", finding a way to invent in her own language the explorations of her authors.

Of these authors, in "*UBU ROI*: a brilliant debut", Jill Fell takes us back to Alfred Jarry, to the beginning of Barbara's work and to a founding moment, not just originally for modern French avant-garde literature, but also for independent publishing history in Britain during a very particular time for Franco-British cultural exchanges, the immediate post-war period. Using many of Barbara's own words, Fell retraces the early steps taken to becoming a translator and of working with the Themersons and Gaberbocchus Press. One key moment is the translation of the song *La Chanson du Décervelage* (the "Disembraining" is the translation coined by Barbara), with which the Themersons wanted to close the book (although not actually a part of *Ubu Roi*), and which they insisted must rhyme; it was Barbara's first apparently "impossible" translation. She was immediately welcomed by the Collège de 'Pataphysique in France, which leads to the second key moment of this essay and Barbara's spirited, and erudite (although not delirious . . .), defence of her opening "*Shittr!*" for Jarry's French neologism "*Merdre!*", a defence written "in the sharpest, wittiest and most elegant French". The correspondence is quoted here in full, translated and analyzed with an insightful commentary by Fell for the reader less aware of the context and less linguistically adept than Jarry's now formidable translator, ready to defend her own work, and indeed that of others if admired by her, with her mercilessly aimed, but always civilized, "barbs".

Proceeding then chronologically from the authors' point of view, if not in the order in which Barbara translated them, we move to Pierre Albert-Birot and the *Six Books of Grabinoulor*, begun in 1917, and of which Barbara translated the *First Book*, published in 1986. In "Grabinoulor has Fun with Language and Makes New Friends: *The First Book of Grabinoulor* and beyond", Debra Kelly shows how Barbara came to choose one of her authors (or perhaps, it was rather that her authors chose her . . .) and the resulting success of her translation of his work. Pierre Albert-Birot's work displays all the erudition, pleasure, playfulness, inventiveness, skill and wit that were previously identified as more general themes of avant-garde French literature in the early to mid twentieth century, and it is no wonder that Barbara became interested in *Grabinoulor's* multi-faceted and complex linguistic universe. Barbara wrote a knowledgeable short preface to the English translation, and she has an unerring eye for the brief details that bring Albert-Birot and his world to life for the as yet uninitiated reader, as she does for the personage of Grabinoulor himself. One focus of the essay is the notion of "excess", connecting us directly back to the delirium of erudition with its attendant threats and pleasures of continual proliferation, as Grabi pursues his unhindered appetite for life and travels ever on in perpetual movement. In a text which may appear at times "chaotic, sprawling, unmanageable", Albert-Birot maintains the balance, and it is, argues Kelly, in fact structured with great precision, even "coded geometrically". In a testament to a friendship with Albert-Birot which endured long after his own death through that with Arlette Albert-Birot, a translation of Albert-Birot's earliest collection of poems, *31 Pocket Poems*, was one of Barbara's final projects.

In the very middle of these scholarly essays comes, quite properly, Raymond Queneau and Barbara's *Exercises in Style*, still regarded by many as her greatest achievement, although it might be argued that to consider her work so often in the light of this one "performance" does a disservice to other works and types of texts that she undertook. Nonetheless, Queneau's *Exercices* presented a particular and formidable challenge for the translator. David Bellos in "The Artist on her Trapeze: Barbara Wright's 99 variations on a theme by Raymond Queneau" takes his own translator's eye to Barbara's *Exercises*, questioning the process of their translation as she may have done, following her methods and eventual renditions in which her own erudition becomes startlingly clear, and using some of her correspondence with Queneau to throw light on their relationship, on their mutual admiration and on their work. The importance of this stage of Barbara's career is described by Bellos: Gaberbocchus Press and the Themersons "did the book proud", with music commissioned by Barbara for the Exercise entitled "Ode", "illuminated, witty, anthropomorphic initials for the title of each Exercise, and [. . .] a photocollage permutation of Queneau's face for the frontispiece", making Barbara's *Exercises*, "visually [. . .] a more accomplished book than the Gallimard original". It is, Bellos writes, "also a historic moment": Barbara's fame as a translator spreads, bringing new friends in France and beyond, but her work also: "conserves texts that have effectively disappeared in France", given Queneau's re-issue of the text in 1973 with some new texts replacing the originals. Barbara did not follow Queneau's choices in the English re-issue in 1981, and so, having apparently grown apart from its source text, "it stands now not only as a perfect example of the creative translator's art, but as a trace of otherwise vanished fragments of Raymond Queneau". An essential, and perhaps unexpected role of the translator in literary history is therefore also made clear.

In "Translating Beckett before Beckett: the translation of *Eleutheria*", Régis Salado presents a quite different challenge taken up by Barbara, not least that of "the unusual situation in which the translator found herself, committed to work for a non-authorized cause, given that Beckett consistently opposed translation of the work" (this alludes to the "lively history" of the publication of *Eleutheria*, his first attempt at writing a play in French, written before the plays which made Beckett famous, and one that he did not want to come to the notice of the public). This problematic situation is then compounded by the fact that Beckett translated his plays from French into English himself; as Salado points out: "Beckett's own English translation of *Eleutheria* does not exist, but this non-existent text necessarily haunts whoever undertakes a translation of play". In his analysis, Barbara's translation is compared both with Beckett's original text, and also, in detail, with the first English translation of it by Michael Brodsky. The very fabric of the linguistic process (a notion suggested earlier) is revealed here in a meticulous textual analysis which shows both the quality and qualities of Barbara's work. This is also apparent in the challenge she set herself when she decided that she "must never use a word that Beckett would not have used", based on her own analyses of the self-translations, while avoiding the trap of mere imitation and the temptation to "Beckettize" her text. This essay reveals the "translator at work", and indeed the literary/

translation critic at work, as does the following essay.

Further close textual analysis shows very different aspects of the translation process in Martin Mégevand's "Barbara Wright translates Pinget's *Le Chrysanthème*: which voice in English?", moving therefore to Robert Pinget, with whom Barbara again enjoyed a sustained working relationship and friendship. She translated several of his books and, like that on Queneau, the work on Pinget is key to Barbara's own "translation as art" (although the two writers are, of course, very different). The aim here is a different one, to show the ways in which, Mégevand argues, the English translation enables, or even compels, the reader to return to the source text: "for clarification, and to raise questions about it translatability". In this penultimate essay, we are returned then, to a question that began Barbara's career. Here, what Mégevand terms "the negotiations of meaning" which are involved in translation are demonstrated with clarity in a suggestive structure of "restoring the tenor", "making explicit", and "transposition". The conclusion is that, this time, the English version is rather an accompaniment to the French text, as long as this term is not understood as the accompanist remaining in the background, but "on the contrary, highlighting, underlining, intervening"; for Barbara had, as her work shows, "temperament".

The set of scholarly essays closes with Celia Britton's "Nathalie Sarraute and the Strangeness of Language", and continues the investigation into language, the very fabric of literature (again, a notion suggested earlier), but once again in other and different ways. Language is, as Britton makes clear from the outset, a major theme of Sarraute's writing, and much commented on. Barbara worked closely with Sarraute on three of her fictional texts, and also her autobiography which is the text from which the examples here are taken. This reveals yet another choice of Barbara's in how to approach a particular text; for this time the translations stay very close to the original French texts, with an "almost mechanical fidelity rather uncharacteristic of Barbara Wright's usual approach to translation". This can result in distinctly stilted English, and as Britton notes, raises the question why "such an experienced and accomplished translator as Barbara Wright might have chosen to render Sarraute's text in this way [. . .] what seems a classic case of an over-literal translation".

Britton's closely argued conclusion is that it is because this approach "corresponds to and expresses something of the peculiar status that language has in Sarraute's writing". Indeed, Sarraute as a writer also endlessly grapples with the problem of finding the right word to express something, an interesting parallel, Britton suggests, with the process of translation itself. Since the "subtle strangeness of language" is already present in the French text, then the translator must not "betray that strangeness", and a "strange complicity" is achieved between author and translator. A complicity achieved between the translator and each of the authors presented here; each time the relationship developing a new and different form appropriate to each one.

After this series of analyses, this collection then takes two different routes: one into the past and into the archive, the other into the future of the continued potential of Barbara's work (despite Barbara's cry "Posterity! Yuk" as noted here by Breon Mitchell). Clothilde Roullier, together with the help of other archivists and scholars, provides an annotated overview of Barbara Wright's archive sources (in the USA, in France and in the United Kingdom) as an invaluable resource for any scholar of literary translation studies, of literary publishing history in the twentieth century, and of avant-garde French literature. This is, as she notes, necessarily an on-going process, but the richness of the material is abundantly clear. Then Breon Mitchell, Director of the Lilly Library at Indiana University, Bloomington gives a further personal insight into Barbara and her work, as well as into the Barbara Wright archive itself with examples of the correspondence there. He begins with a conversation in which Barbara expressed her (characteristic) surprise that anyone would be interested in her and in the "seemingly modest" part she had played in literary history, before then going on to chart how the archive came into being. The archives in the Lilly Library (now housed with over thirty other world-class literary translators) and elsewhere, and indeed this book, contradict by their very existence their subject's own initial views, but the needs of literary and cultural memory are served by acts that eventually received the translator's acceptance.

The future is represented by a previously unpublished translation of a filmscript written by Robert Pinget, *15 Rue des Lilas*. It is preceded by three different types of presentation by Alistair Whyte, by Madeleine Renouard, and by Robert Pinget and Barbara herself, each written for a different purpose and for a different audience in order to contextualize the scenario, its "characters" and "plot" (although anyone familiar with Pinget's work knows that the idea of "character" and "plot" is not really applicable). The familiar reader will also, nonetheless, recognize elements of the setting and of the foibles of those who populate it, of dramatic events and everyday concerns as Pinget's universe is vividly brought to life for the screen.

The book draws to its close with a bibliography of Barbara Wright's principal translations, and a timeline of Barbara's life. The bibliography is not an exhaustive list, since the task proved to be complex and proliferating (further erudite delirium . . .), but it is more complete than any previously produced; nor is the biography complete, for Barbara remained a private, and sometimes, elusive subject. We finally offer a selection of photographs and of extracts from varied and various appraisals and reviews of Barbara's work in order to end, not only on the word in print, but on the human interactions and responses that guarantee Barbara's legacy, whatever she herself may have professed to think about posterity.

Barbara's house in Hampstead, North London, had doors each painted a different colour, but the whole, rather than clashing, presented a pleasing (if not entirely harmonious) whole, all coming together to create one home. Each door was rather like each of her authors; each one different but interconnecting, delivering unexpected new encounters and ushering in old friends. It is our hope that this collection too achieves such a home for translators, and writers, and literary discussion.

Barbara, a Portrait Sketch
Nick Wadley

As I write, I have in front of me two photographs of Barbara Wright. In the first (in the rarefied world of the Collège de 'Pataphysique) she sits between Arrabal and Baudrillard, on the occasion of her elevation to the rank of *Satrape*. In the second (in our house in Belsize Park) she is face-to-face with her lifelong friend, Stanley Chapman. In the first she smiles, almost shyly. In the second her expression is uncompromising, as if waiting—neither particularly patiently nor with much concern—for something that may or may not deserve her attention.

These extremes form an autograph pair of parentheses to contain the range of images and thoughts of Barbara, from the self-deprecating to the acerbic, that I carry around in my head. I nearly wrote "in my memory", but they feel less like memories than resident traces of Barbara, parts of the mental fabric which from time to time appear centre-stage without having to be called. She still echoes around, either sharing some thoughts with me (not least about stupidities of the world and its words), or as a yardstick by which to measure others.

I have read again through all the surviving letters, cards and—latterly—e-mails that she wrote. Her range of signatures, from *Barbara* to *B*—via *Babar, Bar, Barab, la barbe*, and "*la barbare (would-be)*" —is touched by the light mockery with which she viewed the world and her place within it. One might gather from it, too, the lightness with which she wore successive literary prizes and exotic designations (from *Commandeur* to *Satrape*) by which her art of translation was celebrated. One convalescent letter of 2002 is signed "*Rorschach blot*".

It's easy to guess from this that she would identify readily with the gravity of aspiration and levity of means whose blend formed the signature of the Gaberbocchus Press, founded by Stefan and Franciszka Themerson in 1948. Barbara became a key player in the enterprise from the late 1940s into the early 60s. It was there that she learned to translate. Few of her trade can have cut their teeth on such works as Jarry's *Ubu Roi* (1951) and Queneau's *Exercices de Style* (1958). By the time of this latter book, she was already into the fluent breadth of her mature working style. Jarry hadn't survived to enjoy her, but Queneau's appreciation developed into friendship and the sort of close working relationship that she was to establish with many of her authors. It was a means of getting inside the work she was translating, and a formative source for her own hierarchy of values. Reviewing her translation of Queneau's *Pierrot Mon Ami* (1987), Updike wrote that she "has waltzed around the floor with the Master so many times by now that she follows his quirky French as if the steps were in English".

Barbara had a good line in quirky English—both in her oral delivery, broken as it was into a stream of breathless phrases and punctuated by percussive noises, and in the conversational dialect of her letters. Her affection for the colloquial—a key attribute in her armoury as translator—permeated it all. Her correspondence is littered with phrases from popular song lyrics, the Liverpool poets, puns and jingles from the radio; and she used an archaic childish slang that I had grown up with during the war, and which [*natch*] established common ground between us. She extemporized constantly—*ekcetra, ridickerless, probly, hideosity, self-ecstasing*. She looked things up in the *diksh* and posted them in an *ombelope*. We started openly to share such tastes and cultural flaws through her enthusiastic patronage of and the enjoyment she took in my silly drawings, mostly pictorial/verbal puns, that I started making into postcards in the 1990s. (Some that I made with Sylvia Libedinsky were published then, as weekly cartoons in the *Daily Telegraph* and later in the *Financial Times*) A cartoon-like language was familiar territory to Barbara, and it was second nature to her to celebrate the silly and the absurd. Her generous eulogies, full of percussive adjectives like *époustouflant*, were almost without reservation. She ordered and re-ordered a dozen cards at a time of many images, and commissioned from me a letterhead and, every year, a personal Christmas card (usually 100 copies), complaining only about the inertia of my *phynance* department. She distributed the postcards to friends worldwide and designed her own letterhead for the office of *Direcktor of the Number One NW*

Post-Card Consumer Research Consultancy, always finding bouquets to report or award, for lampoons that she endorsed or for qualities she valued in the pictures—from their authentic expressions to their moral attitude. The eye of this beholder was an open-handed, all-seeing phenomenon.

Only occasionally did she offer any criticism of the drawings. Once she asked if two polar bears couldn't smile a bit (but later wrote to the bears personally, apologizing). One pun was just a little too *owchish*; one Ubu "*looks too much like a hell's angel*"; and generally, there weren't enough women being mocked. Another time she was "*only too happy to join you in taking the piss out of intellectuals, but couldn't you do the same to academics?*" Once or twice she edited a caption ("*do you welcome or despise pedants?*"). And then, in 2005, there was a more serious moment when she confessed that "*Nick cards don't seem to be silly any more. Their wit had a silliness that got my wavelengths flowing. The recent batch seems to be more metaphysical, more serious, even sad. Which seems to me totally and utterly reasonable.*"[7]

The immediate context was probably a long series of pictures I was drawing about doctors and hospitals. In fact, subjects related to that world—waiting rooms, consultants, aches, medication, side effects—had long since become another world shared between us. In another letter of the same month she signed off saying "*yes, melancholy is around. All we have to do is kick it in the pants.*" In 2002 she had commissioned me to make a drawing of her pace-maker (*Percy*), an image which she then distributed to all her doctors and surgeons, of course. And a few years later she asked for a picture of herself as a lame snail, which when received was welcomed as "*the best portrait I've ever had. Could I have six of them please—no! call it ten.*"

I think her very favourite drawing, one she often went back to over the years, was "*status crow*", a typically painful pun, which she celebrated as a stand against the hypocrisy and inhumanity of hierarchies, a very Barbara-like cause to champion. From things she wrote, it was obvious that she plagued her correspondents with explanatory notes on its multi-nuanced expression (she told me how Sarraute would have loved it, and regretted she wasn't around to see it).

---

[7] Barbara's description—a "Nick card" was a card designed by Nick Wadley.

Transitions from light relief into more serious matters weren't uncommon in her letters, and conversations. Many of the serious matters were complaints—against medicines or ailments and against the technology of *blankety-blank* word-processors, in equal measure. She condemned snobbery of any sort, especially the intellectual variety. She railed against clichés, bossiness, verbosity, inaccuracies of language and Americanizations. I was her last literate English friend, she said, who used *hallo* not *hello*. She felt the same about "*like*" used for "*as if*", and was delighted with an American equivalent of Fowler that agreed with her. She was a mentor for me, as for many of her friends and working associates, in the fields of language, its usage and its translation, always there to advise with a word or phrase, and enormously missed, for that too, since she isn't on the end of a phone any more. By the end of her life her tastes were resolute. Shortly before she died, I remember how, reading Proust the second time around, she felt relief that awe had dissolved ("*he does go on and on and ON*"). Around the same time she commended Ivy Compton Burnett to me, unreservedly—rather shocked I hadn't read any. Her colourful tastes in paperback fiction are common knowledge.

To return to my opening comparison, Barbara, for a star in so many private firmaments, could appear surprisingly self-deprecating. I recall, for instance, being surprised when she twice solicited company to a *TLS* event, which might otherwise daunt her into not going, and when she expressed self-doubt about holding her own in company elsewhere. I can see more clearly since she's not here that these were less manifestations of self-doubt than a reluctance to spend time and energy dealing with some of the pretensions abroad that she found either unpalatable or hostilely unfamiliar. At the centre of her world, both as translator and as a social being, was an orientation towards dependable authenticity, almost in the sense of the commonplace—the authenticity of an obviously, ordinarily, knowable, touchable *real*, without pretence or pretension. It was neither naïve nor as simple as this may sound. But during the years that I knew her, something like it seemed progressively to become a lodestone for her values, in tune with both her modest and her uncompromising, assertive selves. In any portrait of her, such a sense of the real should be visible, grasped in her hand.

A Tribute to Barbara Wright
John Calder

Barbara started her career as a musician and accompanist, but her enquiring mind, growing interest in France and its civilization, and intellectual curiosity in general, led her into the world of literature, largely through those she met. Soon she turned to translation, which she was to claim was exactly the same in essence. She was always a wise woman, discreet and modest, and she never let me into her private life, although I knew she must have had one. Like many intellectuals I have known, she tended to compartmentalize her life, knowing many people who did not know each other or of other interests of hers. She was rarely outgoing about activities and interests that she did not in some way share with me. That is not to say that she was not always extremely interesting to be with both socially and professionally. I could only guess at what lay behind her discretion from the odd chance remark.

In her professional life she was uncompromising. Nothing she undertook could be done in a hurry, nor could there be two ways of translating a sentence or a thought. There was only one way, the right way and she would find it. She was undoubtedly the finest translator of her generation of French to English. Authors learned to trust her, both as a friend and a colleague. Her understanding of their work made her a collaborator on an equal basis, and often her English version was better than the original. Some, like Raymond Queneau, even allowed her to imitate and add to their inventions, as in the *Exercices de style / Exercises in Style*.

The celebrity of an author, who might be for the time being out of fashion, was unimportant to her. Some will come back and be better known because of the excellence of her renderings. She produced an amazing amount of work. The few lines that follow I wrote as a tribute on the day she died.

For Barbara Wright (d. 03/03/09) [8]

What is translation? Sharing
words, ideas and turns of phrase.
Accompaniment is also caring
for notes of music. Lieder, plays:
all need that other close-knit mating
of the mind that's translating.

She took her time. It must be perfect.
Some work was slight: she made it better.
No effort ever was too great.
A publisher must wait and let her
take her time to get it right
before it finally came in sight.

Authors loved her: she was their friend;
tirelessly they worked together.
To her instinct they would bend
to see French word in English tether,
and come to life in another tongue
just as in music her notes were sung.

For Barbara started as musician.
Accompanying she always said
was just like making a rendition
of plays and novels which she wed
into complex English forms
and now she rests in other dorms.

---

[8] John Calder, *Being—Seeing—Feeling—Healing—Meaning*, London: Herla Publishing, Alma Books Ltd., 2011, p. 37.

Working with Barbara Wright
Madeleine Renouard

"Barbara's absence is still as severe and shocking as ever."
—Stanley Chapman
(In a postcard to me, sent on April 7, 2009; he died a few weeks later)

Since the mid-eighties Barbara and I had a ritualized, but far from conventional way of working. We used to meet at her house in Hampstead on Sunday, late afternoon or early evening. That was in term-time, as most of my other evenings were spent at Birkbeck College (University of London) where I was teaching. Barbara was often there to attend the French public lectures and seminars where she met postgraduate students working on the writers she had translated or was translating, namely Pierre Albert-Birot, Raymond Queneau, Robert Pinget, Nathalie Sarraute . . . She would carry a pocket note book and ask questions about problems she'd met in whichever text she was translating, or about anything French which had interested or puzzled her. She was always ready to invite students to visit her and to discuss their research. When Robert Pinget and Nathalie Sarraute visited the department (March 1986, January 1987), she not only attended their public lectures but came to the seminars they held.

Then, on the Sunday we would catch up on the events of the week, which may have been a series of encounters at Birkbeck, or at the French Institute or somewhere else. We would then move on to the practical issues of the day (the fax machine, the blood pressure monitor, a bulb to replace . . .). That was followed by a glass of white wine ("*l'apéro pour madame*") and *the* question: "Are you hungry?" My answer would usually be: "Not yet!" Barbara would then produce the list of queries she had prepared or the version of a text she wanted us to go over.

Then we would *get on with* some work until we moved to the kitchen to have supper. We would talk essentially about *meaning*, which did not exclude other stylistic, psycho- or socio-linguistic issues raised by the text she was working on. The more familiar I was with the text she was translating (Queneau, Sarraute, Pinget), the

27

longer we would discuss her translation. For these three writers, language is an issue in itself; its arbitrariness is always exhibited ("*Rien n'est dit puisqu'on peut toujours le dire autrement*," writes Pinget).

Over the years it was at this particular moment of the evening that we returned again and again to our fundamental issues and arguments about translating: how to render the ambivalence of a text in another language, how to render this quixotic attempt to track down emotions, thoughts, fleeting impressions. Is there any way for the translator to put into another language what is being said in an avant-garde text about the world? And—when all is said and done—the translator may well ask if indeed *anything* is being said about society, about the power game between speaking subjects. Being faithful to the text means—for the translator as well as for the critic—being aware of all of these undercurrents. Both Pinget and Sarraute were lawyers; they both knew that language can kill or condone. What may be taken as trivialities in their texts are assertions: the verbal reality exists, it is written or spoken by others but its true meaning remains elusive; be it stilted or witty and amusing, it is a ping-pong game which literature endlessly replays. In a letter of June 4, 1987 Barbara wrote, "I can't tell you how reassuring it is that you too have to hesitate over so many *songeries*" (she was referring to Pinget's *Monsieur Songe*). "I think you have now given me enough information, support, encouragement etc. to enable me to make up my own alleged mind." At the time she had been working on *Monsieur Songe* for a while. On December 30, 1986, for instance, she wrote "I have almost finished the revision of *Monsieur Songe* with enormous lacunae—well, not exactly enormous, *mais il y en a*, and in spite of Pinget's ever willingness to help, I feel some of my ignorance is really too elementary to confess to him, so I hope I'll be able to take you up on your offer one day."

Indeed she did—as she always did—, as soon as I resumed teaching after the Christmas vacation. What was striking in Barbara's working methods was her infinite patience. She would focus all of her energy in an obsessive manner to decipher what the text was saying, how it was saying it and why it was saying it as it did. Again while translating *Monsieur Songe*: "I'd spent days—well in a manner of speaking—over your and Pinget's explanations, and the more

I cogitated, the less I arrived at any decisions. Did *you* realize that *Monsieur Songe* was the most dastardly, densely hermetical thing Pinget has ever written? I certainly didn't at first and second and etc. readings, and it even seemed so relatively light hearted *par-ci par-là* [. . .]. In spite of what Pinget says about logic and Monsieur Songe's lack of it, this has got to make some *sense* [. . .]. If M.S. is never where he wants to be, how will he be in the place where he would rather not be? It will become the only place M.S. can't escape from. In other words, if he always wants to be somewhere other than where he is, and he finds himself somewhere where he doesn't want to be, then he wants to be somewhere else but can't be, therefore he's stuck where he doesn't want to be??? Yes but why should he never express the slightest wish? Because he never gets what he wishes for???" This series of questions found a satisfactory answer after a few sessions rereading Pinget's early texts like "Ubiquity" and "Velleities" in *Between Fantoine and Agapa*. In the meantime, Monsieur Songe had acquired the status of a genuine character—quite a person—and had become the old melancholic retired man, rather eccentric and forgetful but quite likable.

Finally the time to eat would arrive. No sooner had Barbara served us the salmon and two veg, than she would be back making notes, crossing out certain remarks and questions in her notebook. And then back to the text. For her second or third version, she would read her rendering, I would have the French text in front of me and we would stop whenever one of us was unhappy or unsure about the translation. Dictionaries were to hand, of course, but most of the time we discussed what the word, sentence, passage might mean. Theorizing was not on the menu; Barbara hated any type of "jargon". She remained faithful to what she wrote in a review of Louis Kelly's book, *The True Interpreter: A History of Translation Theory and Practice in the West*, where she said "He writes simply, extremely well, and with plenty of light touches and humour. Never a trace of that excluding jargon of excruciating ugliness which so many 'experts' love to use to try to prove how superior they are to the rest of us." In spite of her anti-theory stance and her scepticism about the validity of the academic discipline called "Translation Studies," Barbara was willing to share her experience as translator with students and scholars. She was regularly invited to do so in British universities. Likewise she would attend academic conferences and seminars on "her" authors. She was a member of the French Association of Literary Translators and was regularly asked for advice by her authors' translators in other languages: "I have had a letter from E. Badinter's Dutch translator[. . . .] She must have asked Mme Badinter for help with all those appalling footnotes" (July 31, 1987). I remember Barbara going to the British Library to check all those references, and our passionate discussions about "feminism" on either side of the Channel. On a related topic and on the same book, which it should be said, the author, Elisabeth Badinter, found "improved" in English, Barbara wrote to me quoting the text: "*Par son sexe, la famille attire . . .*", underlining *sexe*, "She (E Badinter) uses the same word for 1) penis 2) vagina 3) sex. C'est un monde!" Barbara was such a free spirit that she did not feel that she had to admire all the writers she was translating. Although she could never be persuaded to translate a text she did not have an interest in, she did not hesitate to call some writers "windbags". She was particularly appalled when some of them showed a total indifference to justified and legitimate questions like "What do you mean in this passage?" "Where does this quotation come from?"—she asked them "very politely", I may add. But she never lost her sense of humour, as is shown in this letter of January 17, 1994: "I have sent Tournier *Vices and Virtues*. And just this evening, an American with a Finnish name—a photographer—has phoned from New York, asking will I translate 5 pages of M.T.'s immortal prose to go in a book of the chap's photos. No doubt it will be extra immortal, he gets extra poetic when he's describing photos. But you can't do better than that as *fidélité* towards his *traductrice!*"

Barbara was an avid reader; she reread her classics at regular intervals, and was always keen to discover new writers. She kept a notebook of her readings in French: Jacques Prévert, Francis Ponge, Georges Bataille, Maurice Blanchot, Roland Barthes, Roger Caillois, René Char, Cioran, Pierre-Jean Jouve, Henri Michaux, Boris Vian, together with Sartre and others, are on her lists. She was well-read in contemporary French literature and keen to know more. In a notebook, among her suggestions as copy editor to one of John Calder's projects, she notes "*Histoire d'O*. I thought that just a few years ago, not long before she died, D. Aury admitted authorship of *Histoire d'O*, and let it be known that she wrote it to intrigue Paulhan." Her professionalism is on full display in this notebook: errors of punctuation, spelling mistakes, awkward turns of phrase, approximations, inconsistencies, inaccuracies, as well as her disapproval of some content ("Chapter 12, I'm getting bored with all the sex") are noted scrupulously. Barbara was extremely precise in all she did. Her training as a musician may account for this but, more importantly, when she wrote the final version, she treated the text as a musical score. She would somehow forget about meaning and context on which she had been spending weeks and months, and perform as a musician does. She would match the musical texture of the original by finding the right tone, the right register, the right rhythm; she could play in all registers in French (pompous, clichéd, formal, colloquial, vulgar . . .). Having translated Raymond Queneau's *Exercices de style* so brilliantly and so creatively, she was attuned to the music of a literary text and able to recreate it in another language. She also wisely accepted that some problems had to remain unresolved.

"'Vin d'honneur' translation 'Drinks'. Explain that écart if you can." Barbara left me that task; I shall do my utmost to take up this challenge and leave to others the translation of "*mise en abîme*" and other rhetorical niceties which annoyed Barbara so much.

Working with Barbara was an extraordinary adventure. I can think of no better way of ending than with her own words sent to me on October 10, 1998, together with a copy of her work in progress: Robert Pinget's *Traces of Ink*. She writes, "I take it for granted that I may take it for granted that you will willingly (???) resupervise my efforts. I think this one is quite a bit better but any further comments will only be seen in accordance with the motto of my first educational establishment, Worthing High School . . . THE UTMOST FOR THE HIGHEST! Hrrmph. Merci."

Writing Erudite Delirium
Nathalie Piégay-Gros

Erudition, a method of learning based on the study of texts, is at first sight poles apart from delirium. The knowledge arrived at by such a method is erudite; so too is writing that demonstrates the objectivity of learning by an apparatus of notes, indexes, comments, quotations and references, or that relates how such knowledge was built up (discoveries and the constructions of resources in book form, establishing of texts, identification of texts as genuine, explanatory commentaries, etc.). Erudition is, therefore, both an epistemological process and a critical method, employed in the areas of religious, historical and literary studies. An erudite person is someone learned who researches precise, specialized objects of knowledge, backed up by a patiently amassed store of previous learning. Because of this, an erudite person, especially when featured in books, is often seen as someone struck down or at least threatened by madness. One would have to be mad to read so much, and to read so much cuts one off from the world and sends one mad. Nevertheless, an erudite person is not suffering from the same type of delirium as Don Quixote. The disease of the erudite is not brought on by confusing the fictional world of romance with the real world, but by their passion for studying. Wanting to learn so much, even for the sake of being able to write novels, for the sake of invention, can send someone mad. In the French tradition, Flaubert is undoubtedly the most extreme example of this ambivalence: "So as not to live, I plunge myself in desperation into Art; I get drunk on ink as others do on wine."[9]

Flaubert's correspondence is full of such laments, alternating with moments of exaltation, as when the author of *Madame Bovary* and *Salammbô* deplored the quantity of books he still had to read in order to represent this or that scene, or highlight a detail:

---

[9] Gustave Flaubert, Letter to Mademoiselle Leroyer de Chantepie, December 18, 1859; *Correspondance*, Paris: Gallimard, "Folio", p. 388.

I have indigestion from books. I belch folios. I have made notes on 53 different works since March; now I am studying the art of war, plunging into the delights of counterscarp and cavalryman, digging into slings and catapults. In the end I think I'll be able to draw new effects from the ancient infantrymen.[10]

Archaeology, medicine, surgery, agronomy, history of religion— every discipline and branch of learning was called upon by Flaubert. This is because he aimed not so much to represent Carthage as to make it be born anew, almost from scratch. *Salammbô* is a somewhat melancholy-mad undertaking: "No-one will ever know how sad I had to become in order to try and revive Carthage."[11] On re-reading *Salammbô*, Paul Valéry did understand the fearsome nature of Flaubert's project:

An overweening concern to astonish by the multiplicity of episodes, apparitions, switching of viewpoints, theses, and ramifications, engenders in the reader a growing sensation of being attacked by a library that has suddenly, dizzyingly, gone on the rampage, with all its volumes yelling out their millions of words at the same time, and all the boxes spewing out their prints and drawings at once in rebellion. "He's read too much," one might say of the author, as one says of a sot that he's drunk too much.[12]

This sort of intoxication of reading and references confuses the reader's understanding of what is represented, and threatens to derail learning. It is required to fill the void, to shore up the writing, which would be powerless without it. But the excess of learning threatens the whole edifice; the pressure of texts and references risks bringing the invention tumbling down:

---

[10] Gustave Flaubert, Letter to Jules Duplan, May 1857, quoted in G. Bollème, *Préface à une vie d'écrivain*, Paris: Le Seuil, 1963, p. 191.

[11] Gustave Flaubert, *Correspondance*, op. cit., letter dated 29-30 November 1859 to Ernest Feydeau.

[12] Paul Valéry, "La Tentation de (saint) Flaubert", *Œuvres*, Paris: Gallimard, "Bibliothèque de la Pléiade", volume I, 1957, pp. 616-617.

I am truly overwhelmed by all my reading and my poor eyes can't cope any more. I still have a dozen books to read before starting on my final chapter. I'm now on phrenology and administrative law, not counting Cicero's *De Officiis*, and the coitus of peacocks.[13]

Erudition is, then, a defence against imprecision, against possible failures of representation and invention, but also against the void that fiction always threatens to lay bare. It is also a defence against the present: to fight against oblivion, with erudition and knowledge, to explore old texts and make a lost world "live again" with Carthage, is also to fight against the present.

If erudition sends people mad, it is because it drives them beyond any normal plan of reading (by excess) and mode of learning (it researches minority subjects, sub-sections that could seem ridiculously trivial). It takes people outside the traditional range of books, leads them along byways, the reserve stacks of libraries, hidden fields of learning and the past. Judith Schlanger rightly noted the haphazard nature of the connection with the past implied by erudition, which leads to defying the authority of texts, the authority recognized by tradition; according to her, the sphere of erudition is:

the lands of absence, the sleeping-place for what is not in use— books that are never consulted, ideas that have come to a dead end, lifeless constructions, dead reports of what someone once said. It is an intangible sphere where any movement is astonishing, where one cannot always say which is more faded, the page that has been retrieved or the reader who has got lost. These things which were once, perhaps, powerful and influential, are now unknown and buried. They no longer have the authority to demand attention; they depend on the chance, proximity, error and needs of a random event.[14]

---

[13] Gustave Flaubert, *Correspondance*, Paris: Conard, vol. III, p. 99; quoted in Michel Schneider, *Voleurs de mots*, Paris: Gallimard, "Connaissance de l'inconscient", 1985, p. 384.

[14] Judith Schlanger, *La Mémoire des œuvres*, Paris: Nathan, 1992; republished by Verdier, "pocket edition", 2008, p. 181.

This margin of tradition is what Barbara Wright explored in some of her translations, choosing authors whose vocabulary is both rare and difficult such as Jarry,[15] both bizarre and precise, such as Queneau, and authors who were fascinated by a particular type of marginality such as Pinget and Quignard. Translating these erudite, fantasizing authors meant plunging into writing that was often exhilarating but also inclined to madness, aware of its precariousness and of the possibly derisory content of the work being done. Pinget's stories, which present the convoluted transmission of an unfinished, unclassifiable, spurious work, proclaim this concern, and defy the kind of writing that produces an over-full archive for an uncertain destination. Yet one knows that their author loved nothing so much as unusual reading-matter and rare or ancient texts, from which he would draw out images and vocabulary that lay outside current fashion and its expectations.[16] Writing feeds on them because absolute language does not exist, because one single phrase cannot hold everything together, so the writer has to resort to lists, accumulations, second attempts and variations:

> That we haven't yet found a phrase, from time, to get over nature, a phrase that retains everything together, we'd say it in the morning with a full stomach, until the evening when, in front of the sunset, we'd repeat it with a stale mouth, no more need for either sleep or pleasure, a nourishing, soothing phrase, a panacea, while weeding the meadows, washing other people's Ps, nutritious, absorbable,

---

[15] A good example is cited by Michel Arrivé in the Introduction to the first volume of Jarry's *Œuvres complètes*, Paris: Bibliothèque de la Pléiade, Gallimard, 1972): "When, in *Gestes et opinions du docteur Faustroll*, Jarry describes the vegetation of the Sounding Isle, he makes reference to the musical instruments of the works of Claude Terrasse, which one could easily take to be the plants of this learned island: "The lord of the island [. . .] led us to his plantations, protected by aeolian bamboo markers. The most common plants there were the tarole, the ravanastron, the sambuke, the archlute, the bandore, the kin and the che, the turlurette, the vina, the magrepha and the hydraulus" (p. XVII)." Knowledge is diverted from its destination, exploited by fiction, and enchants both the lexis and the reader's memory.

[16] For more on this subject, see the article by Jean-Claude Liéber and Madeleine Renouard about Pinget's library and reading in *Bibliothèques d'écrivains*, eds P. D'Iorio and D. Ferrer, Paris: CNRS, "Textes et manuscrits", 2001, especially p. 227.

enlightening, until the day . . .[17]

Writing or translating erudite delirium means plunging into a world of learned, rare words, to translate which, as one can well imagine, with their cohorts of literary references, is an uncomfortable but exhilarating task.

With *Children of Clay* (translated by Madeleine Velguth) Queneau gives an especially striking example of madness at work in erudition. Chambernac and Purpulan (the Bouvard and Pécuchet of the 1930s) are composing an "Encyclopaedia of the Inexact Sciences" subtitled "To the limits of darkness". Made up of biographical and bibliographical notices, which are amply quoted in the novel, this vast undertaking sums up the fate of learned men with no affiliation: the "literary lunatic" is "a published author whose wild imaginings [. . .] diverge from all those professed by the society in which he lives, either by this society as a whole, or by the different groups, even the minor ones, that compose it," and which "are not related to earlier doctrines" nor "taken up by anyone else".[18] As stipulated at the end of the novel, the "texts quoted by Chambernac in his Encyclopaedia are, *naturally*, authentic".[19] These are, in fact the erudite notes collected by Queneau in a book called "Literary Lunatics" which was rejected by Gallimard and Denoël. Queneau traces, for example, the story of all the "mad squarers" (who wrote to prove the squareness of the circle); or, again, those who are afflicted by language troubles such as Jean-Pierre Brisset, or etymological delirium. He quotes writings of "learned men" who set off in search of a primitive language or a universal language. Such is the case of the "literary lunatic" who starts from the figure of Thoth, the ancient Egyptian dog-headed god of writing, arrives at the Great Dog constellation, and then at the etymology of the word *toutou* (doggie or bow-wow), which comes, of course, from Thoth . . . Here the erudition is both obvious and delirious. Obvious, because it builds up a novel on the basis of a

---

[17] Robert Pinget, *Passacaglia—a novel*, tr. Barbara Wright, New York: Red Dust, 1978, p. 83.

[18] Raymond Queneau, *Les Enfants du Limon*, Paris: Gallimard, "Bibliothèque de la Pléiade", 2002, p. 728. *Children of Clay*, Los Angeles: Sun & Moon Press, 1998, p. 171.

[19] *Ibid.*, p. 912.

knowledge that is very personal, private, *idiot* in the etymological sense of the word. To write his "Literary Lunatics", Queneau accumulated over 700 index-cards at the Bibliothèque Nationale in Paris. Delirious, in that it is all about "lunatics", but also because it devotes itself to storing up their writings, only to recognize, after having put together over 700 unpublishable pages, that "it was merely reactionary paranoids and doddery old chatterboxes who were exhumed."[20] Both positive and *idiotic*, the learning gathered by Queneau was reworked by fiction and imagination.

The madness of erudition can be still more radical, in that erudition threatens our relationship with the world, our certainty that it is very different from the ways in which it is represented. Ever since Don Quixote, it has been recognized that books are purveyors of illusions and madness, and that libraries can be fatal (the library must be destroyed, preferably by fire). This kind of madness consists of believing that the world of books is the real world, or that the world exists to lead to a library, to books. Kien, the eminent and learned Sinologist in Canetti's great novel *Auto da Fé*, is mad in that he believes that the world is in his head, a head that is itself a library. Erudition becomes fantastic. And this is because a person's connection to a book destabilizes his or her connection with reality. The real world is no more than the reflection of the books that have accumulated in libraries; people are the phantoms of fictional characters. Literature is not a parasite of the real world, but, just the reverse, reality ends up as a parasite of its representations.

Concerning Flaubert, in 1964 Foucault rightly noted this dimension of fantasy in our relationship with libraries: "Henceforth, the visionary experience arises from the black and white surface of printed signs, from the closed and dusty volume that opens with a flight of forgotten words; fantasies are carefully deployed in the hushed library, with its columns of books, with its titles aligned on shelves to form a tight enclosure, but within confines that also liberate impossible worlds."[21]

---

[20] Raymond Queneau, *Bâtons, chiffres et lettres*, Paris: Gallimard, "Idées", 1985, p. 261.

[21] Michel Foucault, "La Bibliothèque fantastique", *Dits et écrits, I*, Paris: Gallimard, "Quarto", 2001 [1964], p. 323.

These are the impossible worlds explored by Jorge Luis Borges. The metaphysical fantasy that characterizes his universe is strongly linked to the pathways of erudition, which, far from testifying to and authenticating objective, solidly-grounded learning, blurs the dividing-line between reality and invention by putting spurious and genuine references on the same level. The reader doubts both the authenticity of the quotations offered, and the reality of the world itself ("The Approach to Al-Mu'tasim", "An Examination of the Work of Herbert Quain", *Fictions*, or "A Universal History of Infamy"): this is the main point of imaginary erudition in Borges. The world, and representations of the world, end up being the same thing. Books and libraries have the power to create worlds, such as Tlön, which arose from the fraudulent interpolation of an article in the Anglo-American Cyclopaedia (*Fictions*). But in return, the world can be robbed of its reality by an accumulation of fictions. Learned notes and references, authentic and spurious quotations, bibliographies where pseudo-references alternate with genuine ones, disparate lists of names of authors or titles: all of them call into question our relationship with the world.

The question of the possibility of transmission—and translation as one of its principle vectors—is at the heart of the passion for erudition. Accumulating learning, objectifying it, and preserving it so that it will reach future generations of readers and thinkers: such is its main aim. And nevertheless it is sometimes a disease of memory and a pathology of transmission that make erudite delirium available to be read. Thus Perec, in *Life: A User's Manual*, collects with near-maniacal care all traces of the past, all signs of what has been: tickets, posters, bibliographies, newspaper cuttings, etc. . . . Collectors, sometimes rather crazy characters, supply the novel abundantly with lists, catalogues which carefully store up everything that needs to be kept and tracked. The novelist himself builds up his novel with multiple learned and pseudo-learned references. He puts true and false quotations on the same level. Through his intellectual education and his work at the CNRS (Centre National de la Recherche Scientifique, the French National Centre for Scientific Research) as well as his membership of the OULIPO (Ouvroir de Littérature Potentielle, the experimental writing group to which Perec belonged, founded by Raymond Queneau and François Le Lionnais), Perec was always in close contact with erudition. From 1967 onwards, each meeting included, as Marcel Bénabou has recalled,[22] the heading "erudition". It centred mainly on "anticipatory plagiarists" because its main concern was to blur the boundary between true and false, spurious and genuine. This blurring of boundaries was followed up in the whole of Perec's work. It should also be recalled that Perec's work at the CNRS brought him into direct contact with learned publications and the research tools of genuine erudition—indexes, catalogues, etc.,—which he would put to hilarious use in *Life: A User's Manual*. These areas of learning (especially neurophysiology and bibliographical documentation) served him as a reservoir of words, a lexical storehouse, perhaps even a thesaurus, where incongruity and precision lived happily together, where the power of science over imagination was unscrupulously expressed. He said to Jean-Marie Le Sidaner:

> The only branches of learning that I have knowingly drawn upon in my work are those whose language was really familiar to me for professional reasons: neurophysiology and bibliographic documentation ("information retrieval"). Neurophysiology provided me with a certain number of words that I have used judiciously or injudiciously (for instance: in Berman's monumental atlas of the cerebral trunk, there occurs the Kölliker-Fuse nucleus, known to all respiratory neurophysicists; it provided me, in *Life: A User's Manual*, with the character of the physicist Kolliker, cerebral trunk-man, inventor of a missile that was the ancestor of Berman's Atlas rockets). The documentation techniques enabled me to build up the whole pseudo-erudite structure of *Life: A User's Manual*.[23]

Erudition is both a way of exercising mastery over learning, and a kind of manipulation. This is because it is also a defence against that learning, against the threat it poses to invention and memory.

---

[22] Marcel Bénabou, "Vraie et fausse érudition chez Perec", *Parcours Perec*, London conference proceedings, ed. M. Ribière, Lyon: Presses Universitaires de Lyon, 1990, p. 41 ff.

[23] Interview with Jean-Marie Le Sidaner, *L'Arc*, no. 76; included in *Georges Perec, Entretiens et conférences, 1965-1978*, critical edition established by Dominique Bertelli and Mireille Ribière, Paris: Joseph K., 2003.

There is something in the nature of a defensive spell about the way Perec takes genuine erudition and adds fictional erudition to it, most obviously expressed in his imaginary catalogues or libraries. Imaginary erudition, which leads to the invention of non-existent books or even whole libraries (like Saint-Victor's Library in Rabelais' *Pantagruel*), holds the passion for erudition up to ridicule. Thus Chapter 84 of Perec's *Life: A User's Manual*, offers the list of books deposited on Cinok's little table:

> *Des Raskolniki d'Avvakoum à l'insurrection de Stenka Razine.*
> *Contributions bibliographiques à l'étude du règne d'Alexis Ier, par Hubert Corneylius*, Lille, Imprimerie des Tilleurs, 1954;
> *La Storia dei Romani*, G. De Sanctis (vol. III);
> *Travels in Baltistan*, by P. O. Box, Bombay, 1894;
> *Quand j'étais petit rat. Souvenirs d'enfance et de jeunesse*, by Maria Feodorovna Vychiskava, Paris 1948;
> *The Miner and the Beginnings of Labour*, by Irwin Wall, off-print from the magazine *Annales*;
> *Beitrage zur feineres Anatomie des menschlichen Ruckenmarks*, by Goll, Ghent, 1860;
> Three numbers of the magazine *Rustica*;
> *Sur le clivage pyramidal des albâtres et des gypses*, by Otto Lidenbrock, Professor at the Hamburg Johannaeum and Curator of the Mineralogical Museum of M. Struve, Russian Ambassador; extract from the *Zeitschrift für Mineralogie und Kristallographie*, vol. XII, Suppl. 147;
> And *Mémoires d'un Numismate*, by Florent Baillarger, formerly Prefectural Secretary of the Département of Haute-Marne, Chalindrey, Librairie Le Sommelier, undated.[24]

Accumulation, precision, disorder, arbitrariness and incongruity: are these the characteristics of the passion for erudition? Is it a maniacal passion that accumulates without sorting, indiscriminately, merely laughing at traditional priorities? And when a novelist adds to the already numerous libraries which he used to write his own

---

[24] Georges Perec, *La Vie mode d'emploi*, Paris: Hachette, 1978, p. 502. *Life A User's Manual*, tr. David Bellos, London: Collins Harvill.

fiction, with a supplementary one of his own invention, is he merely laughing at erudition's passion for preservation? Here fantasy brings Perec into the Rabelaisian humanist tradition. Erudite delirium is an enchantment of language, arbitrary and incongruous linkings are sources of comedy; the list shows both the infinite, dizzying character of learning, but also the telescoping, sudden switches of subject, and syncopes that it produces in the perception we have of reality. From the dry seriousness of the erudite writer we slip towards fantasy and comedy. It is worth mentioning Perec's pastiches, which provide an outlet for his own erudite practice. They show his schoolboy humour, and how he aims to manipulate learning and its authority. *Cantatrix Sopranica L.* is significantly sub-titled "and other scientific writings". He parodies learned research and the hazards encountered by painstaking enquiry—thus researches in Fitchwinder University Library led Mortimer Fleisch to discover five unpublished leaflets by Raymond Roussel, and this is the starting-point of a short story about the (spurious) thesis of a (fictional) student, which deals with French playwrights and involves drawing "the sketch of a melancholy geography" (the title of the story). Learning is placed entirely at the service of the spurious invention of documentary sources, parody and pastiche being, probably, in the nature of an outlet. Perec thus satirizes his own tendency to take refuge in erudite, weird lines of research. These pastiches are not marginal to his work, and they fall within a more general context of blurring the boundaries between truth and invention, manipulating the notion of origin (of the text, of learning, and of oneself) and authority (true and false are often indistinguishable). The point at issue is the trustworthiness of language and of memory. Once true and false, copy and original, are put on the same level (as in the fable of *An Amateur's Studio*, and the destiny of Plassaert the forger), once the novel demolishes the dividing-line between spurious and real, the power of language and fiction is affirmed.

As Claude Burgelin says in his accurate analysis, saturation is an expression of the mastery exercised over memory and reality invaded by printed characters. The novel is constructed by building up memory and controlling it so that it allows nothing to escape. Perec said about the preparatory notebook for his novel, which as we know contained numerous long quotations, that it was a "framework", "a scaffolding [. . .] which merely served as a pump for the imagination."[25] But this scaffolding that constricts both the imagination and the awareness of the writer also serves a defensive purpose: it forearms him against the invasion of his memory and affection, by welcoming everything that comes, mingling true and false stories, erudite passages that are pure invention with others that are rigorously correct. For Perec, the need to classify and categorize signifies that he does not want to be taken in by anything. The stronger the structure is, the more chance is highlighted; life and the user's manual are for ever in opposition, the work of classification and ordering being always subverted by accidental happenings.[26] The memory is healed by the memory; the act of gathering defies loss and protects against "letting go"; "he has to keep things, because conservation offers an image of a life that is maintained. The written trace offers survival, it is the past perpetuated into a lasting present."[27] This is where the tendency to accumulate is checked by the work of sorting and coordinating, the supreme expression of mastery and orderliness. Memory, as is well known, works on the random-access system. The work of sorting and coordinating contributes movement and enjoyment, thus neutralizing whatever deadliness may lie in memory and erudition.

Learning that is so painstaking that it becomes microscopic, so scrupulous that it becomes maniacal, so specific that it becomes *idiotic*, is mocked and held up to ridicule by writers, set in opposition to intelligence, used as proof of narrow-minded mean-spiritedness. And so a great number of contemporary novels poke fun at erudite writers (*La Télévision* or *Monsieur* by Jean-Philippe Toussaint; *Démolir Nisard* by Eric Chevillard). Annotating, compiling, comparing texts, trying to distinguish between spurious and genuine, marking affiliations, tracing influences, identifying sources—all these are the practices of erudition that are ridiculed and make a learned man into

---

[25] Interview with J.-J. Brochier, "La Maison des romans", *Le Magazine Littéraire*, October 1978, quoted in *Georges Perec, Entretiens et conférences, 1965-1978*, op. cit., vol. 1, pp. 239 ff.

[26] Interview with Franck Venaille, "Le travail de la mémoire", 1979, in *Georges Perec, Entretiens et conférences, 1965-1978*, op. cit., vol. 2, pp. 52-53.

[27] Claude Burgelin, *Les Parties de dominos chez Monsieur Lefèvre*, Paris: Circé 1996, p. 74.

a failed writer. A scribbler, as Pinget puts it:

> As our uncle used to say, to spend your whole existence scribbling, to sweat blood and tears gathering your ideas together, numbering pages, reading over what you've written, rewriting, crossing out, cutting out, and finally suffering torments about the result, you can't call that a blessing, the poor man had done it all his life and towards his end he was asking himself what could have got into him, they say it's the muse that guides your pen, ah but it's penury for you she's aiming at.[28]

The erudite person is a real madman (Kinbote in Nabokov's *Pale Fire*), deranged (Professor Goodman in Jacques Roubaud's *L'Abominable Tisonnier* . . .), a socially inept and determined recluse (Sebald's Austerlitz, or Professor Klein, the Sinologist in Canetti's *Auto da Fé*). Erudition is diametrically opposed to experience—such people read and write on books because they do not live; to intelligence—this is the main theme of the criticism directed against erudition, as in the Encyclopaedia and the Enlightenment, that people collect facts instead of thinking (the Bouvard & Pécuchet syndrome); and to invention—a work of erudition is seen as a lack of imagination, denoting an inability to create anything new.

Beneath its airs of rationality, writing then becomes delirium. It is no longer a case of writing excess, the novel as a global form embracing all branches of learning and functioning as a kind of hyper-memory, but of the extreme condensing of learning, true or false. Borges plays at being learned, and still more at manipulating learning and imagination. But his imaginary erudition raises fundamental questions: what ought we to do with all the accumulated learning in libraries, which is now in the process of being dematerialized? What has it got to offer us? What does it teach us about the past and about

[28] Robert Pinget, *L'Apocryphe*, Paris: Minuit, 1981, p. 51. *The Apocrypha*, tr. Barbara Wright, New York: Red Dust, 1989, p.33. I developed these points in my article, "Le récit mélancolique de Robert Pinget", in *Traversée de la mélancolie*, eds E. Grossman and N. Piégay-Gros, Séguier, 2002. On the question of transmission, see also N. Piégay-Gros, "Domesticité et subalterne", in *Robert Pinget, Marges, matériau, écriture*, eds Martin Mégevand and N. Piégay-Gros, Paris: Presses Universitaires de Vincennes, 2011.

ourselves? Situating it in fiction and linking it with fantasy point to a crisis in our relationship with accumulated knowledge and any line of epistemology founded on the patient study of texts that have stood the test of time. When accumulation threatens to become saturation, when it endangers the very possibility of forgetting and hence of a healthy, well-managed memory, learning is cause for concern. The writing of Pascal Quignard,[29] which Barbara Wright also translated, bears the indelible mark of this concern for oblivion, what is immemorial, burying itself in the rubbish-heaps of history to reconnect with what has been spurned by tradition; his narratives feed on what he calls the "sordida".

Fiction that presents erudite delirium, in whatever form, serves to dismantle these fears by objectifying fantasies (the burning of libraries, the return of the past in the present, the fusion of the real and the imaginary, spurious and genuine, interference in or even inversion of the relationship between the real and its representation . . .). Fiction, and especially novels, is especially suitable for representing the way the imagination can catch fire on contact with learning.

The objectivity of erudition is sought after by novelists to explore the madness that pursues learned people and writers. Imaginary erudition shows how much the positivism of learning (represented by notes, bibliographies, painstaking quotations) is linked to obscurity; how scrupulous precision is surrounded on all sides by the shapelessness that is explored and defied by the writing of fiction; and also how tradition, symbolized by the library that preserves and sorts books and branches of learning, not only has its reserves to which writers can come to draw out new sources of inspiration and hitherto unpublished subjects, but most importantly crevasses, traps, filled full of things that were rejected and forgotten by their own era. And a whole swathe of modernity (one thinks of Nabokov, Canetti, Sebald, Umberto Eco . . .) writes and invents under the injunction of this margin, which borders on delirium and the enchantment of language. On the alert for this enchantment, Barbara Wright found a way to invent in her own language the trajectories and explorations of the authors she translated.

Translated by Helena Scott

---

[29] See my book *L'Erudition imaginaire*, Paris: Droz, "Titre courant", 2009, for a closer study of Pascal Quignard.

UBU ROI: a Brilliant Debut
Jill Fell

I first came across the name of Barbara Wright and her translation of Alfred Jarry's *Ubu Roi* in my final year as an undergraduate at Bristol University. Donald Watson, the leader of our seminar on twentieth-century French Drama was also Ionesco's translator. For our dissertation he set us a competition to compare two dramatists of our choice. The winning essay would be published in the journal, *New Theatre Studies*. I chose to compare Jean Giraudoux and Jarry, but could not find much on Jarry in the university library. It was in Bristol Public Library that I discovered Barbara's *Ubu Roi*, the text hand-written by her on bright yellow pages overdrawn with cartoonesque doodles by Franciszka Themerson—rather different from my other set books. It confirmed me in my half-formed opinion that Jarry too must be a different sort of writer if he could have inspired an edition like this.

I intend to use Barbara's own words wherever possible in this chapter, and I will start by summarizing her account of how she became a translator, published in the journal *Pix*.[30] Around 1947 Stefan and Franciszka Themerson, Polish founders of the Gaberbocchus Press, were introduced to Barbara, at that time a professional musician. Stefan asked her if she would work with him on translating a tiny book he had written for very young children (*Pan Tom buduje dom*, Warsaw: Mathesis Polska, 1938), but at which two professional translators had failed. Barbara's musical training helped them to find the right pace and rhythm, and the book duly came out in 1950 as *Mr Rouse Builds His House*.[31] "One thing leading to another," Barbara wrote, as the Themersons knew she had done some of her musical studies in France, they asked her if she would like to take on the translation of Jarry's *Ubu Roi*. "And sure, why wouldn't I?" she apparently replied.

Barbara described the translation of *Ubu Roi* almost as a collective enterprise, during which she would submit her drafts and the Themersons would "come up with constructive criticism and the occasional bizarre word which nobody else would have thought of."

[30] "How the Themersons turned me into a translator," *Pix*, 1, pp. 115-17.

[31] London: Gaberbocchus Press, 1950.

But when it came to the macabre song, *La Chanson du Décervelage*, not actually a part of *Ubu Roi*, but with which the Themersons wanted to close the book, Barbara admitted to being stumped.[32] She announced to the Themersons that nobody could be expected to make the translation rhyme. The Themersons apparently told her not to be silly, to go home and bring the poem back with rhymes. Perhaps this was the first time that she faced what seemed to be an impossible translation and was absolutely on her own to produce a result. She did.

To begin with there was Jarry's term *Décervelage*. "La Machine à Décerveler" is operated by the Palotins, the rechargeable, boxed rubber robots that Ubu kept to torture and kill his victims. Jarry described it as a superior and more entertaining killing instrument to either the guillotine or the Bomb, which would provide a spectacle to amuse the populace on a Sunday.[33] Barbara may have been inspired by an illustration that Jarry published in an early 1895 version of *Ubu Roi*[34]—an old woodcut depicting "quartering", where each of the victim's limbs is tied to a different horse, then ridden in opposite directions. Rather than mundanely translating *décervelage* as "debraining" (as have other translators), she coined the word "disembraining", connoting the barbaric mediaeval practice of disembowelling, as in the practice of hanging, drawing and quartering.

Here is a sample verse in Barbara's translation, taken from the middle of the song plus the refrain. It is sung by the *Ébeniste*, (the cabinet maker), who has taken his family to watch the *Décervelage* as their Sunday outing:

Soon we were white with brain, my loving wife and I.

---

[32] *La Chanson du Décervelage* with Jarry's amendments was included in *Les Paralipomènes d'Ubu*, published in *La Revue Blanche*, December 1, 1896. The original version, titled *Tudé*, had its origins at the Lycée de Rennes, and was written down by Jarry's schoolfriends, Henri and Charles Morin. Cf. Charles Chassé, *D'Ubu-Roi au Douanier Rousseau*, Paris: Éditions de la Nouvelle Revue Critique, 1947.

[33] Alfred Jarry, "Visions actuelles et futures," in Jarry, *Œuvres complètes*, eds Michel Arrivé, Henri Bordillon, Patrick Besnier and Bernard Le Doze, Paris, Gallimard, Bibliothèque de la Pléiade, 1972-1988, vol. 1, pp. 337-8.

[34] See untitled illustration to *Ubu Roi*, "L'Acte Terrestre, *César-Antechrist* (1895)", in Jarry, *Œuvres complètes*, op. cit., vol. 1, p. 303.

The brats were eating it up, and we were merry as hell
At the sight of the Palotin waving his blade sky high
And the knives all different sizes, and all the wounds as well.

......

Look, look at the Machine revolving
Look, look at the brain flying,
Look, look at the Rentiers trembling[35]

The Gaberbocchus translation of *Ubu Roi* came out in 1951. Barbara recalled that it was snubbed by the British establishment; not, however, by the Collège de 'Pataphysique. This had been founded in 1948 by a group of French intellectuals as a kind of impudent alternative to the French academic establishment, defining itself as *"une société de recherches savantes et inutiles."*[36] (A society for learned and useless research.) It was Jarry's philosophy of 'pataphysics that united them. In 1894, in his first published piece, *Guignol*, Jarry had launched the notion of 'pataphysics[37] through the character of Ubu, who introduces himself as "a great Pataphysician" and declares that he had invented the science of 'pataphysics simply because there was a sore need for it: *La 'pataphysique est une science que nous avons inventée, et dont le besoin se fait généralement sentir.*[38] The Collège would follow a more sophisticated definition of 'pataphysics formulated by Jarry four years later for his novel, *Gestes et Opinions du docteur Faustroll, pataphysicien*, as "the science of imaginary solutions" and "the science of the particular . . . that will study the laws governing exceptions, and will explain the universe supplementary to this one; or, less ambitiously, will describe a universe which can be—and perhaps should be—envisaged in the place of the traditional one, since the laws that are supposed to have been discovered in the

---

[35] "The Song of the Disembraining" in Alfred Jarry, *Ubu Roi*, tr. Barbara Wright, illustr. Franciszka Themerson, London: Gaberbocchus Press, 1951, n.p.

[36] *Les très riches heures du Collège de 'Pataphysique*, compiled by Raymond Fleury, Paul Gayot and Thieri Foulc, Paris: Fayard, 2000.

[37] The notion of 'pataphysics also had its origins at the Lycée de Rennes.

[38] Jarry, *Œuvres complètes*, op. cit., vol. 1, p. 182.

traditional universe are also correlations of exceptions . . ."[39]

Barbara's translation of *Ubu Roi* was welcomed in the third number of the *Cahiers du Collège de 'Pataphysique*, although the writer not only misspelt her name but, unforgivably, misread her translation of Ubu's opening word *Merdre!* as *Shitts!* instead of *Shittr!*

Enfin vient de paraître à Londres la première traduction d'*Ubu Roi* par Barbara Wrigt (*Merdre* = *Shitts*) dont la splendide présentation fera date.[40]

(The first translation of *Ubu Roi*, whose sumptuous layout will serve as a high-point in book design, has finally been published in London, translated by Barbara Wrigt [*Merdre* = *Shitts*].)

A physical description of the edition follows, detailing the grey pages of the preface, then the text *calligraphié en noir sur un très beau jaune bouton d'or* (hand-written in black on a beautiful yellow-gold ground) with Franciszka Themerson's *excellents et légers griffonnages tirés en sous-impression du texte même* (excellent swift sketches printed underneath the actual text). Finally congratulations were offered to the publisher, *l'honorable Monsieur Gaberbocchus of 31 King's Road, Chelsea*. As far as the Collège was concerned Stefan Themerson would continue to be known as *Sieur Gaberbocchus*.

The subsequent London production of *Ubu Roi* by William Jay at the Institute of Contemporary Arts on February 18, 1952, with masks by Franciszka Themerson, was also reviewed in the *Cahiers*. The Collège reviewer admitted not being able to judge what the English equivalents for Jarry's special expressions would mean to an English ear, however he praised Barbara's exactitude: "*En tout cas la traductrice me semble n'avoir rien négligé, omis ou travesti*" ("At all events the translator seems to me not to have overlooked, omitted or distorted anything").[41]

---

[39] *Selected Works of Alfred Jarry*, trans. Roger Shattuck & Simon Watson Taylor, London: Jonathan Cape, 1965, pp. 192-3.

[40] *Cahiers du Collège de 'Pataphysique*, 3-4, p. 98.

[41] *Cahiers du Collège de 'Pataphysique*, 5-6, pp. 105-6.

In year 80 of the pataphysical Era, which began in 1873, the year of Jarry's birth, (1953 according to the so-called *vulgar* calendar), Barbara was elected to the rank of Regent, simultaneously with Eugène Ionesco and with Noël Arnaud, Jarry's future biographer. Her exact title was *Régente de Zozologie shakespearienne*. She would later be promoted to *Définiteur suprême* and then to the rank of Transcendent Satrap, as Raymond Queneau, Marcel Duchamp and Jean Dubuffet had been, Louise Bourgeois briefly was and Fernando Arrabal currently is. But long before the official elevation, she was thought of as a *Satrape*. As early as 1962, Maurice Saillet had sent her his Livre de Poche edition of *Tout Ubu* with the handwritten dedication, "*à la Satrapesse Barbara Wright, translatrice incomparable des Écritures Saintes, hommage très cordial*" ("to the Satrapess Barbara Wright, peerless translator of the Sacred Writings, sincerest homage").

Barbara did not brook challenges to her translations, however affectionate her relations with the Collège intellectuals from early days. Probably her most ardent defence was of her translation of the opening word of *Ubu Roi*, "MERDRE!" which she translated as "SHITTR!" on the first page of the Gaberbocchus edition. The letter quoted below dates from 1955, or year 82 in the pataphysical Era. In it, Barbara lays out the reasons for her choice of SHITTR in the sharpest, wittiest and most elegant French. Her letter was in reply to a postcard from Jean-Hugues Sainmont, one of the founders of the Collège de 'Pataphysique. Sainmont wanted to sound Barbara out before publishing an argument for an alternative translation of "*merdre*", by a young American academic, Roger Shattuck, who was working on his book *The Banquet Years: The Origins of the Avant-Garde in France*,[42] which was to focus on Satie, Rousseau, Jarry and Apollinaire.

The Collège was about to devote seven pages of their Cahier no. 20 to Shattuck's article, *Anglifications de Jarry: Translation, Traduction, Transposition*.[43] Here Shattuck set himself up as arbiter of the, by now, two English translations of the full text of *Ubu Roi*, the second by two Americans, Beverley Keith and G. Legman, which

---

[42] New York: Vintage Books, 1968.

[43] *Cahiers du Collège de 'Pataphysique*, 20, pp. 37-43.

he rules out as completely useless, while condescendingly describing the London translation as "*en gros préférable*" ("preferable on the whole"). The nub of his article rested on the difficulty of finding an equivalent for Jarry's *merdre* in English. He rejected Keith & Legman's *pshit* beginning with a "p" as being too light a sound, whereas the sound to justify *merdre* needed to come from the very base of the lungs, he wrote. He observed that in adding an "r" to the English word "shit", *s-h-i-t-t-r* "*Mlle Wright suit avec modestie l'orthographe de Jarry.*" "*Ce n'est point une exclamation qui roule avec énormité dans la bouche*", he declared, and went on to offer his own solution. "*En anglais, ce n'est pas une consonne, mais une voyelle qu'il faut ajouter, ce qui ouvre et prolonge le son. Répétez onze mille fois, confrères et concitoyens, répétez après nous, SHITE et encore SHITE*" ("Mlle Wright modestly follows Jarry's spelling . . . It is not an exclamation that rolls preposterously in the mouth . . . In English it is not a consonant but a vowel that needs to be added, one that will open and prolong the sound. Repeat eleven thousand times, colleagues and fellow-citizens, repeat after us, SHITE and again SHITE").

In his postcard to Barbara, Sainmont refers to Shattuck's further argument in his article that "shite" was not only in current use by American schoolboys, but had received the support of James Joyce in *Ulysses*. "*Qu'en pensez-vous?*" ("What do you think?") queries Sainmont gently, and, unaware of the formidable response he was about to unleash, signs flirtatiously, "*Votre dévoué et affectionné cannibale*" ("Your devoted and affectionate cannibal"). Barbara cut out of the postcard whatever form of endearment the "Cannibale" Sainmont chose to address her with.

Barbara did not give a fig for Shattuck's "SHITE". Nor was she disarmed by the flirtatious tone of the eminent *Provéditeur-Rogateur* of the Collège de 'Pataphysique. Her authority and professionalism were at stake. The Wright typewriter flew into action. Sainmont got his reply almost by return of post, quoted here in full:

Cher Monsieur,

Nous remarquons que vous estes mangeur de régentes en travesti, ce qui nous fait penser (nous nous excusons infiniment) au diable, *passionné collectionneur de hannetons célibataires,*

d'aubergistes gras et de jeunes fiancées . . . (Œuvres Complètes,
Vol. VI, p. 245).[44]

Barbara is here quoting a passage from *Les Silènes,* Jarry's then
little-known translation of the play *Scherz, Satire, Ironie und tief-
ere Bedeutung* (1827) by the German dramatist Christian-Dietrich
Grabbe (1801-1836). Her quotation refers to a scene in which the
devil approaches a young man and persuades him to sell him his
fiancée. Through this apt citation, Barbara demonstrated her close
familiarity with the full range of Jarry's oeuvre—this piece being in
volume 6 of a massive eight-volume edition of Jarry's works. She
had, in fact, decided to investigate Jarry's skill as a translator by making her own English translation of the play from the German. She
continues:

Nous vous remercions de votre aimable carte postale au sujet du
mot; nous en pensons ce qui suit.
   Quoiqu'on ne saurait mettre en doute le respect que nous
éprouvons à l'égard de James Joyce, nous ne voyons pas ce que
feu ce maître vient faire dans la petite question en délibération. Il
s'agit de fabriquer un mot nouveau, et non de se servir d'un mot
déjà employé. (D'ailleurs, en les parenthèses que vous voyez, dans
notre édition d'*Ulysses,* [Bodley Head,1937], le mot en question,
à la page 740, s'écrit simplement SHIT.)
   Mais tout en acceptant que le mot ainsi amplifié se trouve
dans les œuvres du dit maître, nos recherches nous portent à
croire que ce mot là, ce n'est pas lui qui l'a inventé. Le mot, que
vous écrivez si élégamment, et si sûrement, *chaillte,* se trouve dans
tous les dictionnaires qui jouissent d'une certaine considération,
comme: *shit, shite.* C'est à dire que *shite* n'est qu'une alternative
à l'autre mot, laquelle alternative date de l'an 1308. Quel rapport
y a t-il donc entre l'usage que fait le Père Ubu de ce nouveau
et sanctissime mot MERDRE et celui que font maître Joyce, le
satrape Shittuck, et autres de cet archaïsme SHITE?

[44] The reference is not to the three-volume Pléiade *Œuvres complètes* but to the
earlier edition of Jarry's works edited by René Massat; Montecarlo: Editions du
Livre and Lausanne: Henri Kaeser, 1948.

En cette année 82 de l'ère pataphysique, il reste, sans doute, peu d'éloges à faire sur le mot par une modeste régente britannique. Mais il nous semble qu'une partie de la beauté de ce mot, qui sonne comme venant de la trompette de l'archange, réside en ceci: que d'abord l'auditeur innocent doit imaginer qu'il s'agit d'un mot assez courant et qu'il connaît par cœur, pour se rendre compte une seconde plus tard, avec étonnement et volupté, qu'il s'agit réellement de tout autre chose. C'est cela qui rend inenvisageable toute déformation au commencement du mot et toute modification de la voyelle. Essentiel aussi est le "r" sonore et savoureux, à ajouter, en mille façons variées au choix—crescendo, diminuendo, martelé, etc. etc., *après* le mot. MERD...RRR— SHITT...RRR. *Shittr*—ce mot divin, qui nous était révélé de Là-Haut, répond exactement, parfaitement, *simplement,* aux conditions requises—est-ce à inférer que les haut[e]s dignitaires du collège de 'pataphysique s'élèvent contre la simplicité? Il faut ajouter que ce mot, si doux, si explosif, si menaçant (au choix)— nous nous en servons nous-même[s] quotidiennement, et nous pouvons rendre témoignage qu'il est facile à employer, ne manque jamais de produire l'effet voulu, et est entièrement inoffensif pour qui l'emploie.

Quant aux us des écoliers amerdicains de nos jours, ça nous laisse plutôt froide. Qu'ils emploient un mot qui date de l'an 1308, ça nous fait simplement conclure que l'originalité et l'imagination dont jouissaient les écoliers français du dix-neuvième siècle leur fait défaut.

Nous vous prierons, finalement de vous souvenir que la tâche que nous nous imposâmes fut de rendre *l'opus sanctissimum* en langue shakespearienne (tâche digne, il nous semble, d'une future régente de zozologie shakespearienne), et de ne point nous laisser choir dans les abîmes des patois amerdicains ou autres.

Croyez, cher Monsieur, à l'expression de nos sentiments les plus pataphysiques et zozologiques,

(Dear Sir,

We note that you are a devourer of lady regents in disguise, which reminds us (deepest apologies) of the devil, *keen collector*

of bachelor May Bugs, plump inn-keepers and young fiancées
. . .(*Complete Works*, Vol. VI, p. 245).

We thank you for your kind postcard on the subject of the word; our thoughts on the matter are as follows.

Although there can be no doubting the respect we feel for James Joyce, we do not see what that late master has to do with the small matter under discussion. What we are dealing with here is the invention of a new word, not the redeployment of a word already in existence. (Moreover, in parenthesis in our edition of *Ulysses*, [Bodley Head, 1937] the word in question, on page 740, is written simply SHIT.)

But even accepting that the word thus magnified can be found in the works of the said master, our researches lead us to believe that he was not the one who actually invented it. The word, which you spell so elegantly and surely as *chaillte*, is found, in any respected dictionary as: *shit, shite*. In other words, *shite* is merely an alternative form of *shit*, an alternative that dates back to the year 1308. What connection, then, is there between the use that Père Ubu makes of this new and most holy word MERDRE and that made by Joyce, the master, the satrap Shittuck, and others, of the archaism SHITE?

In this the 82nd year of the pataphysical era, what further praise can a modest British lady regent heap upon the word? And yet it seems to us that half the beauty of this word, which sounds forth as if from the archangel's trumpet, lies in this: that the casual listener should at first think it to be a fairly ordinary word, familiar to him, only to realize a second later, with astonishment and delight, that it is in fact something totally different. That is what makes any deformation at the beginning of the word or any modification of the vowel unthinkable. Equally essential is the sonorous, savoursome "r", to be added in a thousand different ways according to taste—crescendo, diminuendo, staccato, etc. etc., *after* the word. MERD...RRR—SHITT...RRR. *Shittr*— that divine word, revealed to us from On High, fits the required conditions exactly, perfectly, *simply*,—are we to infer that the high dignitaries of the Collège de 'Pataphysique are rising up against simplicity? We should add that this word, so gentle, so explosive, so threatening (according to taste)—is one that we ourselves use on a daily basis, and we can bear testimony to the fact that it is easy to employ, never fails to produce the desired effect, and is entirely inoffensive to the user.

As for the current usage by Amer(d)ican schoolchildren, it leaves us pretty well cold. If they use a word dating from 1308, then we can only conclude that they lack the originality and imagination enjoyed by French schoolchildren in the nineteenth century.

We would beg you, finally, to remember that our self-imposed task was to render the *opus sanctissimum* into the language of Shakespeare (a task worthy, it seems to us, of a future Shakespearian regent of zozology), and not to fall into the abysses of Amer(d)ican or any other slang.

We beg you to accept, dear Sir, our most pataphysical and zozological compliments,)[45]

At the end of the same *Cahier* 20 in which Shattuck's article was published, we read of a *Banquet Grand-Breton* held in honour of *la Régente de zozologie shakespearienne, Barbara Wright and Sieur Gaberbocchus, Stefan Themerson*. The account of the banquet states that "*Barbara Wright donna une interprétation vocale de sa traduction de Merdre, Shitttrrr, (en roulant le 'r')*" ("Barbara Wright gave a vocal rendition of her translation of *Merdre*, 'Shitttrrr' (rolling the 'r'").[46] We can therefore assume that Shattuck's argument was demolished. Barbara emerged triumphant.

Barbara had an instinctive feel for what sounded right. She did not slavishly stick to the same translation for a word if it appeared in different contexts or with a different grammatical function. *Il n'est pas bête, ce bougre* says Ubu. "This fellow's no fool", translates Barbara. *Bougre, c'est mauvais!* he says about Mère Ubu's cooking—"Hell, it's awful!" translates Barbara. One of the most frequent mistakes made by translators of *Ubu Roi* has been to use too contemporary an idiom for Ubu's pompous or archaic terminology. Franciszka Themerson's

---

[45] Please note that the English version is only a rendering. The original French must be referred to in order to hear Barbara's voice. My translation.

[46] *Cahiers du Collège de 'Pataphysique*, 20, p. 85.

drawing shows the "*Voiturin de phynance*" (Act III Scene 4) that carries the taxes that Ubu personally collects with the help of the Palotins or Salopins. *Voiturin* is an archaic word. "*Allons, messeigneurs, voiturez ici le voiturin de phynance*," commands Ubu. In her translation, Barbara captures Ubu's vain and laughable aspiration to speak in what he believes to be an aristocratic idiom: "Come on, my Lords the Salopins of Finance, convey here the phynancial conveyance." This is quite different to Simon Watson-Taylor's tough guy idiom: "Come on in my lords of phynance, you sons of whores, wheel in the phynancial wheelbarrow."[47] Barbara's version subtly captures the weakness that underlies Ubu's bombast. What makes his braggart behaviour amusing is the knowledge that it will evaporate at the very first hint of danger or injury to his precious person, as when he trips and falls in front of King Wenceslas at the beginning of the play: "*Oh! Aïe! Au secours! Je me suis rompu l'intestin et crevé la bouzine*". And in Barbara's translation: "Oh! Ow! Help! I've ruptured my intestine and busted my *dungzine*" (*bouzier* being a dung-beetle).

Barbara was probably at her superb best when riding to battle. Her letter to Sainmont demonstrated to the dignitaries of the Collège de 'Pataphysique that she was a master of their language as well as her own, that her rapier-work in French equalled theirs in sophistication and virtuosity. Her letters, whether in French or English, were works of art in themselves.

Barbara did not only go into battle on her own account. In 1975 I had spotted a letter from her to the editor in the *TLS*, headed "I and myself".

Sir,—Is no one going to defend you from Norman Knight's amazement, horror and accusation of having perpetrated "an appalling grammatical solecism" with your heading to Rosemary Dinnage's review of *Private Chronicles*: "Between I and myself"? Miss Dinnage quotes Barbellion's "Now I and myself are on comparatively easy terms with one another": in my understanding, "I" and "myself" here have nothing to do with grammatical nominatives or accusatives, they simply refer to two sides of the

[47] *The Ubu Plays*, tr. Cyril Connolly and Simon Watson Taylor, New York: Grove Press, p. 43.

same person. As it were, "Norman" and "Knight." Is Norman Knight equally amazed and horrified by Rimbaud's "Je est un autre"?

At the bottom of the letter Barbara gave her London address. I was living abroad at the time, but I determined to conserve this piece of information and cut the letter out. When I got back to England a few years later, I wrote to Barbara about my interest in Jarry. She invited me straight over. From that moment I benefited, totally undeservedly, from her hospitality, her generosity and her unique letters, latterly e-mails, and I suspect that is the case for many people who came in contact with her.

I was going to end on that note but decided to look up the diarist, Barbellion, on the question of "I and myself". The fact that he and Barb-ara shared the first four letters of their names to make the word "barb"* will not have escaped her. Here is the 28-year-old Barbellion's most famous passage, concerning death:

> To me the honour is sufficient of belonging to the universe . . . nothing can alter the fact that I *have* lived; *I have been I*, if for ever so short a time. And when I am dead, the matter which composes my body is indestructible—and eternal, so that come what may to my "Soul", my dust will always be going on, each separate atom of me playing its separate part—I shall still have some sort of a finger in the pie. When I am dead, you can boil me, burn me, drown me, scatter me—but you cannot destroy me: my little atoms would merely deride such heavy vengeance. Death can do no more than kill you.[48]

*Barb A sharp process curving back from the point of a weapon rendering extraction difficult. (Shorter Oxford English Dictionary)

---

[48] W. N. P. Barbellion, *The Journal of a Disappointed Man*, London: Chatto & Windus, 1920, p. 72 (Bruce Frederick Cummings, September 7, 1889–October 22, 1919).

Grabinoulor Has Fun with Language and Makes New Friends: *The First Book of Grabinoulor* and beyond
Debra Kelly

Part I: Making Friends With Your English Translator

Barbara Wright's preface to her 1986 translation of *The First Book of Grabinoulor* stresses aspects of the multi-faceted epic *Les Six Livres de Grabinoulor* which provide a telling entry into the complex linguistic universe created by Pierre Albert-Birot and into the translator's relationship with it.[49] She opens on the character of Albert-Birot himself, already eighty-eight when they met, giving the reader a few details of his life at the time (with his much younger wife Arlette, a key figure in bringing his work to new readerships) and then long before he met her, stretching back to his childhood and adolescence in the late years of the nineteenth century.[50] Arlette Albert-Birot's postface is similarly tellingly entitled "Making friends with Grabinoulor", and the introductory section to this piece exploring aspects of *Grabinoulor* within the context of its structure and dexterity with language takes its cue from the pre- and post-faces of that English translation.

Pierre Albert-Birot was born in Angoulême, near Bordeaux, in 1876 and died in Paris in 1967. A painter and sculptor by training, and only an occasional poet until 1916, Albert-Birot had lived alongside the adventure of modernity, seemingly unmoved by the artistic revolution of Cubism and untouched by the poets who were to become some of the contributors to his avant-garde revue *SIC*, until his meeting in 1915 with the Italian Futurist painter, Gino Severini

---

[49] *The First Book of Grabinoulor by Pierre Albert-Birot*, translated by Barbara Wright, London: Atlas Press, 1986. Pierre Albert-Birot, *Les Six Livres de Grabinoulor*, published for the first time in its entirety by Editions Jean-Michel Place (Paris), 1991 (with a new print run in 2007). There were partial publications of either chapters (in numerous *revues* from 1918 to 1988) or of books, notably *Grabinoulor, épopée* (Books I and II), Paris: Denoël et Steele, 1933 and *Grabinoulor* with a preface by Jean Follain, Paris: Gallimard 1964 with selections from Books I, II and III.

[50] For details of PAB's life see Pierre Albert-Birot, *Autobiographie*, suivi de *Moi et moi*, preface by Arlette Albert-Birot, Troyes: Librairie bleue, 1988; and Marie-Louise Lentengre, *Pierre Albert-Birot. L'Invention de soi*, Paris: Jean-Michel Place, 1993.

and through him, with Apollinaire.[51] Out of this paradoxical situation for a poet and editor who would find himself for a few years in
that second decade of the twentieth century at the forefront of the
Parisian avant-garde, has been spun a web of personal mythologiz-
ing, as well as a selection of anecdotes retold in more or less similar form by Albert-Birot in interviews and in a short autobiography
which conceals more than it reveals.[52]

After briefly introducing us to Albert-Birot the man both in old
age and in youth, Barbara next picks out the importance of *SIC* and
specifically a key moment in the life of the Paris-based literary and
artistic revue of which Albert-Birot was the founder and editor for
54 issues from 1916 until 1919. This is the first staging in 1917 of
Apollinaire's play *Les Mamelles de Tirésias*; Barbara thereby deftly
provides the reader with an artistic and historical context, and an
essential reference point, for Albert-Birot's personal aims as an artist,
and then as poet and editor. These aims and principles had origi-
nated in a different perspective from that of the dominant currents
of the avant-garde of the period. They then begin to run parallel
around the time of the First World War, converge during the war,
and finally diverge once again with the rise of Surrealism as a "movement" rather than as the creation of the "sur-real" as conceived by
Apollinaire (the term was in fact used for the first time by him to
describe *Les Mamelles de Tirésias* on which Albert-Birot was to be
such a close collaborator). The title of *SIC* provides an initial insight
into an understanding of Albert-Birot's entire poetic project as well
as of his literary and artistic revue from the moment of its conception
onwards. In later interviews the poet was explicit about the title's
significance: "It means that it is 'thus', it's the absolute cry, of course
the initials stand for sound, idea, colour, but what it really means is

---

[51] For details, see the books referenced above. *Autobiographie* also details the
"birth" and life of *SIC*.

[52] Again, see the books referenced above. It should also be noted that the original
research for the reading of PAB's work here was a PhD thesis on Albert-Birot
conducted at Birkbeck College, London University (awarded in 1992) under the
supervision of Madeleine Renouard. The analysis of Grabinoulor presented here
forms part of Chapter 5 of the book based on that thesis: Debra Kelly, *Pierre
Albert-Birot. A Poetics in Movement, A Poetics of Movement*, London: Associated
University Presses, 1997.

a desire to affirm something."[53] *SIC* is indicative, then, of Albert-Birot's philosophical position, and of his perception of and relationship to the world around him: positive, affirmative, joyful. It is revelatory, too, of his artistic relationship to word and image. In his own accounts of *SIC*'s gestation and birth, Albert-Birot remains categorical on the constructive aspects that he continued to consider the propelling force behind the revue, and by extension behind his whole creative enterprise. This emphasis on the positive, on the constructive nature of his aesthetics and of his artistic principles was to bring him into conflict with other forces in the avant-garde. The notorious evening of June 24, 1917, picked out by Barbara to situate Albert-Birot within the artistic ferment of the First World War avant-garde, proved to be the apex of *SIC*'s activity. The programme for the play carried a sketch by Picasso on the cover; inside there were poems by Max Jacob, Jean Cocteau, Pierre Reverdy and Albert-Birot, and also a woodcut by Matisse. The uproar created by the staging of the play was documented and celebrated by Albert-Birot and his contributors in the pages of *SIC*.[54]

Barbara's preface to the English translation also brings to the reader's attention—the reader of course who is likely to be encountering PAB (as he was generally known by those around him) for the first time—the immense range and quantity of Albert-Birot's creative output. His artistic production covers a whole range of possible modes of expression: figurative paintings and sculptures, still life, landscape, cubist and abstract canvases, experimental forms of what he called "*la peinture absolue*" ("absolute painting"), traditional versification, punctuated and non-punctuated poetry and prose, sound-generated poetry, visual poetry, translation, theatre, autobiography. And then, as Barbara writes: "Grabinoulor sprang, fully armed, from

---

[53] Pierre Albert-Birot, Interview with Pierre Berger, *Les Lettres françaises*, 1057, December 3, 1964. There are several variations on this explanation in interviews with Albert-Birot.

[54] A whole issue of *SIC*, no. 18, June 1917 is dedicated to covering aspects of the staging of *Les Mamelles de Tirésias*, and the following one features selections from the critical (often in both meanings of the word) reaction in the press; Albert-Birot seems to enjoy the hostility it provoked from the "establishment". The facsimile edition of *SIC* provides in its accompanying "Documents" a reproduction of the programme for the play. *SIC* (54 issues, Paris, January 1916-December 1919), Paris: Editions Jean-Michel Place 1980, 1993.

his creator's brain (and heart) in a forest in Royan in 1918 [. . .] Gra-binoulor himself—the *person*" [note Barbara's term and emphasis] "– among all his other talents 'can naturally travel at the same time in the past and the future'. Actually, he can do absolutely everything he wants to, yet to my mind he is only slightly more marvellous than his creator". Both PAB and Grabi had made a new friend in Barbara—and with that friendship, a voice (however incomplete, given the six volumes of this epic on which Albert-Birot would continue to work until the 1960s) in English.

Grabinoulor, begun in 1918 and worked on more or less contin-uously for the fifty years of poetic creation that followed, is the key to the universe created by Pierre Albert-Birot. It is constantly present, simultaneously informing and informed by the other texts within its orbit, a process of constant movement rather than a fixed point of reference, a work that is both structuring and perpetually being constructed. *Les Six Livres de Grabinoulor* hold an enigmatic status, lying at the very heart of twentieth-century artistic preoccupations, yet denying rupture with the past. Resisting facile categorization and mechanical theorizing, its complexity and density stimulate a ques-tioning into the nature and processes of literary creation—and hence into the processes of language.

Barbara's final point in her short introduction is indeed linguistic and concerns Albert-Birot's non-use of punctuation throughout the six volumes of *Grabinoulor*. The use of free verse in poetry was, of course, by 1918 a well-established form, but even amongst the avant-garde the conception of an extended work in prose such as that which *Grabinoulor* would become was new and little, if ever, practised, and certainly not developed to the extent that Albert-Birot would do. In her postface to the English translation Arlette Albert-Birot adds further insights into the "parthenogenesis" of *Grabinoulor* and its unpunctuated narrative form. She particularly notes PAB's own care-ful recording of dates and precisions concerning the fact that the first published "fragment" of *Grabinoulor* (in *SIC* in June 1918) and of the twenty-four further chapters which made up the original "First Book" (composed between 1918 and 1920, published in the Editions SIC in Summer 1921) predated Joyce's *Ulysses* (and its famous non-punctuated soliloquy) which was published in French in early 1922, and heard for the first time in public in 1921. Barbara is sensitive to the necessity of the "one continuous flow" of *Grabinoulor*, and it is on what this uninterrupted flow of energy brings to the work, what it "allows" to happen within the narrative, that I will focus for the remainder of this piece dedicated to Grabi's adventures in language and the friends he makes there (as well as those he avoids).

Part II: The "Excessive" Grabinoulorian Epic and the Nature of its Quest

Although the English translation provides only a short glimpse into the vast textual universe constructed in the full six volumes, this *First Book* holds the essential keys to an understanding of what would follow. Amongst the key chapters in this opening volume is the second chapter, "Grabinoulor tries to find perpendiculars and parallels"—in which, typically, due to some imperfection in his current world (in this instance the fact that a small statuette does not sit perpendicular on its plinth), Grabi sets about re-fashioning a shelf, his apartment, his apartment block, his street, Paris, the centre of the Earth and then its continents, the rotation and shape of the Earth . . . . causing chaos, but marvelling at all the new things that are created until, under pressure, he returns home and the world resumes its usual shape and functions. Grabinoulor "*l'ubiquiste*" is himself a poet-creator (and frequently assimilated by Albert-Birot to God, with irony and humour; Grabi is usually unimpressed by the universe created by the "Old Decorator") and frequently contemplates his own restructured universe admiringly. Grabinoulor inhabits a new space, the space that comes into being between two worlds: one world which is "real", that of daily, lived experience and one which is "imaginary", a world of endless, limitless possibilities created in language by the writer. This is a space which, once transcribed, becomes the text, a space which may appear at times chaotic, sprawling, unmanageable, but which is in fact structured and coded geometrically—hence the need for the perpendiculars and parallels of Chapter 2 in this *First Book*. In *Grabinoulor* and in PAB's work more generally (both on canvas and in poetry), geometry is linked not only to structure, but to the quest for truth and knowledge. Just as abstract art may appear to be intensely subjective, but can only be truly apprehended by rigorous analysis and an understanding of its internal "language", so geometry plays a crucial role in Albert-Birot's epic narrative. One problem explored already by Albert-Birot in this *First Book*, then, is the transposition of how we apprehend what we perceive to be "real"; another is how we (re)structure space according to our desire. And the theme of desire and its generating force runs all through this opening *First Book*, taking form in the expression of Grabi's appetite for the multiple pleasures of life (food, sex, love, nature, luxury, beauty . . .). Yet for all this often excessive, rampant and apparently unhindered (by morals, by social mores, by time and space) desire, the poetic space of *Grabinoulor* is assembled with geometric precision and the narrative is constructed according to a logic that holds within it a "geometric chaos", an apparent chaos that simultaneously engenders it and contains it. It opens out ceaselessly into a more vast space (a space of the imagination).[55] Just when the surface structure threatens to fragment, at a "limit point", an order is re-established. The narrative of *Grabinoulor* proliferates (in subsequent books, the chapters become much longer than in this *First Book*), but returns always to the one "fixed point" of the narrative (if a "fixed point" itself can be in perpetual movement . . .), that of the body of Grabi himself in a quest for a return to wholeness, completeness. The limitless space of the narrative of *Grabinoulor* allows a reorganization of time and space. It is paradoxically in prose, in an apparently linear narrative aimed usually at its conclusion (the straight line identified elsewhere in Albert-Birot's work with the mortality of man) that the poet finds the most perfect figure of his desired geometric figure, the circle (identified with the curved line of God, representing "immortality" and a release from the tyranny of human time). The immensity of the narrative of *Grabinoulor* strives to dissolve external temporal and spatial limits and to construct a space where the reign of the inner time and unlimited space of creation are assured. One way in which this is achieved is through the unpunctuated prose identified as so important by Barbara in her preface. The textual mobility of

---

[55] The idea of "geometric chaos" comes from Book IV of *Grabinoulor* when the Angel Gabriel on a visit to Paris, admires a painting on Grabi's wall—it is in fact Albert-Birot's own *La Guerre (1916)*—and Grabi describes the abstract canvas in this way (IV, 13, 528).

the unpunctuated prose allows a structure that retains a form while allowing mobility—right up to the final full stop which the editors of the definitive version of *Les Six Livres de Grabinoulor* chose to end on, although in another version of PAB's own typescripts the final line actually curls back up onto itself, in the form of a "full stop" that is actually yet another concentric circle that refuses any ending.

The system of excess that operates in *Grabinoulor* has been commented on by several critics, most notably by Marie-Louise Lentengre, who suggests that food and sex keep the text moving, to which Nicole Le Dimna perceptively added "walking", for Grabi and the text itself are indeed perpetually *"en promenade"*.[56] The first two are certainly the obvious, outward, surface figures of excess especially in the first two volumes. From *The Third Book* onwards the chapters themselves lengthen, and carnal and alimentary excess tend to give way to proliferating discussion and debate in the many encounters between Grabi and the other protagonists, some recurrent, some making one, often unforgettable appearance. However, there is another way of considering the excess of the narrative. A close, in-depth reading of the narrative as a whole suggests that it is fundamentally motivated by a quest for knowledge—knowledge about history and myth, artistic creation and human existence, the nature of humanity and of the divine. The quest is necessarily, therefore, proliferating, self-perpetuating, excessive, for its aims to be "total", all-encompassing, and that excess is double-edged, for the nature of excess is both having and losing, the quest for knowledge is simultaneously a gathering-up and a dissemination, accumulation and loss. The quest for truth, for all quest for knowledge is a quest for truth, opens onto the infinite and the eternal; it is never-ending, perpetually present yet also always incomplete, the goal constantly escaping out of reach. The discourse of excess, necessarily limitless and multiple, also risks disintegration; the state of excess is problematic.

However, the positive side of this economy of excess is the dynamic *"joie de vivre"* commented upon by virtually every reader of *Grabinoulor* and certainly much appreciated by his English translator.

---

[56] See Marie-Louise Lentengre, "Les appétits hyperboliques de Grabinoulor", *Lectures* 2, 1979, 143; Nicole Le Dimna, *Jeux et enjeux chez Pierre Albert-Birot*, Chieti: Marino Solfanelli Editore, 1989, 73-94.

Grabi is born of PAB's early poetic work *La Joie des sept couleurs* and infused with the positive and vitalist "Esprit *SIC*". This becomes a philosophical, ethical and almost political position of the eponymous protagonist who takes a stance against all the inhibiting forces that oppress human nature as he transgresses any natural laws which normally prevent humankind taking total pleasure in the cosmos, enjoying every moment, every journey, and every chance encounter.

Part III: Making New Friends and Avoiding Others

It is on those chance encounters that we will bring this excursion into the adventures of Grabi with his English translator to a close (an open-ended close, it should by now be apparent). Many of Grabi's most joyous encounters entail, it will come as no surprise, food and sex: from the two girls on bicycles and his ravenous hunger in the very first chapter to his childhood friend Eugénie on whose amorous adventures the *First Book* closes, complete with cream puffs and chocolate éclairs. In a later volume, one of the most memorable episodes involves a visit and an outing with the Angel Gabriel whose appetites turn out to be of Grabinoulorian dimensions. Another is when Grabi meets Adam and Eve, but the list can go on and on . . . Conversations with PAB's favoured writers, philosophers, artists . . . With the Eiffel Tower, with figures from History and from Myth and Legend . . . With his favoured companions, his alter ego Furibar and later the little demon Bôfrizé, descended from his gothic cathedral to accompany Grabi . . . With those with whom he enjoys debating (and always gets the better of) such as M. Keskedieu (literally "what is god?") and M. Lérudi (literally a "learned man"). The recurrent questioning of M. Keskedieu forces Grabinoulor to take his own position with regard to the "Creator", and that position is a critical one. When M. Keskedieu asks Grabi "don't you think that he's the greatest poet in the world" (III, 11, 229-30), Grabi can only reply that this may be true: "but rather unfortunately he let himself become a playwright". M. Keskedieu never abandons the challenge, and Grabi never fails to find a rebuff, just as he always successfully escapes the threat of immobility, which for him would mean ceasing to exist. The ubiquity and perpetual movement of *Grabinoulor*, continually recurring as a definition of Grabi himself, is also what defines the narrative. The immobility that is considered to be the most dangerous situation that Grabi can experience is also a threat to that narrative. The immobile would appear to be not merely an absence of life force, but equivalent to a state of non-being, of void, of nothingness. Creation is generated from chaos, flux . . . Grabi does not appear to be in such grave danger, for he is a creature of language, and the nature of the material from which he is made allows for endless variation, repetition, profusion of meaning, an infinity of forms. In a glorious encounter with M. Lérudi, Grabi demonstrates the endless proliferation of language (in which the writer luxuriates, but which may cause endless problems for the translator, of course . . .) and which needs to be rendered in its original language (followed by a translation for meaning only, and certainly not as Barbara would have done it justice):

> comme vous le dites Lérudi capitales mais n'oubliez pas qu'il y a aussi les grands capitaines les grandes capitales les gros capitaux les beaux chapiteaux les petits chapeaux les grands chapeliers les gros capitalistes les lourdes capitations les vieux capitols les lâches capitulations les interminables chapitres les vins capitaux les gens bien capités et mêmes les rois décapités (VI, 3 828-29)
> (as you say Mr Learned capital [questions] but don't forget that there are also great captains great capitals great amounts of capital lovely capitals little caps large cappers fat capitalists heavy capitations old capitols cowardly capitulations interminable chapters capital wines people well-capped and even decapitated kings)

Paradoxically, it is a process of language—the writing down of events and discussions—that threatens movement with immobility; the immobile may be on the tip of the narrator's pen. Grabi somehow always manages, as a creature of language within the text, to remain in a state of ever-becoming. Nonetheless, from time to time an unease sets in, becoming gradually more apparent, a state of uncertainty where the "divine" qualities with which Grabi is invested may no longer continue to function, and there are two recurrent figures for whom Grabi never has time to stop and talk: M. Stop himself, and M. Oscar Thanatou, and he courteously avoids them and moves on his way. These are encounters and "friends" that it is best to avoid. Indeed, if there can be no unquestionable certainty in life (as the continual debate in *Grabinoulor* attests), then logic would suggest that death does not exist either and therefore human-kind must be immortal. Already in *The First Book of Grabinoulor* Grabi is amazed, after his unsuccessful quest to find the "Empire of the Dead" despite consulting Virgil and Dante, that mankind has believed in death for so long, and instead a belief in the continu-ing life and interrelationship of all the elements in the cosmos is affirmed. In Barbara's translation:

> and Grabinoulor was knocked sideways by the thought that so many men over such a long time had been able to believe in death and had been pleased to drive themselves to despair by imagining a dead world opposite the living one as if such a thing were really possible and Grabinoulor saw very clearly that his mother was the rose blooming beside him and the forest he was walking through and the birds flying and the children playing the lovers passing by the light illuminating them and then he was filled with joy and he admired the world

The proof of death as a definitive state is constantly refuted: Poire as a mature person may be "dead", but Grabi can still meet him as an adolescent. Contradictions constantly surface concerning death, and its nonexistence does not prevent Grabi conversing with those who are apparently dead, most notably with that most famous of the dead, the Unknown Soldier who turns out to be a childhood friend of his. If humanity would only recognize this fallacy and stand together against the illusion, the concept of death would be abolished. As the narrative progresses, Grabi becomes more despairing of his fellow men, alien as they often are to his ability to make the ordinary extra-ordinary. Creation may not be such a salvation, merely an addition to the excess already in production that finally serves no purpose, and is merely another form of the excrement of living matter, less a hope than an expression of inevitability. Finally, however, the salvation, if salvation there is within *Grabinoulor*, is that we continue to cre-ate, not without despair and disillusion, but with them, and despite the knowledge that: "we have this thing death under the skin we so desire this ideal-nothingness" (IV, 11, 494) as Furibar expresses it. Grabi disagrees, but Furibar is not the antithesis of Grabinoulor; he is one and the same just as being and nonbeing, excess and nothingness, truth and illusion are not opposites but situated just each side of a thin dividing line. The life force with which all the works of Albert-Birot reverberate—and which Barbara so admired—pulses not because they are written against death (even if Oscar Thanatou is never given the time of day by Grabi . . .) or the void, but as an attempt to encompass and embrace it, perhaps to fill it, to nullify it. An impossible quest perhaps, for at any moment excess may topple over into nothingness. The value of the work lies finally, nonetheless, in this sustained quest, not to deny those aspects of existence that we habitually think of as opposites, but to reconcile them because they live so closely together. Grabi's unlimited adventure is undertaken not only in the knowledge that the line at any moment risks being broken, but that the attempt to find meaning constantly escapes us in a universe where the ultimate "*point de fuite*", the point where the parallels coincide, can never be reached:

> Grabinoulor happy to have legs a strong heart and a good spleen was going along and going along with such gusto and his mind so "elsewhere" that he took at this pace the path of Infinity what a walk even for a man who walks well and still will he ever reach this unique point where parallels meet (III, 17, 364)

We leave Grabinoulor walking out, on a quest for the point where the parallels meet, the point where being and meaning are one, and which can never be reached. Little wonder that Barbara the translator is a friend of Grabinoulor in his adventure in language.

In 1986 Barbara ended her preface to *The First Book of Grabinoulor* with a translation (for the first time in English) of the final poem of PAB's first published book of poems *Trente et un Poèmes de poche* dating from April 1917 (Editions "SIC"):

Nature has no full stops
Day isn't separated from night
nor life from Death
enemies are united by their hatred
Vae soli
Why? Because he doesn't exist
This book is not
separated
from those that will follow it
and I'm going to stop
using full stops

Seventeen years later, in one of her final projects, Barbara would return to the *31 Pocket Poems*, translating them all in an edition for Paul Rosheim of Obscure Publications (2003). In that preface Barbara writes: "I called Arlette that evening, to communicate my enthusiasm, and left a garbled message on her mobile phone. When she called back later it was to tell me that she was in Cherbourg, where she was surrounded by a group of PAB fans to whom she had just given a talk—on *Trente et un Poèmes de poche*! And one day soon we are going to meet, and go over every single word of the translation, as we did with Grabi, until we are satisfied that we can do no better. And this we have just done, in July 2003."

The point where the parallels meet is never reached, for the journey is circular.[57]

---

[57] The translated edition of *31 Pocket Poems* is dedicated "to PAB and Arlette": *31 Pocket Poems. Pierre Albert-Birot*, translated by Barbara Wright, Wisconsin: Obscure Publications, 2003. This piece on Barbara and Grabi is dedicated to Barbara, PAB and Arlette. Arlette Albert-Birot died in July 2010.

The Artist on Her Trapeze: Barbara Wright's 99 Variations on a Theme by Raymond Queneau
David Bellos

Some time in 1957, Barbara Wright took a school exercise book in which she had been writing out some personal thoughts in Italian, opened a new page and wrote in capital letters in blue biro: EXERCISES IN TRANSLATION. There followed a pencil version of the first of Raymond Queneau's already famous *Exercices de style*, later overwritten in blue biro.[58]

Barbara had already translated two short stories by Queneau, as a commission: *At the Edge of the Forest* and *The Trojan Horse*. But as she said to a Belgian scholar in later years, once she had translated some Queneau, she was hooked.[59] She had corresponded briefly with the writer in 1954 over those first translations, but did not yet know him personally. So it was with obvious trepidation that she dared to send him the first batch of the *Exercises*, to see what he would think, in the early summer of 1957.

Barbara was a meticulous translator, and I guess a meticulous person altogether when it came to words and facts. She always consulted friends in France and elsewhere on obscure or difficult points,[60] and only pestered her authors as a last resort, with queries that nobody else seemed able to answer. But the *Exercises in Style* was an exercise in a different kind of translation. The work consists of 99 variations ranging in length from a paragraph to three pages on the same trivial, futile story of a man who treads on toes in a Paris bus and then some time later gets upbraided for having his overcoat button in the wrong place. The variations play with a range of different literary devices, from rhetorical techniques such as homoteleuton, apocope and synchysis, to poetical forms (sonnet, haiku, alexandrines), games with language register (pompous, vulgar, bureaucratic), and with

---

[58] Lilly Library, Bloomington, Indiana, Wright.mss, folder "Exercices de style". All further quotations from manuscripts and correspondence are from this archive.

[59] Draft English typescript of a reply in French to Andrée Bergens, dated February 21, 1972.

[60] A couple of years later, Jean Queval commented on the mysteries that she had flagged in *Zazie dans le métro*. He provided her with a fascinating and far-reaching set of linguistic and cultural notes.

languages themselves (Italianisms, sound-translation into English), and to changes in effect (reactionary, apologetic, hesitant). The initial question in Barbara's mind was, very obviously: can such a language-based, formally structured and apparently nonsensical work be translated? What is the meaning of a translation of such a work? Would the author even want it to be translated? That is why she sent her first trial versions to Queneau himself, asking him if he wanted to see more. He took a long time to answer. She must have been pretty encouraged to get this reply in tiny neat handwriting on a tiny sheet of paper with the *nrf* letterhead:[61]

23 août 1957
Chère Madame,
Je suis très impressionné par votre entreprise. Je ne suis pas moins curieux de voir le résultat. Aussi, s'il vous était possible de me communiquer non pas "some of the translation", mais l'ensemble, ce serait pour moi d'un bien grand intérêt. Je suis impatient de voir comment vous avez résolu les problèmes de traduction qui se posaient.

[Dear Madam, I am very impressed by your enterprise. I am equally curious to see the result. So if it is possible for you to send me not "some of the translation" but the whole of it, it would be of the greatest interest to me. I am impatient to see how you have resolved the translation problems that were raised.]

Within a few weeks Barbara had finished a substantial draft and sent it to Queneau in two batches. He took a while to reply this time as well:

13 novembre 1957
Chère Madame
. . . Il me semble que tout cela est excellent. Je dois dire même que je suis saisi d'un inexprimable saisissement devant la réussite de ce travail. Je me permets de vous en faire de bien immenses compliments. J'avais toujours pensé que rien n'est intraduisible,

---

[61] Nouvelle Revue Française / Gallimard publishers.

j'en vois là une nouvelle preuve.

[Dear Madam, [. . .] It seems to me that all of this is excellent. I should even say that I am seized with inexpressible astonishment at the result of this work. Please accept my immense compliments. I had always thought that nothing is untranslatable, and here I see a new proof of it.]

Barbara continued to polish off exercise after exercise over the winter and by the spring she was down to her last few queries, which she finally sent to Queneau in April. For each piece, she carried on writing her drafts by hand in follow-on exercise books—the red ones you used to get at the post office in England with the shiny back cover printed with tables of Imperial weights and measures, including furlong, chain, scruple and fathom (the last two at least well-suited to the translator's task)—on the right-hand page only, in pencil first, then overwriting in blue biro, and annotating herself in red and blue crayon, especially when she had to count up occurrences and repetitions.

Barbara knew French very well, of course, but there were a great number of things in Queneau's erudite and playful games that pushed her towards the resources all translators use—dictionaries, encyclopaedias, and reference works. From her notes on facing pages we can see that she used the OED for definitions, the *Gradus ad Parnassum* for information on rhetorical figures, and Harrap's for French words she didn't know. We can see that she didn't know *funambules*, *acculer*, and *canicule*—rather odd gaps for a scholar of French such as she was, but reassuring to the rest of us, for we all have to look things up some of the time.

Barbara translated the majority of the 99 exercises "straight", that is to say, playing exactly the same game as Queneau. A text in French telegraphese can be represented pretty directly in English telegraphese, and a begging letter in French makes a begging letter in English, it's just the words, the rhetoric, the formulae and the tiny linguistic touches that constitute the tone of whining that have to be exchanged. Indeed, the most striking thing about the work and its translation—we now have to say, its translations, because the

Exercises have appeared in dozens of languages—is just how transposable nearly all of it is. In fact, unbeknownst to Barbara, a German poet, Ludwig Harig, was proceeding along exactly the same lines as she at almost exactly the same time, in Saarbrücken. But for some of the texts, Barbara struck out on her own. And this is where it begins to get really interesting.

Exercices 29, 30, 31 and 32 are retellings of the story in the main French tenses in which a story can be told: *passé indéfini, présent, prétérit,* and *imparfait.* As the distinction between preterite and imperfect is barely grammaticalized in English, Barbara decided to replace this set with her own variations on English story-telling verb forms: *past, present, reported speech* and *passive.* The last two are therefore in effect Barbara's own variations, and do not correspond directly to anything Queneau invented (though he could have, of course: there are many more exercises than the 99 in the book, but on that, more later).

It was when she was faced with Queneau's exercises in hybridized prose—when the object of the exercise was to show French so to speak in bed with Latin, Italian and English (exercises 70, 81, 83, and 84)—that Barbara followed her own natural and stupendously witty bent. For Queneau's Anglicism exercise (70), she showed how English can play the same game in a mirror:

Un dai vers middai, je tèque le busse

is replaced by:

One zhour about meedee I pree the ohtobyusse

Even more curious and clever is her rewriting of Queneau's macaronic, *Sol erat in regionem zenithi.* Why, you might ask, should a text written in Latin need to be translated at all? Because Queneau's bad Latin is a mask for French, and Barbara has to turn it into a mask for English. So the original *Autobi passebant completi* turns into *Omnibi passebant completi.* Even better: *Sancti Lazari stationem ferrocaminorum passente devant . . .* has to be turned into *Sancti Lazari stationem ferramviam passente by . . .* , since it is not *chemin de fer,* but *railway*, that requires misrepresenting. In fact, Queneau was particularly interested in the transformation of the Latin text and provided Barbara with various famous examples of nineteenth-century English macaronics, one of which, in view of the winter that preceded my writing this piece,[62] really needs to be quoted:

> *Anno incipiente happinabit snowee multum*
> *Et gelu intensum streetas coverabit wislidas . . .*

The most famous and spectacular of Barbara's reinventions are exercises 83, 84, and 96, where she replaced, respectively, Queneau's *Italianismes* with "Opera English", his homophonic translation *Pour Lay Zanglay* with "For Ze Frrench", and Queneau's *Paysan* with "West Indian". These are real "Exercises in Translation", as the whole original manuscript is called: Barbara sought and found a target language functionally equivalent to the object-language of the original exercise, and trained herself to write in that register, dialect, or discourse, depending on the jargon you want to use.

Reading the manuscript of the *Exercises* is for me personally a fascinating experience, because I see in it an example of something I myself experienced many years later: faced with a paradoxical, strenuous linguistic challenge, the translator, by dint of trying, and then of letting go, actually learns to write and to become himself or herself, from the very process of learning to translate a given text. I do not think Barbara would have learned how to free herself from the original sufficiently to write "Opera English" if she had not already been formed by the practice of translating the preceding 82 exercises, which serve exactly as Queneau intended them to: as *exercices*, training routines, and practice.

Barbara's exertions were nearly over by the summer of 1958. The book was published by Gaberbocchus Press, a small London publishing house run by the extraordinary Polish poet, novelist and film-maker Stefan Themerson, with whom Queneau was in fact well

---

[62] Winter 2009–10, which was particularly severe with very heavy snowfalls across Europe and North America.

acquainted. Themerson did the book proud.[63] He allowed Barbara to commission a French composer, Pierre Philippe, to write the music for the Exercise entitled "Ode", which is something you will find in the English edition but not the French. Themerson illuminated witty, anthropomorphic initials for the title of each Exercise, and devised a photocollage permutation of Queneau's face for the frontispiece. Visually, Barbara's *Exercises in Style* is a more accomplished book than the Gallimard original.

It is also a historic monument. It marks the start of Barbara's fame as a translator, the start of a warm and fruitful relationship with Queneau and his many chums in the Collège de 'Pataphysique and the OULIPO, and through them, her acquaintance with Eugen Helmle, Queneau's principal German translator, who helped her with later Queneau volumes . . . and who also helped me, many years later, when I started to translate Georges Perec. But it also preserves texts that have effectively disappeared in France. That is because Queneau reissued the *Exercices de Style* in 1973 and replaced a number of the original pieces with new exercises. Specifically, *Exercices* 61, 63, 66, 67, 69 were dropped and replaced by those now printed as *Ensembliste, Définitionnel, Tanka, Translation,* and *Lipogramme* So Barbara's English translation is now the only place (apart from scholarly libraries) where you can read two of the permutation exercises (61 and 63), and those entitled "Reactionary", "Haiku" and "Feminine". When the English translation was reissued in 1981, Barbara chose not to follow Queneau—she did not translate the five new pieces and left the old ones where they were. So the English *Exercises in Style* has as it were grown apart from its apparent source text. It stands now not only as a perfect example of the creative translator's art, but as a trace of otherwise vanished fragments of Raymond Queneau.

In fact Queneau did not write only the 99 *exercices de style* that are in the published book (or the 104, if you add the extra five of the 1973 edition). In a 1963 luxury edition of the work, he appended a list of "123 imaginary exercises", a list which paradoxically includes all the 99 published in his 1947 first edition—but excludes two that

---

[63] "Je suis enchanté" (I am delighted), wrote Queneau to Themerson in a letter dated December 9, 1958.

he wrote in 1954 especially for the launch of a record of the musical version of the texts sung by the Frères Jacques. The idea of the *Exercices*, once invented, has endless potential.

Translating Beckett Before Beckett: the Translation of *Eleutheria*
Régis Salado

Translation is a discreet art in more senses than one. Firstly because it can only be done by virtue of an original text, which, albeit as a rule inaccessible to the reader or listener of the translation, still comes first. This is apparent from the book covers, which feature the name of the translated author, relegating that of the person who actually wrote the words that are about to be read, to the inside, normally in small letters. Discreet, too, because it relies entirely on choices left "to the discretion" of the translator, that strange double agent of Literature whose ancillary character, "at the service" of another, is compensated for by the freedom offered to him or her by the language itself, which is always prodigal in alternative solutions when it is a question of transferring an act of writing from one language to another. Studying a translation, then, means appraising the discreet liberty that has been exercised in the narrow framework of services rendered to the original text.

In the case of Barbara Wright's English translation of *Eleutheria*, the first thing that needs to be recalled is the unusual situation in which the translator found herself, committed to work for a non-authorized cause, given that Beckett consistently opposed publication of the work. Only after that will I turn to specific aspects of her translation, published by Faber and Faber in 1996. It appeared after Jérôme Lindon took the decision to publish Beckett's original text with Editions de Minuit in 1995, pressured by Barney Rosset, Beckett's American publisher, who had commissioned a first translation from Michael Brodsky.[64] To give a better idea of the quality of Barbara Wright's work, her translation will be compared both with Beckett's original text and also, in detail, with the first English translation of it. In this way, on the basis of some telling examples with no pretensions to systematic treatment, the art of the translator will, it is hoped, be made apparent.[65]

Before Beckett, despite Beckett

The phrase "Beckett before Beckett" means, firstly, that he wrote *Eleutheria* before the plays which made him famous in the 1950s. Although written in January–March 1947, and thus preceding *Waiting for Godot* by only a few months, this work with its cast of 17 characters and complex decor is separated from the plays which would make Beckett's name famous by a bigger distance than that of strict chronology. It was his first attempt at writing a long play in French, and *Eleutheria* differs from his later works in several decisive ways, notably in its less rigorous writing and composition, the fact that the social milieu it portrays, albeit a fantasized caricature, is identifiable (a bourgeois family), and finally in the explicit nature of several

---

[64] For the lively history of the publication of *Eleutheria* and the preceding manoeuvres, see Jérôme Lindon's *"Avertissement"* dated January 23, 1995, pp. 7–11 of the Editions de Minuit edition. See also the "Foreword" by Martin Garbus (Barney Rosset's legal representative in the *Eleutheria* case) and S. E. Gontarski's "Introduction", pp. iii–vi and vii–xxii respectively of the Foxrock Inc. edition of *Eleutheria*. (Foxrock Inc. was a publishing company set up in view of the forthcoming publication of *Eleutheria* in English, after Barney Rosset was fired by Grove Press, which he had founded and where he had published Beckett's works for over thirty years). The story is further documented and contextualized by Marius Buning in "*Eleutheria* Revisited", a lecture given at Ciudad Real, Spain, on December 2, 1997 (Buning was then President of the Dutch Samuel Beckett Society; the lecture is available at www.samuel-beckett.net/Eleutheria_Revisited. html). Buning gives a detailed account of the stormy career of Beckett's play from 1947 when it was written, to the reception of its various published versions in 1995–96. Additionally, he offers a close examination of some aspects of Brodsky's translation, highlighting several major faults and harshly criticizing certain gross errors. While sharing unreservedly his judgment that Barbara Wright's translation is superior to Michael Brodsky's, the present essay does not reproduce either the choice of examples subjected to analysis or the focus of Buning's study, concentrating instead on Barbara Wright's work.

[65] Editions referred to here are: Samuel Beckett, *Eleutheria*, Paris: Les Editions de Minuit, 1995; *Eleutheria*, translated by Barbara Wright, London: Faber and Faber, 1996; *Eleutheria*, translated by Michael Brodsky, New York: Foxrock Inc., 1995.

passages where Beckett explains his great themes—wanting things to come to an end, waiting in vain, or putting life in the dock—in a more didactic way than he ever did again. Evidently, in *Eleutheria* Beckett had not yet completely found his dramatic voice. The traits of social satire, the use of elements close to popular comedy, and the inclusion of sometimes explanatory monologues, indicate that Beckett's dramatic aesthetic was here partly compromised with a type of realism that he would reject radically from *Waiting for Godot* onwards. So it was not by chance that after some efforts to get it read and performed in 1949–1950, Beckett did not want *Eleutheria* to come to the notice of the public. Apart from the defects of a work which he considered imperfect, Beckett may have had two more reasons for sidelining *Eleutheria*: on the one hand, the over-personal nature of certain aspects of the play (Victor Krap, the young protagonist who has "gone on strike from life" and cut communication with his family and friends, has more than one point in common with Beckett), and on the other, the fact that several of the play's situations and some fragments of its dialogue were re-used in later plays, especially *Waiting for Godot* and *Endgame*.

The translating of *Eleutheria* into English not only contravenes Beckett's prohibition on publishing it, but goes on to aggravate the offence, in that if it seems already illegitimate to make this text available, bearing in mind the author's clearly expressed desire, translating it into English "before Beckett" compounds this problematic legitimacy in view of the fact that Beckett translated his plays from French to English himself, and insisted on this practice of self-translation by virtue of a rigorous writerly ethic. It was a painful process for him, but the ordeal of translating himself was, for Beckett, the price to be paid in order to preserve the integrity of his work in both the languages in which it was written. In the light of all this, the English *Eleutheria* is "unauthorized" twice over, both as a text published against the author's will, and as a translation of a work that Beckett could and would have translated himself if he had wanted a translation at all. Barbara Wright was not ignorant of the difficulties of her position in translating a text by Beckett "despite Beckett", as she makes clear in the "Translator's Note" that prefaces her translation of *Eleutheria*:

It was in no spirit of hubris that I agreed to translate *Eleutheria*, it was rather with a feeling of apprehension. Who am *I*—who is *anyone*—to claim to be able to translate Beckett? We all know how he suffered in translating his own work, and that the only reason he did so was that he couldn't accept other people's even most dedicated efforts. And *Eleutheria* is a play he refused to translate himself, and said he wanted to jettison. (Wright, v)

Beckett's own English translation of *Eleutheria* does not exist, but this non-existent text necessarily haunts whoever undertakes a translation of the play. How would Beckett have proceeded if he had decided to translate *Eleutheria* into English, as he did most of his other plays originally written in French? And what is the right way to translate the style, which is still in a state of becoming, not recognized as an integral part of his oeuvre by the writer? How can one reproduce this text, which is in some respects unfinished, without giving in to the temptation to project onto it, by a sort of loyalty to Beckett's oeuvre, the retrospective shadow of the great plays that followed it? There are so many questions like these, posed here in general terms, but which must have resonated in the actual work of translating it. This at least is what Barbara Wright seems to imply, when she declares in that same "Note":

I studied all Beckett's self-translations, and decided that I must never use a word that he would not have used. On the other hand it was out of the question to try to imitate him. I was tempted, for a time, on the very first page of *Eleutheria*, to write: "Immobility of Madame Krap", and "Incomprehension of Jacques"—a formulation Beckett often uses, as, for instance, "Impatience of Willie's fingers". (Wright, vi)

In the light of these factors the path followed by the translator seems to have been a steep and arduous one, beset on one side by the danger of using a word that Beckett would not have used, and on the other by the danger of merely mimicking Beckett's own translations. While it seems possible to avoid the trap of mere imitation by studied vigilance (and the examples given in the "Note" show that the translator was able to resist the temptation to "Beckettize" her text), the first temptation presents greater problems. By basing her work on an analysis of Beckett's self-translations in order to discard from her version any term that he would not have used, the translator must, surely, have run the risk of diminishing something that did belong to the text: its dissimilarity to Beckett's later plays. Since *Eleutheria* was not recognized by Beckett as worthy to figure among his works, it would not be surprising if the price of the translator's stated resolution to be loyal to the author was a degree of unfaithfulness to the particular character of the text she was translating. As can be seen, translating Beckett before and in spite of himself is not a straightforward undertaking.

The difficulty of this situation was, however, lessened by the existence of the American translation by Michael Brodsky. His translation was both defective (as we shall see later) and solely responsible for breaking Beckett's ban on publishing *Eleutheria*. In other words, had Barney Rosset not forced his hand, Jérôme Lindon would almost certainly have respected Beckett's wish; but in view of the American publisher's insistence on bringing out the translation, Lindon's decision was the only way to remedy the absurd situation in which the original text was inaccessible while an unauthorized, and moreover unsatisfactory, translation was available to the public. This is an important point: it was only after Editions de Minuit had brought out the French edition of *Eleuthéria* that Beckett's English publisher, Faber and Faber, asked Barbara Wright to translate it. The harm had been done, and since the American translation had been the "crime weapon", there was nothing wrong in producing another translation to repair the damage. In that sense, Barbara Wright's translation, always scrupulous, often inspired, and remarkably consistent in its translatorly choices, certainly did a good restoration job. It did justice to Beckett's work, providing English-speaking readers with a quality text. What specific choices effected this restoration? It is now time to get inside the translator's workshop, in amongst the words and languages she used as tools for her work.

Translator at work
Reading a text and its translation simultaneously is a bothersome but

enlightening task. At least two viewpoints are superimposed on one another: one is that of the reader of the original text, and the other is that of a particular type of reader—the translator. Any translation is after all firstly a reading, a reading which is made present in the text produced by the translator. Reading this text in its turn, in the light of the original, our vision is enriched: to the first reading is added that of the translator, on the basis of which a return is effected to the first text, which we can then read differently. The interest of reading a translation in the presence of the original is therefore not just the opportunity it offers of evaluating the quality of the translation, but also the comparison, sometimes word-by-word, with another reading of the same text whose meaning and effects are redeployed in the translation. Such redeployment is revealing because of the choices that have produced it, the difficulties, sometimes insurmountable, that it has encountered, and the solutions found for these difficulties. When two translations of the same text are available in one language, as is the case with *Eleutheria*, the comparison between original and translations is admittedly harder work, but the profit derived from going backwards and forwards between them all increases likewise. In the acrobatics involved in this double or triple comparison, the possible meanings contained in the first text are seen under different lights, obliging the reader to home in on words just as a camera can home in on images. The following sections will attempt to do this in detail.

Opening

On frappe. Silence. On refrappe.

Mme KRAP, *avec un sursaut.*—Entrez. (*Entre Jacques. Il présente à Mme Krap un plateau sur lequel se trouve une carte de visite. Elle prend la carte, la regarde, la remet sur le plateau.*) Eh bien? (*Incompréhension de Jacques.*) Eh bien? (*Incompréhension de Jacques.*) Quel abrutissement! (*Jacques baisse la tête.*) Je croyais vous avoir dit que je n'y étais pour personne, sauf pour Mme Meck.

JACQUES.—Oui, madame, mais c'est madame la sœur de madame, alors j'ai cru . . .

Mme KRAP.—Ma sœur!

JACQUES.—Oui, madame.

Mme KRAP.—Vous êtes impertinent. (*Jacques baisse la tête.*)
Montrez-moi cette carte. (*Jacques présente à nouveau le plateau,
Mme Krap reprend la carte.*) Depuis quand ma sœur s'appelle-t-
elle madame Piouk?

(Beckett, acte I, 21-22)

A knock. Silence. Another knock.

Mme Krap (*with a start*)—Come in.

*Enter Jacques. He holds a tray out to Mme Krap; it has a visiting
card on it. She takes the card, looks at it, puts it back on the tray.*
Well?

Jacques doesn't understand.

Well?

Jacques doesn't understand.

What an idiot!

Jacques hangs his head.

I thought I told you that I wasn't at home to anyone but Madame
Meck.

Jacques—Yes, madame, but it is madame's sister, madame, so I
thought . . .

Mme Krap—My sister!

Jacques—Yes, madame.

Mme Krap—Impertinent fellow.

Jacques hangs his head.

Show me that card.

Jacques holds out the tray again. Mme Krap takes the card again.
Since when has my sister been called Madame Piouk?

(Wright, 9-10)

The opening scene of a play is obviously a strategic site. The first
lines of dialogue evoke a tone, an atmosphere, a situation, while at
the same time the audience is discovering the setting and characters.
The bourgeois interior of the Kraps' house, described in the stage
directions coming just before the above dialogue ("*corner of the little
sitting-room* [. . .] *round table, four period chairs, armchair, lamp-
stand, wall-light with shade*"), provide an identifiable setting, which

suits the opening scene between mistress and servant. Their dialogue would lie within the conventions of popular theatre except that the names mentioned, Madame Meck and Madame Piouk, introduce a touch of fantasy from the start, at odds with the realist setting.[66] It should be noted that these comic-sounding names are plays on words in both the languages spoken by Beckett, since Meck sounds like *mec*, "guy" in French, and Piouk sounds like "puke" in English,[67] the starting-point for a lexis of bodily waste-products that includes, of course, Krap.[68] What is more, Beckett was to reuse this suggestive name some years later, with the variation of an additional "p", in *Krapp's Last Tape*. In short, under the trompe-l'oeil appearance of popular comedy, we are introduced into a matter in which "matter" is indeed very present from the first, as will not surprise anyone who knows their Beckett.

Barbara Wright's translation of the first lines invites two comments. The first concerns the Mme Krap's exasperated sigh, "Quel abrutissement!", translated as "What an idiot!" The word Beckett uses, *abrutissement*, is a curious one in this context—one would expect "*Quel abruti!*", which would have been both clearer and more idiomatic. Considering that Mme Krap is stigmatizing Jacques, one may even think Beckett guilty of slight clumsiness in using an impersonal term to apply to a person. *Abrutissement* might be used of an activity, or a spectacle (in the 1920s people talked of cinema as an *abrutissement* for the crowds; today people might say that television

---

[66] The everyday name Jacques is also an obvious one, denoting a domestic servant. "Jacques" is used in classical French to mean a peasant (hence the expression *jacquerie*, peasants' revolt, and *faire le jacques*, play the fool). But the meaning quickly broadened into a general term for a manservant (this gives rise to several exchanges between Jacques and his master in Diderot's *Jacques le fataliste*). So Beckett's choice of the name is understandable as a way of playing with the comedic code: by his very name, Jacques incarnates domesticity, becomes his own name which is also the name of his job, an identification which is labelled as parody by the character's excessive servility.

[67] The possible meanings of the name include the equally unpleasing ones suggested by its closeness to the French word *plouc*—dowdy, bumpkin.

[68] The name of Mlle Skunk, fiancée of Victor Krap (whose name ironically joins victory and excretion) enters into the paradigm of the monosyllabic names that make sense in English, making an effectively noisome contribution to the play. When he tells her, later in the play, that she is "sickeningly ugly" (Beckett, 54), Krap links Mlle Skunk to the "puke" collection.

is a "mass *abrutissement*"), but it is not naturally used to refer to an individual, unless to specify that he or she is in a state of *abrutissement*. If Beckett wanted Mme Krap to comment on the situation, and not, as seems more probable, address her remark to Jacques, he should really have written "*C'est d'un abrutissant!*" The meaning would then have been very different, since in the context of *Eleutheria* the words could have taken on a "meta-theatrical" meaning as a judgment on the play itself (the character of the "Spectator", who appears in Act III, will draw the play in that direction, giving it a Pirandellian touch). But this is a very unlikely conjecture; the context pleads clearly in favour of the first interpretation, that Mme Krap is calling Jacques stupid. So by translating it by "What an idiot!", which leaves no ambiguity about the fact that Mme Krap is stigmatizing Jacques, Barbara Wright both clarifies the meaning and rectifies a slight incongruity in Beckett's French, helping the flow of the dialogue. This choice seems obvious when one reads Wright's translation alone; whereas Michael Brodsky's version shows that he has no idea:

> Mme KRAP. [. . .] (Jacques uncomprehending) What brutishness!
> (Jacques lowers his head)
> (Brodsky, 7)

Closer to the original term in literal meaning, the word chosen by Brodsky, "brutishness", is nonetheless unsatisfactory in that it is a poor rendering of the sense that the context shows to be needed, i.e. a personal insult. In this regard Wright's translation is more convincing because it is closer to the intention of the utterance (its content as an act of language), as can be understood with reference to the situation. The liberty taken by Wright makes sense in relation to the dynamic of the dramatic exchange, and if she opts for "normalization" by choosing to translate it as though Beckett had written "*Quel abruti!*", it serves to improve that dynamic.

The second point bears on the choice Wright made to transform the verbal phrase "*Vous êtes impertinent*" by a noun-phrase: "Impertinent fellow." Comparison with Brodsky's more literal translation— "You're being impertinent"—confirms that it is a meaningful choice, whose *pertinence*, here too, deserves praise. Not only does the syntactical transformation avoid the use of a verbal form which is overweighty in English, but the use of the term "fellow" by the mistress to her servant is entirely suitable in a context in which the conversation is ruled by class distinctions. "Fellow", here, has connotations of contempt and so expresses Mme Krap's wish to mark the social gulf between her and Jacques; a wish also expressed, in Wright's translation, by the fact that Mme Krap no longer addresses Jacques in the second person but relegates him to the state of a non-person, annulling his presence in some sort. The freedom claimed by Wright in adding a word that is not in Beckett's text and in modifying the form of the address, is therefore fully justified with regard to the economy of the dialogue, the more so because it is a text for the stage, and the actress will find the phrase "Impertinent fellow" a useful support for her rendering of the role. Robert Pinget, whom Beckett asked to translate his radio play *All That Fall* (*Tous ceux qui tombent*), stressed the idea of "tone" when asked about his work as a writer. Through this discreet example of the word "fellow" inserted in the English text, we can see that Wright, to whom we are also indebted for some superb translations of Pinget, was also in agreement with him on the question of tone.

Registers

> VITRIER.—Il y a un temps pour le travail, madame, et il y a un temps pour les amabilités. Il faut que Michel apprenne à les distinguer de bonne heure.
> Mme MECK.—C'est votre fils ?
> VITRIER.—Quand je travaille, je n'ai pas de famille, madame.
> Mme MECK.—Vous appelez ça travailler ? Vous ne faites que bavarder.
> VITRIER.—Mon cerveau travaille sans cesse.
> (Beckett, acte II, 74)

> **Glazier**—There is a time for work, madame, and there is a time for amiabilities. Michel must learn at an early stage to distinguish the one from the other.
> **Mme Meck**—Is he your son?

Glazier—When I am working, I have no family, madame.
Mme Meck—You call this working? You do nothing but talk.
Glazier—My brain never ceases to work.
(Wright, 70)

GLAZIER—There is a time for work, Madame, and there is a
time for pleasantries. Michel must learn to tell the difference
between them, early on.
Mme MECK—It is your son?
GLAZIER—When I am working I have no family, Madame.
Mme MECK—You call that working? You just chatter.
GLAZIER—My brain works non-stop.
(Brodsky, 69)

One of the pleasures of reading *Eleutheria* is the way Beckett
entertained himself by playing with the gaps between the social
standing of his characters and the different registers of the language
they used. The most eloquent case is that of the Glazier, who comes
on stage in the second act and invades Victor's bedroom. The flavour
of this character is conveyed by his elaborate mode of speech, so it is
important that the translation brings out this clearly marked idiolect.
The choice made by Wright of the relatively rare term "amiabilities"
to translate "*amabilités*", the careful turns of phrase "learn at an early
stage", "to distinguish the one from the other" for "*apprenne à les dis-
tinguer de bonne heure*", reproduce this effect of "distinction" which is
perceptible in the Glazier's speech. As for the emphatic and definitive
line, "*Mon cerveau travaille sans cesse*", its solemnity is beautifully
preserved by the choice of verb and the syntax of "My brain never
ceases to work". There is nothing really spectacular in these choices,
but their aptness shows brilliantly when compared with those of
Brodsky's translation. His rendering of "*amabilités*" by "pleasantries"
in the sense of "civilities" may be understandable, but the syntax of
the next phrase, which follows on from that of the first in Beckett's
text, is lost in Brodsky's translation. But it is above all the way he
renders the last line in this extract by "My brain works non-stop", a
trivializing formula, poles apart from the measured, weighty effect
sought by Beckett for the character of the Glazier, which enables us

to appreciate by contrast the aptness of Wright's choices.

The second instance of playing on the registers of language is a still more obvious one. It is an extract from Act III where we see Jacques, the servant, going into Victor's room and trying to re-establish friendship with him. Jacques has just been harshly treated by the character of the Spectator, who took offence at the (supposed) fact that Victor should have entrusted himself to him, a mere man-servant, and the Glazier expresses surprise at his lack of reaction. It is at this point that Jacques makes the Glazier a reply worthy of the best traditions of classical theatre (which Beckett parodied in a play written in his youth, *Le Kid*), a reply framed as an impeccable Alexandrian line, with a break duly occurring at the caesura.

> VITRIER, *à Jacques*.—Vous supportez qu'on vous traite de cette façon ?
> JACQUES.—Il vous faut un valet. Souffrez qu'il en ait l'âme.
> (Beckett, acte III, 134)

> **Glazier** (*to Jacques*)—Don't you mind him insulting you like that?
> **Jacques** (*nobly*)—You need a servant here. Let his soul fit the part.
> (Wright, 134)

> GLAZIER—You put up with being treated in this way?
> JACQUES—You need a manservant. Allow him to have the soul of one.
> (Brodsky, 145)

Barbara Wright is manifestly very sensitive to Beckett's parodying intention. She doesn't hesitate to reinforce it in her translation by the addition of a stage direction to the actor: "(*nobly*)", which is not in the original. Above all, she provides a metrical equivalent to the Alexandrian line which perfectly respects the symmetry of its two halves. Finally, she found especially attractive lexical and syntactical solutions to transpose the heightened register and effects of the original ("fit the part" is particularly apt in that it introduces a theatre motif, echoing the reference to classical drama perceptible in the original). Here too, comparison with Brodsky's translation, which sacrifices the verse form and seems not to recognize Beckett's play with classical language, underlines by contrast the quality of Wright's work.

Play on words

Beckett loved playing on words. This is a major ingredient of verbal comedy that he used lavishly in the texts of his French plays, prizing immediate effect over subtlety (see e.g. the play on the words "*coite/ coït*" in *Fin de partie/Endgame*). *Eleutheria* is no exception; it contains plenty of plays on words which sometimes strike one as unlikely to have occurred to a native speaker, either because they are so rough or because they seem a little forced. When Beckett writes in French one sometimes feels that plays on words were a temptation to him, that the language which the writer had learned, mastered and thoroughly made his own, was still enough of a foreign language for him to see it as a form, a material, a territory to explore, so that he saw similarities between words which a native French writer would not perhaps have been aware of in the same way. Ionesco, Adamov and Beckett all wrote for the theatre in French "from outside", modifying it and playing with it.

For the translator, a play on words is an opportunity for extra inventiveness, a challenge to his or her verbal dexterity. But a pun is also a dangerous shibboleth and possible stumbling-block. Four examples, out of many, caught my attention. The first, which I will quote without more ado, shows that the same pun can have two equally successful translations.[69]

Dr PIOUK.—Et vous, cher monsieur, votre rôle est-il bien déterminé ?
M. KRAP.—Il est terminé.
(Beckett, acte I, 40)

Dr Piouk—And you, dear monsieur, is your role well delineated?
M. Krap—It's eliminated.
(Wright, 33)

---

[69] Notice in passing that Barbara Wright retains "monsieur", preserving the French setting of the play.

Dr. PIOUK—And your role, my dear sir, is it very clear-cut?
M. KRAP—It is being cut.
(Brodsky, 30)

The translations of the second example, unfortunately, do not display the same equality.

M. KRAP.—J'aurais voulu être content, un instant durant.
Mlle SKUNK.—Mais content de quoi ?
M. KRAP.—D'être né, et de ne pas être encore mort. (*Silence.*) Je conclus rapidement, car je sens que ma femme approche.
Mlle SKUNK.—Ta fin ?
M. KRAP.—Ma FEMME Cette catastrophe.
(Beckett, acte I, 57)

M. Krap—I would have to be contented, just for a moment.
Mlle Skunk—But contented with what?
M. Krap—With having been born, with not yet being dead.
Silence.
I'll conclude rapidly, because I can tell my wife's descending . . .
Mlle Skunk—Your life is ending?
M. Krap—My *wife*. That catastrophe. Is descending on us.
(Wright, 52)

M. KRAP—I would have wanted to be pleased, for a whole moment.
Mlle. SKUNK—But pleased with *what?*
M. KRAP—With having been born, and with not yet having died. (A silence) I am finishing up quickly, for I have a feeling my wife draws near.
Mlle. SKUNK—The end of life?
M. KRAP—My WIFE. That catastrophe.
(Brodsky, 52)

This passage highlights the talent of Barbara Wright, not only reproducing the partial homophony of the French words (*fin/femme* rendered by life/wife), but takes account of the whole expression which gave rise to the misunderstanding in Beckett's text. Translating "*ma femme approche*" by "my wife's descending" enables her to expand the original play on words, developing it in the following line "Your life is ending?" in which "ending" represents "descending", so that the sound-matching now involves two words twice over (wife/ life, descending/ending) where Beckett only played on one partial rhyme (*femme/fin*). Another masterstroke is her prolongation of this play into the line which concludes the sequence, which Wright completed with a verb separated from its subject by a full stop, giving this addition an inchoative, syncopated sound that is entirely Beckettian in nature. The metaphysical and theatrical way that the motif of "end" is underlined as a catastrophe[70] seems justified since this motif is definitely part of Beckett's text. For the rest, the linking of the theatrical and normal meanings of the words "end" and "catastrophe" is especially brought about in the role of M. Krap, who, like Ionesco's Bérenger in *Le Roi se meurt*, ceaselessly refers to his imminent death as the end of a role (see the foregoing example of the play on the words "*etermine/terminé*" which immediately precedes M. Krap's death at the end of Act I). Wright's initiative in adding words to Beckett's original text should be acclaimed, all the more because reproducing the play on words was not easy, as can be seen from Brodsky's translation, from which it is signally absent.

The next example of a pun that I wish to dwell on is in Act II, in the dialogue between the Glazier and his young son Michel, whom he has asked to fix a light bulb:

MICHEL.—Où qu'il faut la mettre, monsieur ?
VITRIER.—Où qu'il faut la mettre ! Mais dans le . . . dans le . . . dans le truc, quoi, pas dans ton derrière, dans le . . . dans la DOUILLE, voilà, mets-là dans la douille, et grouille-toi, andouille. (*Pause.*) Au fond, il n'y a que les mots qui m'intéressent. Je suis un poète qui préfère s'ignorer.
(Beckett, acte II, 85)

Michel—Where do I put it, monsieur?

---

[70] Technically speaking a catastrophe is the final climax of a tragedy. Beckett was perfectly aware of this, giving one of his final plays the title *Catastrophe* (1982).

Glazier—Where do you put it! Why in the . . . in the . . . in the whatsit, of course, not in your behind, in the . . . in the *socket*, that's the word, put it in the socket, and not in your pocket, either, and don't knock it, idiot. (*pause*) Basically, it's only words that interest me. I'm a poet who prefers not to know it.
(Wright, 82–83)

GLAZIER—[. . .] in the SOCKET, there we go, put it in the socket, and timeclock it, don't half-cock it. Deep down only words interest me. I am a poet who would rather not know it.
(Brodsky, 82)

The way the mechanics of language suddenly take flight in the three terms "*douille, grouille, andouille*" in the French text is distributed twice and over more terms in Wright's translation (socket/pocket, and don't knock it/idiot), while Brodsky's version transfers the play on words to two verb phrases (socket/timeclock it/don't half-cock it). Although both translations differ somewhat from the meanings of the words used by Beckett, it has to be recognized that the divergence is better compensated for in Wright's version, mainly because of the effectiveness of the doublet socket/pocket (what linguists call a minimal pair).

To end this reflection on the art of playing on words, there is an authentic find from Barbara's pen. It is a passage that comes very early on in the play, a sort of expository passage where we learn a certain number of things about the wretched life led by Victor:

Mme KRAP.—C'est lorsqu'il [Victor] n'a plus rien à manger. Alors il fouille dans les poubelles. Il pousse jusqu'à Passy. Le concierge l'a vu.
Mme MECK.—Tu penses, les poubelles de Passy!
(Beckett, acte I, 28)

Mme **Krap**—It's when he has nothing left to eat. Then he rummages through dustbins. He goes as far as Passy. The concierge has seen him.
Mme **Meck**—Fancy! Dustbins in Passy!

(Wright, 19)

Mme KRAP—It's when he has nothing more to eat. Then he digs around in the garbage cans. He pushes on as far as Passy. The concierge saw him.

Mme MECK—When you think of it, the garbage cans of Passy.

(Brodsky, 16)

As in the previous example, we see the logic of the signifier at work in this exchange. The triad "*pousse, Passy, penses*" contain the same consonants,[71] and the assonance is partly taken up by "*poubelles*". This alliterative effect is not easily reproduced in English. However, for once Michael Brodsky almost gets there with "He pushes on as far as Passy", whereas Barbara Wright seems to have given up trying to find an equivalent for the playing with sounds which is so emphatic in the original. But far from giving up, she was merely retreating in order to leap further: she invents the wonderful formula which contains the assonances omitted from the previous line, while losing nothing of the sense: "Fancy! Dustbins in Passy!" In comparison with the ringing "Fancy!" and "dustbins", Brodsky's heavy "When you think of it" and "garbage cans" seem remarkably awkward.[72]

Allusions

Beckett's writings contain numerous literary allusions which the translator is charged with identifying and reproducing. Bearing in mind the change in cultural context it may happen that a given

---

[71] The same consonants are alliterated a few lines earlier in the French when Mme Krap announces straight out to Mme Meck, about her husband, "*Henri ne pisse plus*" (Beckett, 27).

[72] Besides the awkwardness of expression, the American term "garbage cans" is unfortunate because it helps distort the Parisian context, which is still strongly marked by place-names (as well as Passy, Montparnasse is also referred to in the play) and other references (M. Krap declares that his wife "*est restée un après-midi entier sous l'emprise de l'Exposition surréaliste*", Act I, 48, which may refer to the demonstration held in Paris in 1936). Wright's translation preserves this cultural and social context, but Brodsky's drowns it by using a large number of terms that are characteristic of the English spoken in the US (Buning sees this as one of the main problems of this translation).

reference which is straightforward for the reader of the original text, is somewhat obscure for the reader of the translation. In such cases the translator can either add a translator's note, or choose to make the translation more explicit than the source text. *Eleutheria* abounds in intertextual allusions, particularly in the lines given to the Glazier, who, as we know, goes in for heightened language. Three of the four examples given below are spoken by this character, to whom Beckett seems to have attributed part of his own literary culture. The first concerns Dante, whose tutelary shade hovered over Beckett's work for the whole of his writerly career. The example quoted below is relatively unobtrusive, but there are others, more marked, elsewhere in the play. So in Act I, when his wife complains about his posing "*Il se croit au cercle*", M. Krap, a man of letters (he is a writer who has stopped writing) answers, "*J'y suis. Au neuvième*" (Beckett, Act I, 29-30). Hence it is hard to ignore the network of references to the *Divina Commedia* in *Eleutheria*. This is however what Brodsky does when he uses "floundering around" to translate the words "*tourner et girer*", a play on the familiar expression "*tourner et virer*" which Beckett has endowed with a slight Dantesque twist by using a neologism close to the Italian word *girare*, which occurs frequently in the *Divina Commedia*. Wright, on the other hand, brings this intertextual reference to the fore by using the word "circles" (echoing the foregoing allusions) and translating "*âme en peine*" by a technically more exact phrase than Brodsky's ("soul in torment" fits better with the theological context of Dante than "lost soul").

VITRIER.—Qu'est-ce que vous avez à tourner et à girer comme . . . comme une âme en peine?
(Beckett, acte III, 121)

Glazier—What's the matter with you, dancing around in circles like . . . like a soul in torment?
(Wright, 120)

GLAZIER—What's the matter that you're floundering around like—like a lost soul?
(Brodsky, 127)

The second example is similar to the case quoted earlier, of a translation that makes an allusion explicit for an audience which can be presumed to be less familiar with the author referred to than the target audience of the original text. Wright took the decision to develop the allusion to Pascal to render it more readily understandable; and with good reason. However, this option has the drawback of infringing the principle of economy of expression which normally rules literary allusions in Beckett's writings. In this regard, Brodsky's translation, which risks being too elliptical for readers to capture the allusion, is closer to Beckett's own practice. Additionally, it allows the alliteration in the original to be heard better (*"l'espace de Pascal / Pascal's space*).

VITRIER.—[. . .] Silence! On dirait l'espace de Pascal.
(Beckett, acte III, 137)

Glazier—[. . .] Silence! It's like the eternal silence of Pascal's infinite spaces.
(Wright, 137)

GLAZIER—[. . .] Quiet! You'd think it was Pascal's space.
(Brodsky, 150)

The third example of playing with a literary intertextual reference is due to the libidinous and upsetting Dr. Piouk, who woos Mlle Skunk in the course of the play. In the third and last act, a brief exchange between the two characters, which owes its flavour to the knowledge that they have performed another kind of act offstage, is Beckett's opportunity to allude to Juvenal's famous phrase about Messalina—*"lassata (. . .) sed non satiata"*[73]; an allusion that might go unnoticed were it not underlined by the comment *"Souvenir classique"*. The two translations differ and Wright's seems to render the intertextual play more perceptible, because the word she uses is closer

---

[73] Juvenal's famous verse on Messalina, in *Satires* VI, is often quoted in truncated form. It reads: *"Et lassata viris necdum satiata recessit"* ("And exhausted by men, but not yet satisfied, she departed"). It was in reference to Juvenal's text that Baudelaire gave the 26th poem of *Les Fleurs du Mal* the title "Sed non satiata"; a poem which Beckett obviously knew.

to the Latin word which is alluded to (satiated/*satiata*).

Mlle SKUNK.—Je suis fatiguée.
DR. PIOUK.—Sans être rassasiée. Souvenir classique.
(Beckett, acte III, 157)

Mlle Skunk—I'm tired.
Dr Piouk—But not satiated. Classic memory.
(Wright, 159)

Mlle SKUNK—I'm tired.
DR. PIOUK—Without being sated. Classic souvenir.
(Brodsky, 178)

The final example, which comes towards the end of the play, refers back to Shakespeare's *Tempest*. Here two different attitudes to translation can be clearly identified. Wright, by dint of rendering the English text more archaic in flavour than the French original, chooses to quote Prospero's exact words in Act IV of *The Tempest*. She introduces an actual quotation which was not strictly speaking present in the original (at best, "*Notre temps ici est fini*" could be an approximate translation of Shakespeare's verse, which Pierre Leyris, for example, gives as "*Nos divertissements sont finis*"). In doing this, she ratifies the hypothesis that the Glazier is referring obliquely to Shakespeare here—a perfectly reasonable one given that it is entirely in character. She thus enables the English readership to recognize a well-known quotation which the French audience would probably not have perceived so clearly in the vaguer version chosen by Beckett. It could be said that here Wright goes in the same direction as Beckett's text, but goes further than he does. Would it have been better to settle for less, and translate literally as Brodsky does? For this once, the question will be left open, and I will use this eminently conclusive line to put an end to our own "revels".

VITRIER.—Notre temps ici est fini.
(Beckett, acte III, 162)

Glazier—Our revels now are ended.
(Wright, 164)

GLAZIER—Our time here is ended.
(Brodsky, 184)

Journey's end

The art of translation does not fit easily into theoretical systems. It is a matter of sensitivity, intuition, taste, inspiration, and is marked out first and foremost by specific details. That does not contradict the idea of overall consistency; specific choices are made within the context of the whole, and ruled by the rationale which guides every step of the translation and provides the specific principles which underpin the translator's work. Barbara Wright gives one of these principles in her preliminary "Note": not to use words that Beckett would not have used. In the course of my reading I have not caught her out on this point.

But have I not been taking sides in this romp through the three versions of *Eleutheria* open before me? Perhaps so. In any case I have not disguised my preferences, even at the cost of breaking the convention that academic writing should abstain from making value judgments. Rather than feigning neutrality, the choice made here was to express admiration and give free reign to the enthusiasm that takes hold of one when, in tackling a word, expression or turn of phrase, the translation displays its own genius and takes its place, without in any way usurping that of the text it aims to serve, in the rank of creations. And it is fortunate that *Eleutheria*, which began its career under unfavorable auspices, could profit from an English translation that is fully at the level of what one would expect on reading Beckett's own English. If we can today rejoice that this play, which its author disliked and was consigned for more than half a century to the forgotten pile of works destined to remain unpublished, has finally seen the light of day, it is also owed to Barbara Wright's creative talent.

Translated by Helena Scott

Barbara Wright Translates Pinget's *Le Chrysanthème:* Which Voice in English?
Martin Mégevand

The aim of this chapter is to grasp the ways in which the translation into English of a text by Robert Pinget enables or even compels the reader to return to the source text for clarification, and to raise questions about its translatability. I propose to examine the unique features of translating Pinget on three levels: Pinget's *phrasing* (tone, voice, rhythm—Barbara Wright and Robert Pinget both had musical training, and Barbara Wright pointed out the importance of this link with Pinget through music); the *cultural and intertextual content* (translation viewed as transposing a piece of knowledge from one culture to another). This question is naturally connected to that of the decisions involved in translation: to smooth out or maintain the points where the sense of the original is left open, in short, to decide on questions of *making explicit* that are part of the poetics of translation. Between Paul Mazon and Paul Claudel, both translators of the *Orestes* trilogy, Barbara Wright would set herself on the side of Claudel, but would sometimes find herself obliged to resort to Mazon's academic procedures, aiming to clarify the Greek text by explanations, at the risk of spoiling the effects of the original meaning by her efforts.[74]

Le Chrysanthème, a difficult text by Pinget, will serve as a convenient reference point to discuss these three levels of translation, which correspond to three modes of intervention: restoring, transferring and making explicit. I propose, then, to examine the celebrated verse that closes *Cette voix* and *Le Chrysanthème,* and which is presented at the same time as a poetic art and an art of living in poetry. The transition of this text from French to English provides a sort of summary of the negotiations of meaning which are involved in translation.

---

[74] Loraux, Nicole, "La métaphore sans métaphore", *Europe*, 1999, vol. 77, no. 837/38, pp. 242-264.

Robert Pinget's text	Barbara Wright's translation
Le Chrysanthème	**The Chrysanthemum**
Recomposer contre l'angoisse d'où qu'elle vienne ce rêve inoublié (17) . . . pour finalement le laisser bien loin (9), vieux plafond chargé d'oiseaux et de fleurs dans le goût d'autrefois (16), et progresser vers l'inaccessible (9) . . . sans repères, sans ratures, sans notes d'aucune sorte (12), insaisissable mais là (7) . . . auquel croire sous peine de ne jamais mourir (11).	To recompose as a defence against anguish, no matter where it may come from, that unforgotten dream (26) . . . then finally leave it far *behind* (9), an old ceiling cluttered with birds and flowers in the taste of a bygone age (19), and progress toward the inaccessible (11) . . . without *landmarks*, without erasures, without notes of any kind (16), *unattainable* but present (8) . . . which must be believed in for fear of never dying (13).
Remémoration d'instants privilégiés où tout semblait possible sans le secours d'aucune présence, mais le mythe reprend pied, les mots sont impropres à déconcerter la logique, les bouches qui les prononcent retrouvent un visage, on retombe dans l'affabulation primitive, ce conte pour nourrissons indécrottables.	The recollection of special moments when everything seemed possible without the aid of any other presence, but the myth is taking hold again, words no longer suffice to disconnect logic, the mouths that pronounce them find a face again, you fall back into primitive fable-making, this **story** for incorrigible babes in arms.

Martin Mégevand

First move: Restoring the tenor of poetry ("poetic fidelity")

In the translation, we see that the metrical progression is respected by the numerical proportion of syllables in the phrases. In the French version, the numbers of syllables in the phrases are distributed as follows: 17, 9, 16, 9, 12, 7, 11: the long and short sequences alternate in a decrescendo rhythm, and become progressively shorter, by one syllable at a time for the long sequences (17, 16 and then 12, 11). The English version scrupulously respects the progressive shortening and the rhythmical proportion, while the rendering into the other language means that the length of each phrase is significantly greater (26, 9, 19, 11, 16, 8, 13). But there is more to it than that: the internal rhymes (*believed in—never dying*) restore all its poetic force to the last phrase. Phonic unification is achieved through the labials (*no matter where it may come from*). Here, then, the translator's choice is to restore the rhythmic and sound effects in English.

Now this poetic fidelity can sometimes involve letting go of the strict meaning of the original. In practice, the translator has to choose between semantic proximity and phonic proximity. The pair "*inaccessible*" / "*insaisissable*" becomes "inaccessible" / "unattainable". Evidently the choice was to respect the cognate words. Another choice could have been "elusive" (closer in English to the meaning of *insaisissable*), but then the phonic and rhythmic link would have been lost. Now where "inaccessible" bears on the realm of sense (sometimes metaphysically, sometimes with the meaning of non-closure), *insaisissable* refers us to the aesthetic of approximation, i.e. failing to express something, in the realm of words and speech. Choice necessarily entails a loss: here it is a semantic one, compensated for by a skilful restoration of the close matching of the signifiers.

Second move: making explicit

The English version often makes explicit what is left implicit or undetermined in the French text. For instance, "*Recomposer contre l'angoisse*" is glossed as "To recompose *as a defence* against anguish": the writing project described thus by Pinget is understood in the English rendering in a univocal way, as a defensive operation, as a negative warding-off. In the French, by contrast, the ellipsis enables the phrase to embrace both the apotropaic meaning of the act of writing as defence, and the temporal meaning of a reversing of time's arrow to point towards childhood, which is justified here by the nostalgic tone of the passage, especially notable in the brief description of the *"plafond chargé d'oiseaux et de fleurs dans le goût d'autrefois"*.

The French text does not contain modal verbs, and this can be seen in the closing formula: *"auquel croire sous peine de ne jamais mourir"*. The expression can therefore be understood either in the sense "which can be believed" or "which must be believed". Barbara Wright removes the indecision: "which *must* be believed in". Here too, the English is more precise and less equivocal. It inclines decisively towards a moral meaning, and this is confirmed by other passages. Three notable examples: *"je m'en accommoderai"* becomes "I *must* put up with it"; *"au nom imprononçable"* becomes "whose name *may not* be pronounced". Finally, the famous *"conte pour nourrissons indécrottables"*, describing the primitive fable-making—the great account of Revelation—becomes "this story for incorrigible babes in arms". *Indécrottables* becomes incorrigible.

Making meanings explicit has the merit of clarifying the sense, but there is also a disadvantage which is inseparable from the process: it is often accompanied by an axiological orientation which seems difficult to avoid, because the translator is constrained by the practices and linguistic structures of the target language.

Making the sense explicit also leads to localising the meaning in space and time. The English version anchors the text spatially and temporally, thus also giving it a direction. " . . . *then* finally leave it far *behind*" is a gloss on *"pour finalement le laisser bien loin"*, introducing a spatial direction ("behind"); this is found again in "landmarks" for *"repères"*, and in the consecutive "then" for *"pour"*. What is rejected in this process of making explicit is the dimension of hesitation, rewriting, meditation. Second thoughts are discarded in favour of sudden decision, and since this text describes the work of the writer, such modification of the meaning has significant consequences. The text is as it were stabilized by these spatio-temporal ties. A strong effect of contextualization is introduced, where the source text is left indeterminate and fluid. And in the movement of the work of translation, the geometric location of the meaning seems to shift from the metaphysical sphere to the moral and psychological one.

Above all it is the univocal character of the text that strikes one on reading the translation, and it could not be otherwise. The expression *"sous peine de ne jamais mourir"* cannot, for example, be rendered into English without loss; in fact, "for fear of never dying" witnesses to two slight alterations in meaning. It introduces an inchoative, "dying", whereas *mourir* is the full stop which enables the subject to exit from the progressive degradation of his or her being. Likewise, "for fear of" is duly listed by the Collins dictionary as a translation of *"sous peine de"*: proof if proof were needed that the difficulties of translation really do arise from the transferring of one language system into another. Barbara Wright could have used "on pain of", which is semantically closer to *"sous peine de"* than the expression "for fear of". The option "for fear of" maintains phonic homogeneity within the phrase: the fricatives link "for fear" with "believed", and above all, the dominant vowel-sound /i/ is maintained throughout, whereas "on pain of" would have caused a rather too violent phonic rupture, because of its repeated vowel-sound /o/. But the consequence of this choice is to introduce a clear lexical shift instead, from the juridical, theological and psychological register of guilt to the strictly psychological one of fear. The sense of this passage thus moves from anguish to fear, where the French original marks a progression and an openness of meaning.

So this is a work of free translation, which avoids a word-for-word rendering to offer, at its most extreme, an interpretation, an accompanying, of the source text. This overt distancing was expressed by Barbara Wright when she compared her translating to the action of a musician: "translating someone and accompanying them in music is more or less the same thing." [75] That says it all, thanks to the phrase "more or less". Renouncing a word-for-word rendering, Barbara Wright's work ends up as a transposition, often a masterly one, of Pinget's work.

Third move: transposition
The first and most visible transposition is that of transferring one

---

[75] "Traduire quelqu'un, et l'accompagner en musique, c'est plus ou moins la même chose" ("Un auteur de rêve pour le traducteur", in *Europe, Robert Pinget / Jean Grenier*, Jan-Feb 2004, no. 897-898, p.171).

cultural code into another. This is the uncontested kind that leads, for example, to transpose *"jambes en coton"* into "legs like jelly". In this regard a passage from *Abel et Bela* is enlightening. In the French version, the two protagonists try to think of imperfect subjunctives to fill up the programme of the sublime transposition of their wretched lives.

Robert Pinget's text	Barbara Wright's text
Abel et Bela	**Abel and Bela**
Bela: Comme je vous plains, pauvre âme et que ne donnerais-je pour que vous fussiez serein. Ça y est, le subjonctif! Abel: Il faudrait quelque chose en assassiez *(un temps)* Bela: tracassassiez Abel: jacassassiez Bela: décrassassiez Abel: rapetassassiez *(un temps)* ce dialogue est une idée funèbre. On ne fera rire personne.	Bela: How I pity you, you poor soul. What would I not give for this to be a play . . . for this to be a play . . . To ease the anguish of a torturing hour. I've done it! That's Shakespeare! Abel: We'll need some more (Pause) Bela: I speak of peace Abel: A peace is of the nature of a conquest Bela: Expect Saint Martin's summer, halcyon days Abel: Farewell the tranquil mind. This is hopeless, we aren't going to make anyone laugh.

Barbara Wright replaces the play on subjunctives with four Shakespeare quotations. But this freedom with regard to the initial text is not arbitrary. Thematically, it references the Shakespearean leitmotiv of Pinget's original, and it takes up the structure of the four subjunctives by four quotations of equal length.[76] The transposition of one cultural code into another is thus justified, here, by the totality of the context of the French text. Admittedly, the risky choice might seem to add a dimension of quotation (and so learning or erudition) to the original text, and so to invite rejection from a nervous or disdainful translator. But quotations themselves are present in Pinget's original; at least, it seems hard to see mere chance in the occurrence of the word "stuff", which Pinget puts into Bela's mouth as he struggles to express himself, a dozen replies further on from this passage: "*j'entends que les mots, comment dire . . . étoffe même de notre . . . vous saisissez . . .*" In this context, for an ear that has been alerted by the repeated allusions to Shakespeare, this fragment points unmistakably to "such stuff as dreams are made on."[77] Here too, then, the freedom employed by the translator is justified and checked by the integrity of the text.

Restoring, making explicit, transposing, then: these operations are not, of course, always effected without a re-composition of the meaning but it seems that at the most difficult points a choice invariably has to be made between one of the three, the riskiest being to make explicit. Admittedly, making explicit endows the text with fluidity, but it tends to finish it off in and through its specificity.

In favour of these three operations, finally, we must necessarily note a still more decisive transformation of the French text with regard to meaning. This is not strictly speaking the tendency to make explicit, which has been discussed above, but the introduction of multiple linkings which have the effect of narrativization and of producing an account by added precision, where the original text remains undecided or imprecise. We will limit ourselves to a few examples from *Le Chrysanthème*. For instance, "*sans le secours d'aucune présence*" becomes "without the aid of any *other* presence", implying that there is already one presence—namely, that of the

---

[76] "To ease the anguish of a torturing hour": *A Midsummer Night's Dream*, Act V scene 1.

"A peace is of the nature of a conquest": *King Henry the Fourth*, Act IV scene 2.

"Expect Saint Martin's summer, halcyon days": *The first part of King Henry the Sixth*, Act I, scene 2.

"Farewell, the tranquil mind! [Farewell content]": *Othello*, Act III, scene 3.

[77] "We are such stuff / As dreams are made on": *The Tempest*, Act IV, scene 1.

narrator. The addition of this adjective gives the text a more realistic appearance, perhaps; it certainly reinforces a sort of referential illusion. Similarly, the account of the meeting with Théodore is regularly put into the past in the English version, whereas in the French it is in the present ("*ce garçon vient fleurir*" becomes "this boy *has come* to put flowers"). All these procedures tend to give the text a sort of narrative coherence which Pinget did not give to the French version.

A study based on the constraints of translation, and the advantages that can always be drawn from the constraints, would have led us to the same conclusions. Thus, for example, "*le tréfonds*" becomes, for lack of any other option, "the depths", in the plural, which seems a happy occurrence, since the plural implies the dispersing of intimacy, the impossibility of unifying the self, the dissolution of the subject in the depths.

To sum up, the best fate that could be hoped for Pinget's work in the English-speaking world would be publication in bilingual editions, or, at the very least, for the French texts also to be made widely available there. Barbara Wright's work of translation makes the English text into a place of long-drawn-out negotiation among three sometimes contradictory demands, between which a choice has to be made. Because of this, the English version is an interpretation of, an accompaniment to the French text. "Accompaniment", with its musical overtones, is definitely the most appropriate term to describe her work; on condition, however, that it is emphasized that accompanying does not mean remaining discreetly in the background, but on the contrary, highlighting, underlining, intervening. What strikes one on reading Pinget in English is that the translator has what is generally known as temperament—a term that is all the more justifiable in that it too has musical connotations.

Translated by Helena Scott

Nathalie Sarraute and the Strangeness of Language
Celia Britton

Language—its possibilities and limitations, and our attitudes towards it—is one of the major themes throughout Sarraute's writing, and as such has been much commented on.[78] In this chapter, however, I am going to consider it specifically in relation to translation: both the challenges that this thematization of language creates and the opportunities that it opens up for the translator. Working closely with Sarraute herself, Barbara Wright translated three of Sarraute's fictional texts, and also her autobiography, *Enfance* (*Childhood*), which is the text from which I will be taking my examples .[79]

Perhaps the first thing that the reader notices about these translations is simply that they keep very close to the original French texts. Not only is this almost mechanical fidelity rather uncharacteristic of Barbara Wright's usual approach to translation; it also means that in the more colloquial passages (which occur frequently, since much of the language of Sarraute's texts consists of representations of speech) they sometimes appear distinctly stilted. In an incident in *Childhood*, for example, Natasha's father is angry with her for stealing some sugared almonds from a shop, and particularly enraged by her innocent explanation that: "It was because I wanted them so much" (*C* 138); Barbara Wright's translation of his reaction is as follows:

---

[78] See for example Lucette Finas, "Nathalie Sarraute ou les métamorphoses du verbe", *Tel Quel*, 20 (1965), pp. 68-77; Celia Britton, "The Self and Language in the Novels of Nathalie Sarraute", *Modern Language Review*, 77 (1982), pp. 577-84; and Valerie Minogue, *Nathalie Sarraute and the War of the Words: an Introduction to the Work of the Distinguished French Writer*, Edinburgh: Edinburgh University Press, 1981. In her introduction Minogue describes Sarraute's novels as depicting "that war of daily discourse, spoken or unspoken, with its constant collision of personal worlds [. . .] It is the paradoxical task of the writer to overcome the tyrannical forces of words by means of words; the writer is a rebel in occupied territory" (p.1).

[79] *Enfance*, Paris: Editions Gallimard, 1983. *Childhood*, trans Barbara Wright, New York: George Braziller, 1984. References to Sarraute's original text and to Barbara Wright's translation will henceforth be to *E* and *C* respectively. The fictional works translated by Barbara Wright are: *L'Usage de la parole* (Gallimard, 1980) as *The Use of Speech* (London: John Calder, 1983); *Tu ne t'aimes pas* (Gallimard 1989) as *You Don't Love Yourself* (New York: George Braziller, 1990); and *Ici* (Gallimard, 1990) as *Here* (New York: George Braziller, 1997).

- These words make him furious . . . He repeats them: "Because I wanted them! I wanted them! So I allow myself no matter what. So I get caught like a thief, I injure other people . . . I want them, well then, I do everything that comes into my head . . . Can you beat it, I want them . . ." it seems to me that now he is really suffering and in a rage . . . "What about me, then, do you imagine that I do everything I want? What do you think, then? . . . I want them so much that nothing restrains me, nothing counts . . ." (*C* p.138, *E* pp. 157–8; ellipses in original)

Even allowing for the fact that he is producing a sarcastic version of how her attitude might have been put into words, it is hard to believe, I suggest, that this is the speech of a father addressing his daughter, who is probably round about eight years old. Phrases such as "no matter what" (for "*n'importe quoi*"), "I injure" ("*Je fais du mal*"), "well then" ("*eh bien*"), "you imagine" ("*tu t'imagines*"), "What do you think, then?" ("*Mais qu'est-ce que tu crois?*") and "nothing restrains me, nothing counts" ("*plus rien ne me retient, plus rien ne compte*"), are both too formal and unidiomatic in their vocabulary and too awkward in their rhythms to retain any naturalistic credibility. One has to ask, therefore, why such an experienced and accomplished translator as Barbara Wright might have chosen to render Sarraute's text in this way: that is, as what seems a classic case of an over-literal translation which, in the traditional formula defining what we have all been taught to avoid, "reads like a translation". I am going to argue that it is because this approach actually corresponds to and expresses something of the peculiar status that language has in Sarraute's writing.

From her first publication *Tropismes*, with its illumination of the small-scale psychic impulses of attraction and repulsion that subconsciously, she claims, determine our feelings and relationships, one of Sarraute's central concerns has always been with the *barrier* between the verbal and the non-verbal.[80] Her writing conveys an acute sense of a radical separation between on the one hand psychological states—which include perception of the outside world, but focus more especially on emotions, insights and ideas—and, on the other hand, language. Such a separation problematizes the whole notion of verbal expression; it implies that language is never *immediately* expressive, and that there is always a certain disconnect between sign and referent.

Childhood provides particularly striking examples of this kind of barrier, in so far as the persona of Nathalie Sarraute is here divided into three "voices": the child Natasha, the adult Sarraute who is attempting to recapture Natasha's experience, and finally the "alter ego" with whom the latter is constantly in dialogue, and who questions her memories and interpretations of the past. As a result, the non-verbal reality of the child's experience has to pass through a number of filters before it can take on a verbal form. Moreover, this process is not merely illustrated in the text but is actually analysed. At the beginning of *Childhood*, Natasha has gone from Russia to live with her exiled father in Paris; in this new situation she feels that she is being encouraged to forget about her mother, but is determined to remain loyal to her:

> I'm resisting . . . I'm holding out on this bit of territory on which I have hoisted her colours, on which I've put up her flag . . .
> - Images, words, which obviously couldn't have come into your head at that age.
> - Of course not. No more than they could have come into the head of an adult . . . It was, as always, an all-embracing feeling, outside words . . . But it is these words and images that enable us to grasp, as best we can, to retain these sensations. (*C* 9)

---

[80] *Tropismes*, Paris : Denoel, 1939. In the later essay "Conversation et sous-conversation" (in *L'Ere du soupçon*, Paris : Gallimard, 1956, pp. 95-147), Sarraute defines tropisms in terms which stress their non-verbal nature as "ce qui se dissimule derrière le monologue intérieur : un foisonnement innombrable de sensations, d'images, de sentiments, de souvenirs, d'impulsions, de petits actes larvés qu'aucun langage intérieur n'exprime" (115). [what is hidden behind interior monologue: a profusion of innumerable sensations, images, feelings, memories, impulses, little latent acts which are not expressed in any inner language]. Cf. Britton, "Reported Speech and Sous-conversation", *Romance Studies*, 2 (1983), pp. 69-79. My translation.

Here, in other words, the reader is first of all given Natasha's supposed experience, then reads the alter ego questioning the verbal and metaphorical form in which that experience has been presented, and finally the adult Sarraute formulating the rather distant relationship between the child's emotional reaction and the words which try to express it.

In Sarraute's earlier works, the separation was clearly manifested in the split between "conversation" and tropistic "sub-conversation".[81] This resulted in a text that shifted between two stylistically very different discourses: vocalized speech and the imagistic language into which the tropisms are translated. The former is an accurate representation of colloquial, often very clichéd, speech; but the latter, because it is not reproducing speech, is free to be as metaphorically elaborate and emotionally extreme as the author wishes. The difference between the two is often striking—for example between the two paragraphs in this passage from *Les Fruits d'or*:

Bien sûr, tu as montré que tu refusais ce qu'il t'offrait. Tu as refusé de fraterniser. Il a cherché autre chose . . .

Ha, ha, autre chose. Bien sûr. A ma portée. Les voyages: c'était pour moi. Un peu plus, et il se serait mis, pour être à ma portée, à me parler de marques d'auto . . . Mais ça t'a fait trop peur . . . Tu n'as pas pu le supporter . . .

Non, je ne peux jamais . . .

Le sol s'ouvre. Crevasse énorme. Et lui de l'autre côté, lui qui s'éloigne sans se retourner . . . il faut crier, le rappeler . . . qu'il se retourne . . . qu'il revienne . . . ne nous abandonnez pas . . . vers vous, chez vous, sur votre bord, aidez-nous, nous venons . . . [82]

---

[81] See "Conversation et sous-conversation".

[82] *Les Fruits d'or*, Paris : Gallimard, 1963, p. 13.
[Of course, you showed that you wouldn't accept what he was offering. You refused to fraternize. He tried something else . . .
Ha, ha, something else. Of course. On my level. Travel: that was for me. It wouldn't have taken much for him to have started talking about makes of car, to come down to my level . . . But you were too frightened . . . you couldn't bear it . . .
No, I never can . . .
The ground opens up. A huge crevasse. And him on the other side, going away without looking back . . . I must shout, call him . . . make him look back . . . don't abandon us . . . to you, to where you are, on your side, help us, we're coming . . .]
My translation.

But this stylistic opposition between conversation and sub-conversation is no longer apparent in the later work such as *Enfance*, where the whole text is in the form of an inner dialogue between Sarraute and her alter ego—and so is wholly written as speech, sometimes very colloquial. The sense of the gap between language and experience, therefore, in texts such as *Enfance* has to be communicated differently: no longer in the relatively tangible distinction between conversation and sub-conversation, but in a more diffuse quality that inhabits the dialogue—i.e., the text—as a whole. It is difficult to define this quality as anything other than a slight *strangeness*: it is nearly, but not quite, convincing as naturalistic speech. For instance, the very first lines of the book:

> *Alors, tu vas vraiment faire ça? "Evoquer tes souvenirs d'enfance"*
> *. . . Comme ces mots te gênent, tu ne les aimes pas. Mais reconnais*
> *que ce sont les seuls mots qui conviennent. Tu veux "évoquer tes*
> *souvenirs". . . . il n'y a pas à tortiller, c'est bien ça.*

It is this strangeness which seems to me to translate the distance which, as I have tried to show, Sarraute feels towards language (and perhaps especially towards speech). It is as though she cannot just inhabit language automatically and non-reflexively, with the result that even the most ordinary colloquial speech is presented self-consciously, as though it does not belong to her. Moreover, this feeling of estrangement from speech, the slight distance and lack of spontaneity, dovetail exactly with the lack of naturalness of Barbara Wright's very faithful translation:

> Then you really are going to do that? "Evoke your childhood memories" . . . How these words embarrass you, you don't like them. But you have to admit they are the only appropriate words. You want to "evoke your memories" . . . there's no getting away from it, that's what it is.

Psychological phenomena, then, are essentially non-verbal; and the converse is also true: language is a *social* rather than an inner reality. For Sarraute, language always belongs to other people. When

Natasha asks Vera, her father's new wife, if she hates her, and Vera replies "in her curt, peremptory tone, 'How can anyone hate a child?'" (*C* 242), Natasha's reaction focuses initially on the word "anyone" ("*on*" in the original), and the way in which it excludes her:

> Words she went to fetch, and which she brought back from a place where I can't follow her . . . compact, opaque words in which I can only perceive the "anyone" that I recognize . . . "Anyone" . . . normal people, moral people, people who are as they should be, people like her. (*C* p. 242).

"Anyone", in other words, except Natasha herself. Speech thus serves above all to emphasize the gulf she feels between herself and other people: what "normal" people *say* is inaccessible to her. It is also this focus on the social character of language that accounts for the hypersensitivity to sociolinguistic nuances and clichés, and the satirical treatment of the ways in which people use language in order to project a certain image of themselves, that we find in all Sarraute's novels.

This in turn produces that extreme objectification of language which is so characteristic of Sarraute and runs throughout her work; particular phrases that are associated with certain other people are isolated from their contexts, repeated and obsessively analysed until they acquire the opacity and density of objects.[83] They acquire definite sensuous qualities: they can be soft, viscous, slimy—or alternatively hard, sharp and prickly. As such, these pieces of language hardened into objects are usually perceived as weapons attacking the subject. When Natasha hears the maid say to her, "What a tragedy, though, to have no mother", the word "tragedy" "strikes you like a whiplash" (*C* 106), then becomes a predatory animal ("This same

---

[83] Sometimes they even form the titles of her texts: the play *C'est beau* (1975), the novels *"disent les imbéciles"* (Paris: Gallimard, 1976) and *Tu ne t'aimes pas*. Ann Jefferson comments that "Whole plays are devoted to worrying at a single phrase [. . .] The novels *Vous les entendez?*, *"disent les imbéciles"* and *Tu ne t'aimes pas* revolve around the utterances that provide their titles" (*Nathalie Sarraute: Fiction and Theory: Questions of Difference*, Cambridge: Cambridge University Press, 2000, p. 62.) *Vous les entendez* (Gallimard, 1972) and *"disent les imbéciles"* (Gallimard, 1976) are translated by Maria Jolas as *Do you hear them?* (London: Calder and Boyars, 1975) and *"Fools say"* (London: John Calder, 1977).

tragedy has pounced on me, it grips me, it has me in its claws", *C*
106), and finally becomes a trap that she has to escape from: "I tear
off this yoke, this carapace. I won't stay in this thing in which that
woman has imprisoned me" (*C* 106-7).

Natasha's reaction in this particular incident is understandable in
that it occurs when she realizes that she is being moved out of her
bedroom and "thrown into what seemed to me to be a sinister cub-
byhole" (*C* 105) to make room for her new half-sister, Vera's baby.
But it seems to initiate in her a more generalized paranoia about
being "trapped" in other people's words: "But how many times since,
have I not escaped, terrified, out of words which pounce on you and
hold you captive" (*C* 107)—and this includes, strikingly, even apparently quite benign words:

- Even the word "happiness"—every time it came quite close,
ready to alight, you tried to ward it off . . . No, not that, not one
of those words, they frighten me, I prefer to do without them, I
don't want them anywhere near me, I don't want them to touch
anything . . . nothing here, in me, is for them. (*C* 107)

In other words, there is a sense in which Natasha/Sarraute actually has a far more immediate relation to *others'* language than to her
own—but it is a relation of exclusion and vulnerability. Moreover,
it is concerned solely with the pragmatic aspects of language–the
impact of language in and on the real world—as opposed to its semiotic aspects: it is not the meaning of the word "tragedy" or the word
"happiness" that provoke Natasha's response to them, but the way in
which their use by a certain individual in a certain situation trans-
forms them into weapons or threats.[84]

When it comes to the subject's relation to her "own" language,
however, it is the semiotic dimension that dominates, in so far as this
subjective relation is entirely concerned with the difficult struggle for
expression and signification: words cease to be frightening weapons

---

[84] As Jefferson puts it, "If words have this central status in Sarraute it is largely
because their capacity to produce effects on their recipients far exceeds their
capacity to signify." *Nathalie Sarraute: Fiction and Theory: Questions of Difference*,
op. cit., p. 63.

and become elusive, delicate entities that are difficult to track down. Here, rather than Natasha having to "escape" from words that are trying to hold her captive, it is the words that "escape" from her attempts to grasp and use them. This is thus the other implication of the barrier between the verbal and the non-verbal: the urge to overcome it, and hence the concern with what cannot easily be put into words, and the sensation of inexpressibility, of groping for words that is also so characteristic of Sarraute's writing—that is in fact, according to the alter ego, "your element", in which:

> everything [. . .] fluctuates, alters, escapes . . . you grope your way along, forever searching, straining . . . towards what? What is it? It's like nothing else . . . no one talks about it . . . it evades you, you grasp it as best you can . . . (*C* 2)

Here there are interesting parallels with the process of translation, which also grapples with the problems of finding the right word to express something. In the case of translation, the "something" is not of course a non-verbalized or pre-verbal sensation (or perception, emotion, etc.)—it is something which has already been expressed, but in a different language, so that the translator's task is to move from one code to another. Sometimes this merely involves matching up an idiomatic expression in one language with the literally different but idiomatically equivalent expression in another language. But there are also more subtle mismatches between languages, and in these cases, in order to find the right word in the target language, the translator has to as it were retrieve the non-verbal sensation behind the word in the source language and then express this in the target language—an endeavour which is almost identical to that of the original writer.

In the specific case of Sarraute's writing, moreover, the prominence of this theme of "groping for words" also means that the translator of Sarraute is often translating the process of expression rather than the end-product: not translating the "right word" but the *search* for the right word, which is not always successful. For instance, in trying to describe her mother's face Sarraute writes: "J'aimais ses traits fins, légers, comme fondus . . . je ne trouve pas d'autre mot

... sous sa peau dorée, rosée" (*E* 93). Barbara Wright translates this as: "I loved her fine, delicate features, as if they were blended . . . I can't find any other word . . . with her golden rosy skin" (*C* 82). "Blended" here strikes the reader as a slightly odd choice of word, but its oddness simply replicates that of "*fondues*": this is not a clumsy approximation of the original, as we might have thought had it not been followed by "I can't find any other word", but a *translation* of a clumsy approximation *in* the original that serves to illustrate the point that Sarraute is constantly making about the difficulty of language.

I have been arguing that Sarraute's novels and the autobiography are dominated by the duality of the objectified language of other people as against the subject's own attempts to achieve the difficult feat of putting into words an essentially non-verbal reality. I want finally to link her conception of language to another kind of duality: her bilingualism, to which *Enfance* often refers. It recounts how after her father had to flee Russia for Paris Natasha was shuttled from one country to the other and seems from the start to have acquired native competence in both French and Russian (as well as learning German and English at a very early age). While it would be very reductive to attribute all of her acute hypersensitivity to language solely to the fact of her having been raised to speak both Russian and French, I do want to argue that there may be some connection between her unwillingness—or perhaps her inability—to feel unthinkingly at home in language and her lack of a single "mother tongue". In their study of the bilingualism of a very different author, namely Lautréamont, Leyla Perrone-Moisés and Emir Rodriguez Monegal claim that the bilingual speaker has a different kind of awareness of the materiality of the signifier—which they describe in a way that exactly echoes what I see as Sarraute's estrangement from language:

> *Le bilingue maintient, face à la langue, cette attention au signifiant qui est propre aux enfants, au moment où ils apprennent des mots nouveaux, et aux poètes, qui gardent à jamais cette attention et cette jouissance. Tandis que le monolingue associe le mot à l'idée d'une façon indissoluble, le bilingue conserve toujours la "vision"*

et "l'audition" de chaque signifiant, dans sa matérialité et son arbitraire.[85]

(The bilingual in his attitude to language maintains that attention to the signifier that is the characteristic of children when they are learning new words, and of poets, who keep forever that attention and that pleasure. Whereas for the monolingual the word and the idea are indissolubly associated, the bilingual always retains the "vision" and the "hearing" of every signifier, in its materiality and its arbitrariness.)

Thus, for example, when Natasha is "attacked" by her stepmother's telling her "They have abandoned you", this example of objectified speech acting as a weapon depends upon her conscious awareness of the sound of the Russian words and of the image their etymology conjures up:

"*Tyebya podbrossili*" . . . the Russian words came out hard and harsh, as they always did from her mouth . . . *podbrossili*, a verb whose literal meaning is "to throw out" but which also has an irreplaceable prefix which means "under", "from below", and this ensemble, that verb and its prefix, conjure up a picture of a burden that someone has surreptitiously unloaded on to someone else. (162)

Enfance often explicitly juxtaposes French and Russian, contrasting specifically the phonetic differences of the two languages and the physiological articulatory differences involved in pronouncing them. Natasha and her father playfully try to teach each other to pronounce the "r" sound properly in, respectively, French and Russian:

he imitates me comically, purposefully exaggerating, as if he were hurting his throat . . . Parrris . . . He gets his own back when he

---

[85] L. Perrone-Moisés and E. Rodriguez Monegal, *Lautréamont, l'identité culturelle: double culture et bilinguisme chez Isidore Ducasse* (Paris: L'Harmattan, 2001), p. 78. Quoted in Bill Marshall, *The French Atlantic: Travels in Culture and History,* Liverpool: Liverpool University Press, 2009, p. 280.

teaches me to pronounce the Russian "r" properly, I must curl up
the tip of my tongue and press it against my palate, then uncurl
it . . . (36)

Elsewhere she distracts herself from her distress at leaving her mother
after a visit to Russia by repeating in turn the French and the Russian word for "sun", again focusing on the purely phonetic qualities,
exaggerating and distorting them until the movements her tongue
and lips make become an obsessive kind of game:

> I amuse myself by chanting the same two words [. . .] the French
> word *soleil* and the same word in Russian, *solntze*, in which the
> "l" is hardly pronounced, sometimes I say sol-ntze, pulling back
> and pushing out my lips, with the tip of my curled up tongue
> pressing against my front teeth, and sometimes, so-leil, stretching
> my lips, my tongue barely touching my teeth. And then again,
> sol-ntze. And then again, so-leil. A mind-destroying game which
> I can't stop. (94-5)

Her awareness of the different sound patterns of different languages, as distinct from their meanings, is an important version
of the objectification of words. Although this usually applies only
to other people's speech, in the case of foreign words it sometimes
affects Natasha's own speech; when she tells her German governess,
in German, that she is going to rip up the sofa with a pair of scissors
she says: "*Ich werde es zerreissen*", and thinks: "the word *zerreissen*
has a hissing, ferocious sound" (p. 4). It is as though in order to be
sensitive to the force and the sensuous qualities of words, she has
to be "outside" rather than "inside" the language that she is hearing or using; and as a bilingual, she is also always situated *between*
languages in exactly the same way as a translator is. But the importa-
tion of fragments of languages other than French into *Enfance* also
reminds the reader that a certain amount of the original French text
is itself quite literally a translation: we do not know exactly how
much Russian Natasha spoke with her father and Vera, but presumably it is the language she used with her mother in Ivanovo, and
therefore her memories of conversations with her mother have had to

be translated from Russian into French before appearing in the text of *Enfance*. Here again, Sarraute's writing is *already* a translation— and this has important implications for the process of translating it into English.

In so far as this position "outside" or "between" languages affects her writing in general, I am tempted to see in Sarraute an illustration of Edouard Glissant's injunction that one should always "*écrire en présence de toutes les langues du monde*" (write in the presence of all the world's languages).[86] By this he means that my use of my own language is as it were haunted by the awareness of all the other languages that other people are writing in—so that even if I only know one language, I can no longer inhabit it with the unreflexive confidence that normally characterizes the monolingual native speaker; as Glissant puts it: "*Je ne peux plus écrire de manière monolingue*" (I can no longer write in a monolingual way) (ibid). From this point of view one could see a parallel between Sarraute and Glissant's fictional character Amina in his novel *Tout-monde*, whose particular way of speaking Italian leads the narrator to imagine that "*elle était capable de toutes les langues du monde*" (she was capable of all the languages in the world) (p. 40)—not because her Italian is full of foreign borrowings, but because she speaks it with a particular kind of "*hésitation légère au bord des mots*" (slight hesitation on the edges of words) (p. 41)—as though her Italian is shadowed by the ghostly presences of all the other languages she might have chosen to speak instead:

> Amina par exemple, qui était bien italienne [. . .] avait une manière étonnée de commencer ses phrases, comme si l'usage de cette langue italienne lui était difficile, en sorte qu'on pouvait se demander si elle n'avait pas grandi dans les échos d'une autre langue qui pour l'instant dormait ailleurs. (p. 40)
> (Amina for example, who was certainly Italian [. . .] would begin her sentences with an air of surprise, as though the use of this Italian language was difficult for her, so that one might wonder whether she had not grown up in the echoes of another language

---

[86] Edouard Glissant, *Introduction à une poétique du divers*, Paris: Gallimard, 1996, p. 40. My translation.

which for the moment was sleeping somewhere else.)[87]

A translation, of course, is by definition a text which is always aware of the other language that it translates. Conventionally, translators attempt to hide this awareness by producing a text which is as idiomatic and "normal" in its usage as possible. But, as I have tried to show, this is precisely not what Barbara Wright does when she is translating Sarraute. Sarraute's refusal to "write in a monolingual way", her constant "hesitating on the edges of words", creates a strange kind of complicity with her translator: the English translations of Sarraute's French texts will just by virtue of being translations convey the subtle sense of the strangeness of language that is already present in the original French versions. It is because Barbara Wright has the good judgment *not* to betray the strangeness, and at times the awkwardness, of Sarraute's language that her translations are so successful.

---

[87] Edouard Glissant, *Tout-monde*, Paris: Editions Gallimard, 1990. My translation.

Locating Barbara Wright's archive sources
Clothilde Roullier

This is an attempt at locating the original archive documents either produced or received by Barbara Wright and kept in various places. Of course, such an undertaking has to be constantly upgraded, owing to the arrival of new collections and inventories being made. But today we already have a sound basis for work.

I. In the USA

Lilly Library Manuscript Collections, Indiana

The Barbara Wright literary archive. Recorded between 2003 and 2010 and covering the years 1930-2010, it contains approximately 10,000 items. The inventory, which is available online (http://www.indiana.edu/~liblilly/lilly/mss/html/wrightb.html), is set up as follows: I. Personal; II. Writings, excluding translations; III. Individuals: correspondence and translations; IV. Organizations and publications; V. Radio: scripts and correspondence; VI. Miscellaneous notebooks; VII. Conferences and events; VIII. Collège de 'Pataphysique; IX. Clippings by subject; X. Photographs; XI. Honors and certificates; XII. Miscellaneous.

The Calder & Boyars collection, particularly Box 56, f.26-27: Wright, Barbara (May 30, 1967-Sept. 13, 1975). Folder 26 includes a sample translation from *Snapshots* by Alain Robbe-Grillet, corrections for *The Bark Tree* and *Le Chiendent* by Raymond Queneau. Folder 27 includes a review of *Le Maître de maison* by François Nourissier, a brochure on *Le Libera* by Robert Pinget. The general correspondence and the files concerning the creation of the works can also be found there.

The Red Dust mss., ca. 1961-2006, consist of the correspondence, drafts, manuscripts, proofs, business records and book production materials, etc. for Red Dust Publications. According to Joanna Gunderson, author and publisher of Red Dust books, "Red Dust was started in 1961, with the purpose of publishing work thought unpublishable because of length, form or content." See subseries: Barbara Wright, Box 3 (notes, correspondence, manuscripts, publishing agreement, copy of essays and articles on Pinget, clippings, ephemera, 1969-2002); subseries Robert Pinget, Boxes 2 and 3 (correspondence, reviews, playbills, proofs, book design materials, publicity materials, essays on Pinget, drawings, 1978-2002); reviews on Pinget, Boxes 7, 16 and 20 (1970-1991); Box 16, about *Trio* (proof, correspondence, contract agreement, 2001-2006); Box 8, Calder, John and Boyars, Marion (correspondence, 1968-1980).

II. In France

Institut mémoires de l'édition contemporaine (IMEC), Saint-Germain-la-Blanche-Herbe

The Pierre Albert-Birot and Arlette Albert-Birot collection: in the process of classification.

The John Calder collection. It contains correspondence between Barbara Wright and her publisher (December 1975—March 1992); a translation of Sylvia Bourdon's *L'amour est une fête* (107 typed pages), with a rejection card from Giangiacomo Feltrinelli Editore (Milan, Jan. 31, 1978); the collection includes the following translations: *Fable* by Robert Pinget; *Seven Dada Manifestos and Lampisteries* by Tristan Tzara; *Monsieur Klebs and Rozalie* by René de Obaldia; *The Exchange* by Paul Claudel (with Vladimir Mirodan); *The Singular Life of Albert Nobbs*, by Simone Benmussa; also included are *The "trials" of translating Pinget* (April 20, 1982, 3 typed pages) and a notebook for *Une aussi longue absence*.

The Jean Queval collection: 21 letters and postcards covering the years 1967–1986. To quote just one example:

2.9.85

Dear Jean,

Well, I was in France for 2 weeks (only just come back) but only on Very Serious Business (such a trying to teach Pinget's mother cribbage, and handing over (enfin!) the tr. of his *Journal d'Harvey* to Prof. Sir DE L'ACAD. FR...)

Essential question: How much shorter is "a much shorter book"? And how full of *astuces* and puns and *jeux de mots et poésie* ?? At the moment I feel fairly battered what with the prof's infernal Harvey and done 5 chapters of Grabinoulor and with some more Tzara & Pinget in the offing. My ideal would be a book written for 5 year-old children by a foreigner to the French language— they're the only ones who can ever be said to be relatively easy simply because they don't know enough to be complicated!

R.S.V.P

Love to you both,

Barbara

Bibliothèque nationale, Paris

The Nathalie Sarraute collection (NAF 28088): 16 leaves, covering the years 1991–1998. They are cover letters that were enclosed with postings of books, magazines, newspaper clippings, etc.

Bibliothèque littéraire Jacques Doucet, Paris

The Robert Pinget collection: 39 letters from Barbara Wright.

Service commun de la documentation de l'Université de Bourgogne, Dijon

The Raymond Queneau Collection. http://www.queneau.fr
Of particular interest art. 21: Correspondence with Barbara Wright (1967), and a translation of *Science et littérature* (notes, manuscripts, dactylogrammes) (1967).

III. In the United Kingdom

The British Library, London

The archive of Margaret Ramsay Ltd, Add MS 88915. Margaret Ramsay (known as Peggy) was Britain's foremost playwright's agent of the post-war period, best known for spotting new writing talent, but also highly influential in bringing foreign writers to the British stage. She represented a number of prominent Francophone playwrights (Eugène Ionesco, Armand Salacrou, Arthur Adamov, Fernando Arrabal) and some 30 translators whose client files are extant in the archive. Peggy was a personal friend of Barbara, the two having roomed together in the 1930s, and she later represented her for about 30 years.

Barbara Wright's client file (Add MS 88915/1/218) covers the period 1959-1988 and includes 18 letters from Barbara: 15 to Peggy or other members of her staff and others to John Calder, American agent Toby Cole and solicitor Laurence Harbottle. The correspondence covers the commissioning of translations, rights, royalties and publication, including a dispute with Spike Milligan over rights to the English translation of *Ubu Roi*, which threatened to suppress the use of Barbara's translation.

Other correspondents are: Grove Press New York, Ninon Tallon Karlweis, Hector Macquarrie from South African Broadcasting Corporation, Oscar Lewenstein, Terry Lane at Traverse Theatre Club, University of Bristol, Peter Rawley at Associated London Scripts, John Elford at Nicholas & Co, Laurence Harbottle, Michael de Laszlo, John Calder, Nathaniel Tarn at Jonathan Cape Ltd, Toby Cole, BBC, Norma Whittaker, Trevor Nunn and David Brierley at the RSC, Danielle Mignot, Samuel French Inc, Southwest Texas State University, John S Harrison Junior at Image Works, Charles Marowitz at Open Space Theatre. Includes letters from Peggy Ramsay to Rosica Colin, New Directions Publishing Co, International Center for Theatre Research, Micheline Rozan, Peter Brook and Norma Farnes Management.

The file contains the following contracts and agreements:
- drafts and copy contract between Spike Milligan, Barbara Wright and Oscar Lewenstein for rights to *Ubu roi*;
- contract between Barbara Wright and Oscar Lewenstein Plays to translate *Ubu roi*;
- agreement with BBC to broadcast *Picnic on a Battlefield* by Fernando Arrabal in translation by Barbara Wright;
- contract between Barbara Wright and John Calder Ltd to publish translations of *Dada Manifestos & Lampisteries* by Tristan Tzara, *L'Amour est une fête* by Sylvia Bourdon and *Vinci avait raison* by Roland Topor.

Elsewhere in the archive there is a letter from Barbara Wright to Peggy Ramsay, dated January 11, 1965, expressing her opinion on the work of Salacrou, particularly the play *Comme Les Chardons* (Add MS 88915/1/191). This file also contains letters from Salacrou with his opinions on Wright's translations. A report by Jennifer Birkett on Barbara Wright and Terry Hands' translation of Jean Genet's *The Balcony* is catalogued at Add MS 88915/1/99.

The Themerson Archive, London
www.themersonarchive.com

Stefan and Franciszka Themerson were avant-garde artists, filmmakers and thinkers born in Poland. They founded Gaberbocchus Press—of which Barbara was a director (1950-1962)—and published over 60 titles between 1948 and 1979. Alfred Jarry's *Ubu Roi*, translated by Barbara Wright, was published in 1951. There are three main files devoted to Barbara Wright.

File I (May 27, 1950—June 18, 1974) contains 87 items, mostly cards about places visited while travelling in Continental Europe, Poland, India, America and about work. In 1959, she writes about her translation of *Zazie* published the following year. Several items deal with rights and permission fees, some addressed to Peggy Ramsay. There are also the report she wrote on Anne Hébert's *Kamouraska*, a poem by Kasmin dedicated to her and a letter to her from Martin Wiener. Two 1950s photographs of Barbara are included. Additional material is to be found in the following files: Letters, Franciszka Themerson, Stefan Themerson, 1947-1972 / Jim Haynes / Franciszka Themerson reviews / About Stefan Themerson / Gaberbocchus common room / Day to day expenses of the common room / Gaberbocchus royalty agreements / Stanley Chapman / Brillat-Savarin / Collège de 'Pataphysique / Raymond Queneau / Shows and events.

File II (January 1975—February 5, 1993) contains 78 items with more postcards from her travels often signed by friends she visited. There is also a copy of a text—*Epître aux communautés*—that she wrote against a pataphysician who objected to her doing a broadcast on 'Pataphysics for money. For a translator who needed some help, she explains some phrases in Henry Reed's *The Naming of Parts*. In a 1982 letter to John Russell Taylor, she writes that David Hockney's permutational *Portraits* are not as original as it is claimed and she points to Stefan Themerson's permutational portrait for the cover of *Exercises in Style* published in 1958. For the translation of Henri Guigonnat's *Démone en Lituanie*, she asks Stefan Themerson's advice for the translation of Polish phrases. Her text on how she became a translator published in *Pix* no. 1 is also included. There are 11 photographs of Barbara and family and the album of photographs she took in Nepal on a trip with François Caradec and friends, and in India in 1978.

File III contains 39 items; there are some undated letters and cards and financial items (royalties, second rights, book purchases, correspondence about options referring to *Ubu* in particular).

In a letter to Stefan Themerson about Barbara's translation of *The Trojan Horse* and *At the Edge of the Forest*, Raymond Queneau (*Raymond Queneau's file*) wrote "Cette traduction me paraît excellente" (25/05/1954); on June 2, 1958, he wrote "mon meilleur souvenir à mon excellente traductrice", he was then referring to Barbara Wright for her translation of *Exercises in Style*.

Stanley Chapman (*Stanley Chapman's file*) in a letter to Stefan Themerson of 24/08/1956, wrote: "I was delighted, surprised, touched—oh, and many other emotions that I know no words to express—to receive a big letter tonight from our wonderful Barbara, full of comments on (and suggestions for) my Camille Renault translation."

In **Barbara Wright, File II**, there is a selection made by Beverly
Gordey (Doubleday) of extracts from book reviews praising Barbara
Wright's work as a translator. For example, John Weightman wrote in
The New York Times Book Review, May 17, 1981, "This translation
[of *Exercises in Style*] is a reissue of an existing version, first published
in Great Britain and Canada as long ago as 1958, when Queneau
was still alive. He declared himself well pleased with it, and he had
every reason to be, since Barbara Wright has exactly caught the spirit
of the book, and where direct translation was not possible—as, for
example, in the case of the variations in country dialect or *argot*—
she has transposed creatively into such corresponding forms as West
Indian Immigrant speech or Cockney jargon. Her rendering deserves
the highest praise."

The Barbara Wright Archive at the Lilly Library: A Personal Memoir
Breon Mitchell

On a misty day in Manhattan, over thirty years ago, I asked Barbara if she had been saving her own manuscripts and correspondence. "Who would care?" she asked, as the bus pulled up.

Years later, she recalled the falling rain, the question, her own surprise—not that someone might be interested in Raymond Queneau, Nathalie Sarraute, or Robert Pinget—but that someone might be interested in her, and in the seemingly modest part she had played in literary history. Yet toward the end of her life, as self-effacing and unpretentious as she was ("do you really want all this stuff?" she would ask), she finally began to realize how much others valued her work.

The question I put to Barbara, following a pleasant lunch with our editors at New Directions, arose from my delight in her quick mind, the cleverness with which she handled difficult questions of literary style, and her insights into the works of some of the leading writers of our century. Shouldn't this all be preserved in some way? What would happen to the complex record of her life as a literary translator? Was this all going to be lost? I asked as a fellow translator, fully realizing how little, in fact, most people cared about translation, how seldom they realized its possible importance in their own lives.

Years passed, but neither Barbara nor I forgot our conversation. Then, in 2002, as the new Director of the Lilly Library, I finally had a chance to follow up on my question concretely. I wrote to Barbara, told her I was coming to London, and that I would like to see her. She invited me to her home in Frognal, I arrived, and she listened patiently to my ideas.

I told her of our desire to create a broad research archive of translators' papers at the Lilly Library, including correspondence with authors and publishers, drafts of translations, annotated copies of original texts, corrected galley proofs—in short anything that would shed light on both the process and context of literary translation. I told her I feared that this vital material would be lost to future generations if we didn't save it now. Her response was immediate, generous and warm.

From 2002 on, I visited Barbara on a regular basis, first at Frognal, and later in her basement flat in Rylett Crescent, as she gradually shifted major portions of her papers and her books to the Lilly. She had, in fact, kept almost everything over the years—all her correspondence with publishers and authors, her notebooks, her reviews and periodicals, the heavily-annotated copies of each book she had translated. She seemed to take great pleasure in slowly sifting through her past, sharing her memories, and counterpointing them with lively opinions on contemporary culture. The depth of her study for individual translation projects was amazing, and clearly evident in the thick and clearly-labeled files. As her mind moved nimbly from topic to topic, I felt privileged to be in her presence.

As Barbara's friends well know, her letters are a constant delight, flowing easily and openly, sometimes page after page. Here are a few samples from her letters that shed light on her feelings at the time:

April 7, 2002: "I'm also a bit scared because I realise that it's more or less going to be like revealing my whole life to anyone who wants to poke his or her nose into it. (All right, I could have phrased that less scornfully . . .) And that seems to me to be against my nature. I have always refused to be interviewed. A) Because I just don't want to be, and B) because it would bore me—I reckon I know about myself! On the other hand I love being the interviewer and talking to other people about themselves. Some years before I started to translate her, some literary mag sent me to the institut français here to interview Nathalie Sarraute, and she was so lovely and simple and friendly and interesting and prepared to talk . . . Well, she was such a professional that whenever she gave a lecture it was just as if she was talking to close friends. With me, on the other hand, whenever I have allowed myself to be pushed, screaming and shouting (metaphorically) into talking in public, it has had every chance of becoming a disaster."

Barbara's ambivalence about revealing her personal life ran like a leitmotif through our letters, although in the end she left it up to me to draw the line, passing on nearly everything she had kept. Her method of "weeding" her papers provides interesting insights into the process:

> May 14, 2002: "I must have told you that for several years now I have been thinking that I *must* weed out my files . . . And that I go and take a distraught look at them from time to time, and then either make a quick retreat or pick out one or two and consider whether I *really* need to keep them. . . . Usually I start by reading one of the first letters—only reasonable, no?—and then think: Goodness, this is rather interesting........and end up without a decision.
>
> "The most recent one I scrutinised is a good case in point, and I see that it will be invaluable to me to have your advice when we decide what we might pack up and send. I had thought that this huge file could really be dispensed with . . . then I read the first letter, dated June 30 1977......From a very witty, happy-go-lucky American student at a U. in California [. . .] who was in love with words and had ambitions to be a writer. . . . 'Dear Ms [ugh] Wright, Thank you very much for the excellent job you have done in translating Queneau's novels. "The bus ran ovaries head", is the greatest. It is absolutely superb work; a five star rating.'............Well—I don't know about posterity, but, well, I don't *quite* feel like getting rid of that *just yet* . . ."

"Posterity! Yuk!" was Barbara's normal reaction whenever I suggested someone might eventually care about what she had written, and in the same letter she tackles the issue (new for her) of letters read by strangers:

> [A friend said] on a postcard (undated, as usual, but I date them) on 9 April 2002: "Please let's throw out our letters from now on so we can write what we like." Well *me*—I have never not written what I liked, I have never thought of anything or anyone other than my immediate correspondent. Writing a letter is pretty nearly as good as being in the company of the pal you're writing to. [. . .] But when I was told that [a friend] had kept all my letters . . . Well, I kind of woke up. And I realized that *ALL* the things

one does, spontaneously, and just because one is alive..........
are, in a way, there, engraved in stone.
So clearly, the thing to do is to carry on regardless (which was a
saying during the war!), but be aware that God's, or Buddha's,
Databank has got you taped, whether you like it or not. So clearly,
the thing to feel is: So what?? And not to care.

Like many writers and translators, Barbara wanted to hold on
to earlier papers if there was any chance she might still need them.
She would only "institutionalize" things that seemed clearly part of
her past and not her present. But here too, as she moved toward her
ninetieth year, she began to simplify her life:

> May 13, 2004: "It's a year or so since I wrote that long article
> on Queneau for *Context*, and I got piles of RQ books out of my
> shelves to consult and left them lying about, but people keep
> giving me more and now there simply isn't room to put them all
> back. So what do I do? I just think Oh dear oh dear, in a feeble,
> despairing way, and leave them cluttering everything up.
> "But I had an idea the other day: Why don't I pass all my
> Queneauphilia over to Lilly? Now? Only it's not just a few
> portable books and papers like the Hamburger, it's at least a
> crateful . . . Do you think you might be prepared to deal with
> it when you come over Wannsee-bound? There are heaps of files
> which I haven't looked at in years, each concerning different Q
> translations, etc. And there are a few really charming letters from
> him. I wouldn't keep anything back. But there might be a bit of
> sorting out I would probably ask you to help with. What do you
> think?"

The Queneau files in their entirety were soon joined by Pinget,
equally rich in content:

> August 14, 2004: "It will be very good—and therapeutic!—to
> see you in November. I have been thinking a little about what
> I might ask you to take, thank goodness there's no immediate
> hurry to make up that alleged mind. [. . .] Would Pinget be a

good idea? I have what seems like hundreds of letters. . . . And photos, now I come to think of it."

Again and again, early memories would rise to the surface as Barbara contemplated what she wanted to send next:

November 18, 2004: "Maybe some Sarrautiana, too? She hated writing letters but I have one or two. And when I sent her the first draft of *Enfance*—(well, actually probably the fifth or sixth draft, but the first to be submitted to her comments). . . . When she had studied it she phoned me and sounded ecstatic: It was terrific, 'le ton est là, le rythme est là', there were just a few places where she had questions. . . . I was going to Chérence, their country house, to read it to her as usual, but as it was so long it seemed sensible to send her a script first. It was. She wrote down her 'few questions', and sent them to me. And of course I still have the manuscript: I seem to remember the few questions came to about 400. . . . As I did every summer, I was going to be driving through France, so I told her I would find the nearest little hotel and come and talk the translation over with her for as long as we needed. 'There isn't a little hotel anywhere near,' says she, 'you'd better come and stay here. . .'. Well, I had to, didn't I? . . . In the mornings she and I worked, in the afternoons we went for walks or I even took them on tourist trips in the car—which they loved . . . It took us a week to be satisfied with the translation. . . . You certainly know what it is to have an author who appreciates you. I have certainly showed you Nathalie's dédicace to me in her Pléiade edition that she gave me. I cherish it."

By 2006, she still had thick files to be dealt with, and they continued to spark memories:

November 6, 2006: "I've been casting a few eyes on my files, and I came across the Obaldia one, and it all came flooding back to me. As usual, lots of funny and pleasant things happened which culminated in the brilliant—and lovely—Yugoslav director Vlado Habunek—alas, no longer with us—putting *Mr Klebs & Rozalie* on in Scotland at the Pitlochry Festival. I drove up there with my Finnish/French friend Anna, and a very very *very* good time was had by all."

To this letter was attached a blow-by-blow account of the "state of Barbara's thinking" dated December 23, 1980, that begins "John Calder did not commission me to translate *Mr Klebs*," one of a myriad of fascinating documents scattered throughout her files. Even her extensive collection of clippings was preserved as grist to the mill of knowledge:

November 6, 2006: "Among all my frightening files, there were two boxes that I had been *meaning* to examine for years, and years, and years. . . . I knew what they contained, and I thought I would maybe just be able to throw away their contents. They date from the days when I naively thought that I only had to be interested in a subject to be able to learn something about it. They were cuttings about all kinds of subjects that I had cut out and saved from even before 1959, when I came to Frognal. Today I braved it, and opened them. What I didn't remember was that some day—when??—I had been efficient enough to make myself a great long index of their subjects. This one-page index—with three or four-hundred entries—*seems* to be the only one the kindly paper-worms have fed on. And they mostly went for the blank spaces, so nothing much is lost. But before I ditched the papers, two items jumped out at me: 1) A big, interesting article (in the TLS) on October 5, 1962, inspired by Ralph's translation of the Tin Drum, and 2) Two intelligent articles about P. Albert-Birot in August 1966, the year before he died, inspired by the Gallimard reprint of extracts from the first 3 books of Grabinoulor. Then I saw that I also had articles on Astronomy, Brainwashing, Constantine, Danilo Dolci, the Etruscans. . . . So I thought to myself: I won't throw these away just yet. Shall I save them for Lilly?"

Yes, I would say, save everything, still marveling at her enthusiasm for the widest range of topics and ideas. Then, as she prepared to move into the basement flat at her grandson Jim's home, she began to think in earnest about what that would mean. Soon after her arrival at Rylett Crescent she wrote "I'm in the mood to give you just about anything you would like, so as to be able to have a simplified, minimal living space . . . I have gradually been adding texts relating to the books and Mss you already have and putting them into the big LILLY box."

Barbara's final years were not without pain and discomfort, which she faced steadfastly, comforted by the security of her new living arrangement with her family. Her mind remained sharp, as did her determination to ensure that everything, including her own set of her translations, would come at last to the Lilly, along with her cherished Pléiade edition bearing Nathalie Sarraute's warm inscription. I would like to think that comforted her too.

What would she have thought of others, both friends and strangers, reading my own brief memoir based largely on her letters? Just months before she passed away, she wrote this:

June 29, 2008: "Just the other day. . . I thought I should send you a line or two . . . But then I thought that before I did, I should have a look at our correspondence, because I couldn't remember where I'd got to, and I was rather afraid that for some time I had been allowing myself to complain and feel sorry for myself . . . and I'm afraid I had . . . but at the same time I had been telling you all the details of my moving in here, and I'd forgotten them!—so I was interested to read all about it . . . And Breon . . . Someone was showing me Wikipedia the other day, and I think I caught a glimpse of someone saying that Lilly had my letters to Russell—Russell who?—ah yes, Fitzgerald, I think . . . I remember how surprised and even shocked I was when you forbade me to throw those letters away, but now I begin to understand why . . . I wonder what happened to Russell? Did he ever become a writer? I daresay I could find out, if I only knew how to manoeuvre Modern Technology . . . But over the last few days, reading your and my letters from about the last three years, it occurred to me that there might be a case for saving them, too!"

So in the end, Barbara herself began to sound like an archivist! The Barbara Wright archive is at the Lilly Library because, after careful thought, she wanted it to be there, and because, in spite of her intense modesty, she knew how much that meant to me and others. Her archive joins those of over thirty other world-class literary translators, including among others, William Weaver, Leila Vennewitz, Nicholas de Lange, David Bellos, Krishna Winston and Margaret Jull Costa.

Barbara's papers include her extensive correspondence with authors and publishers, notebooks and drafts of her translations, her own essays, and her daily appointment books from 1933 to 2008. Authors and publishers represented include, among many others, Pierre Albert-Birot, Robert Pinget, Raymond Queneau, Nathalie Sarraute, Michel Tournier, Calder & Boyars, Collins, Doubleday, New Directions, and Red Dust. Her working library, including annotated copies of the books she translated, is also held at the Lilly Library. The finding aid for the collection can be found at: http://webapp1.dlib. indiana.edu/findingaids/view?doc.view=entire_text&docId=InU-Li-VAB8803

Fellowships to use the Barbara Wright archive, and other archives at the Lilly Library, are available to scholars around the world. For further information, see: http://www.indiana.edu/~liblilly/fellowships.shtml

Filmscript

15 Rue des Lilas [88]
Robert Pinget

Adapted by Madeleine Renouard
Stage directions by Madeleine Renouard and Philippe Miquel
A film by Philippe Miquel
English translation by Barbara Wright

---

[88] In 1990 Alistair Whyte, Jean-Michel Mullon and Madeleine Renouard, with the collaboration of Barbara Wright, created a production company called SISO Films to develop and promote the film *15 Rue des Lilas*. The initial stages of the project were discussed with Pinget at Barbara's house in Frognal, and with students at Brest University. Pinget was enthusiastic about the project, which came to fruition in its written form, with the support of the European Script Fund, an iniative of the Media Programme of the European Community, but the film was never shot. An opportunity to reach a wider readership for Pinget and to familiarize cinemagoers with his world was then missed. The French version of *15 Rue des Lilas* has never been published. The three presentations of the filmscript that we include here were written to introduce the project to different funding institutions and television companies.

15 Rue des Lilas
Synopsis
Alistair Whyte

The film is set in France, in the Touraine region. Two bachelors in their late forties, Gaston and Fred, own a *pension de famille*, 15 rue des Lilas, which has a number of permanent guests, including a retired couple, Monsieur and Madame Cointet, a writer, Monsieur Songe, an old lady from Eastern Europe, Madame Apostolos, etc. It is a large, elegant but somewhat dilapidated house with a huge garden. On the surface, life at the *pension* is calm and unchanging, but the guests and the owners are all deeply affected by the apparent disappearance or possible murder of a local child. What, if anything, has actually happened is never resolved but the investigation carried out by the police provokes conflicts in the household and each person seems to have a different interpretation of the nature, the circumstances and the motives of the affair. None of the characters is really unpleasant but in the past of all, there appear to be areas shrouded in mystery. Perhaps each of them, each of us, is capable of a brutal crime.

*
* *

15 Rue des Lilas is obviously enigmatic and disturbing but like all Pinget's works it is also comic. The examples of dialogue will give some idea of the way in which the banalities of everyday exchanges can be turned to humorous effect while also suggesting half-suppressed tensions and an avoidance of genuinely worrying issues.

Unlike both certain avant-garde films and many mainstream movies, *15 Rue des Lilas* will provide, thanks to Pinget's great skill with dialogue and his ability to suggest hidden depths of character, not just one or two interesting parts but a whole range of challenging and rewarding roles. There is, therefore, much to attract actors of the highest calibre.

The meals at 15 rue des Lilas form what might be called the spine of the film but, at the same time, sequences in the early autumn landscape of the Touraine will convey both tranquil beauty and a sense of underlying menace, paralleling and extending the atmosphere of the *pension*. This particular combination of interiors and exteriors will offer great scope to the director and the lighting cameraman.

Philosophical, puzzling, but also warm and funny, *15 Rue des Lilas* will appeal not merely to the art-house audience but to a whole range of cinema and television viewers.

15 Rue des Lilas
Note
Madeleine Renouard

The script's aim is to translate the universe of the writer Robert Pinget (novelist, playwright and essayist) into the language of the screen. His universe is simultaneously prosaic (depicting provincial, everyday life) and dreamlike (the reader or viewer is forced to ask: "What is happening in reality? What is dreamed or imagined?").

Pinget's stage plays appear around the world; his radio plays are produced regularly both in France and abroad. The success that his dramas have continued to achieve since the 1987 Avignon Festival is undeniable. The production of *Monsieur Songe* by Jacques Seiler in 1989 in Paris (at the Théâtre de Poche, Montparnasse) was received with universal praise both by reviewers and the public.

To date there is still no film by Pinget. It is high time, we consider, to bring to the screen the imagination of one of the greatest contemporary French writers. He combines humour and tenderness; rigorous structure and verbal creativity; simplicity of form and depth of message—both human and philosophical.

The film will bring together voices and atmospheres from various works by Pinget: *Someone, The Inquisitory, The Libera Me Domine, Monsieur Songe, The Enemy* . . . The dialogues, by turn humorous, tender and violent, demand good, straightforward actors who are capable of moderating their voices. Pinget devoted enormous attention to what is *heard*—noises, rhythms, voices—and the sound-track will need equal care. As a painter, he specified images, colours and movements very precisely.

It would be a mistake to look for an epic-type film from Robert Pinget. *15 Rue des Lilas* is the cheerful, fantasized, banal, sordid adventure of a number of individuals—beautiful, ugly, old, young, honest, dishonest—in the French countryside of Touraine, patterned by *fin de siècle* chiaroscuro. At the heart of each individual lies drama, anguish, guilt . . . A child has disappeared. Has he been murdered?

15 Rue des Lilas
Presentation
Robert Pinget, Barbara Wright

The action takes place in a private guest house in the country, in the province of Touraine, France. Two unmarried men of about fifty, Gaston and Fred, run the guest house, which has about eight boarders. It is a large house with a huge garden.

The boarders' routine is interrupted by tragedy, the murder of a child. The police investigate. Life goes on apparently as tranquilly as ever, but the affair provokes conflicts between the characters and discrepancies emerge with regard to the nature, circumstances and motives of the tragedy. The past of certain people is explored, and shady areas are uncovered in their lives before their arrival at the guest house.

Marie the cook prepares meals and goes out to the shops, where she meets all sorts of people. Madame Apostolos, an old lady who emigrated from Eastern Europe, receives and sends many letters. Monsieur and Madame Cointet, a middle-class retired couple, reminisce about their travels. Johann the gardener has memories of Broy Manor . . .

The schoolteacher, who is also involved in cultural affairs, and the postman, are regular visitors to the guest house.

The enquiry stalls, and several people are suspected. Johann returns evasive answers to the inspector's questions. The conversations between the boarders, stimulated by anonymous letters and articles in the press, become more and more contradictory. To add to matters, Monsieur Songe's nephew is involved in financial complications.

The schoolteacher is seen with a group of children on an outing into the forest. One of them disappears. Johann is seen again at the manor house where he used to be a steward and where the inhabitants' worldly, shameless lifestyle gave rise to rumours.

At the guest house, 15 rue des Lilas, Gaston sees to the day-to-day running of the household helped by Fred, who writes a diary. Monsieur Songe, the oldest inhabitant, also keeps a diary. But the two accounts do not give the same version of events.

We see Monsieur Songe in conversation with his niece, his nephew, and his old friend Mortin, who also knows Gaston and Fred.

None of the characters is really villainous. They engage in ordinary activities, but their pasts, and their dreams, do not seem to match their behaviour. Falsehood has been part of life at the guest house for years. The role of detective is difficult. Nevertheless, a child has been killed. But when?

March 4, 1990

MAIN CHARACTERS

The owners of 15 Rue des Lilas:
GASTON AND FRED: Both about fifty.

The guests:
MONSIEUR AND MADAME COINTET: In their seventies. She is of the so-called "distinguished" type.
MONSIEUR AND MADAME ERARD: In their sixties. Simple people.
MADAME APOSTOLOS: In her eighties. She still has pretensions to elegance. She has rheumatism.
MONSIEUR SONGE: In his seventies.

The servants:
MARIE: The maid: in her late fifties.
JOHANN: The gardener: about sixty.

OTHER CHARACTERS
Monsieur Songe's NEPHEW and NIECE: About twenty or twenty-five.
MORTIN: A friend of Monsieur Songe. In his seventies.
THE JUDGE: In his late fifties.
THE SCHOOLMISTRESS: Mademoiselle Lorpailleur. An old maid. Ageless.
THE GIPSY: About thirty.
THE DUCREUX CHILD: About eight.

MINOR CHARACTERS
The village tradespeople, Monsieur de Broy (the lord of the manor), the trainee teacher, guests at the manor house, the plumber, the gendarme . . .

15 Rue des Lilas

SEQUENCE 1

EXTERIOR. DAY—COUNTRYSIDE

PRE-CREDITS SEQUENCE

Somewhere in the Touraine countryside.
Blinding sun, midday, in July.
General shots of the landscape: in the distance, a forest; in the fore-
ground, a pool. Medium shots and close-ups of the surrounding vegetation and undergrowth, full of wild life. Gradually, however, the
presence of man is revealed: bits of rusty old iron, scraps of dirty
paper, plastic bags, old newspapers, a broken doll . . .
Sounds of insects, bluebottles, wasps, dragonflies, crickets . . .
These are joined by children's laughter as the camera advances towards
the edge of the forest, on the far side of a wheatfield glowing in the
sunlight.
Suddenly, in the darkness of the forest, the shrill cry of a child in
pain, followed by total silence. In a low-angle, backlit shot, the camera approaches a big, rather decrepit building. This is the guest house
run by FRED and GASTON at 15 rue des Lilas.
When the camera finally comes to a halt and focuses on the house, a
man's voice can be heard.

> M. SONGE (off)
> It was in July, a bad month in our parts. Every
> sort of calamity happens to us in July, fires,
> road accidents, hailstorms, drownings, but we
> hadn't had a murder since, since . . . Well, it's
> still there, in the records and newspapers of the
> time . . .

Fade out

CREDITS

SEQUENCE 2

INTERIOR. DAY—CORRIDOR—GUESTS' ROOMS.

Fade in

General shot. The first floor corridor, a sort of long, dark passageway painted brown, on to which all the guests' rooms open.

Sound of lavatory being flushed. At the far end of the corridor, the lavatory door opens. An old lady comes out of it and goes into her room. The camera follows her. She is wearing a short-sleeved flowered dress, her flabby white arms show. Her hair is dyed red, her lips painted violet. She has rheumatism. She limps.

She is Madame Apostolos. She takes some lavatory paper out of one of her pockets and starts cleaning her canary's cage. She finds it hard to separate the bird's droppings from the semolina she feeds it with.

Sideways tracking shot. The camera moves into the adjoining room and focuses on Madame Erard, who is like an old little girl. She makes rag dolls. There is a big pile of them in a basket at her feet.

Not far from her, Monsieur Erard is sitting in an armchair. He is fairly tall, with grey, slicked-back hair. He is looking through a medical journal.

Sideways tracking shot. In the next room there is another old lady, but this one is tall, very gaunt and very pale. She looks like an Englishwoman on holiday. This is Madame Cointet.

Her husband is there too, Monsieur Cointet, a thin little old man with a little beard. Madame Cointet is playing a game of patience. She is getting irritated because he is disturbing her, looking for his handkerchief.

M. COINTET
My handkerchief.

MME COINTET
Jack, ten, what? What did you say?

M. COINTET
My handkerchief, I don't know where my
handkerchief's got to.

MME COINTET
Have you looked under the bed? Ace, king,
what did I say, had I got to eight? Was it eight
or seven?

M. COINTET (shouting)
It isn't there.

MME COINTET
Leave me alone, will you. I've gone all wrong
because of your handkerchief, leave me in
peace, jack, ten, it isn't going to come out, it's
all your fault, my game isn't going to come out!

M. COINTET spits in the bidet.

The camera moves, in one shot, to the ground floor. In the dining
room, GASTON is reading the local paper, while FRED uncorks a
bottle of red wine. Sound of the service hatch. MARIE, the maid,
shouts from the kitchen.

MARIE (off)
It's ready! Will I serve it?

Through the banisters, the legs of the guests are seen coming downstairs, one after the other. MME APOSTOLOS is the last.

SEQUENCE 3

INTERIOR. DAY—GUEST HOUSE DINING ROOM.

The guests take their places at the dining room table. M. COINTET puts a cushion on his chair so as not to look too short next to his wife, but it doesn't make much difference. It's the midday meal in the guest house. The dining room has a provincial look. Louis-Philippe furniture. A big sideboard. A dumb-waiter near the service hatch which opens on to the adjoining kitchen.

Beside a little crucifix on which there is a dried up twig of palm, stands a grandfather clock. The tick of its pendulum penetrates the silence.

GASTON and FRED are sitting at either end of the table, and the guests are in their usual places along its sides. But two places are not occupied.

They all unfold their napkins and help themselves to bread.

It's hot. Flies keep settling everywhere.

The ladies are in summer dresses, the men in their shirt sleeves.

Through the window, JOHANN the gardener can be seen, moving earth about in a wheelbarrow and shoveling it out with his spade. He is perspiring heavily, and he wipes his face with his apron. Children can be heard, playing in the distance.

FRED is the only one who occasionally looks out of the open window.

Long panoramic shot of all the guests, which ends in a close up of M. ERARD. He is sniffing his napkin. Long silence.

> M. ERARD
> What a horrible smell. Couldn't they be
> changed today?

> MME ERARD
> They were changed a week ago. You don't have
> to smell it.

> M. ERARD
> Makes you sick. You'd think I'd been hiding
> chunks of rotten meat in it. What d'you all
> think about yours?

He goes on sniffing at his napkin. Pleasure and disgust can be read on his face.

> MME COINTET
> You know the laundry's closed for a month,
> and our table linen . . .

> GASTON
> Patience, patience, we'll be getting our washing
> machine this winter. No more bothering about
> the laundress being on holiday.

FRED stands up and goes to close the window, as if the bad smells come from outside as well. Before he sits down again he automatically taps a barometer on the wall. The pointer, on Set Fair, doesn't move.

GASTON watches him. The guests notice FRED's movements but make a point of ignoring them. MME COINTET starts speaking before he has sat down again. They speak fairly quickly, their faces follow one another like the cogs in a perfectly adjusted piece of clockwork. They all remain serious, except M. ERARD who is still slightly smiling.

MME COINTET
That machine—don't you think it's an
unnecessary expense? In a small household like
ours?

GASTON
We must keep abreast of the times. And
everyone isn't of your opinion, you know.

M. ERARD
I haven't said anything about the machine, I'd
like to point out . . .

Once again he smells the napkin several times.

M. ERARD
. . . But really, this smell . . .

MME ERARD
Are you trying to spoil our appetites? Pass the
bread please.

M. ERARD
Actually, that would be as good a saving as any
other.

MME APOSTOLOS
That machine, a saving?

M. ERARD
No, to spoil your appetites.

M. COINTET
Charming as usual.

MME COINTET (to M. COINTET)
In your case it wouldn't hurt. You eat far too

much. Remember the doctor.

MME COINTET (to Mme Erard)
Did you sleep well?

MME ERARD
I hardly sleep at all in this heat. The summer
doesn't suit me, and that canteen next door
that gives off all those smells until four in the
morning, I can't imagine what they get up to in
that kitchen.

MME ERARD hasn't been interrupted in time. All the guests show
signs of embarrassment. A heavy silence falls over them.

SEQUENCE 3 (i)

EXTERIOR. DAY—GUEST HOUSE GARDEN.

An old man whom we only see from behind comes out on to the
steps leading down from the house. He turns his head right and left,
as if he was looking for something.

In the background, a few dozen metres away, a black smoke is coming out of the chimney of a grimy building. The old man goes down
the steps with the aid of a walking stick.

Through one of the open windows, the guests can be heard continu-
ing their conversation

M. ERARD (off)
They cook, presumably. And as health is a
question of smell . . .

SEQUENCE 3 (i) (continuation)

INTERIOR. DAY—GUEST HOUSE DINING ROOM.

Back in the dining room, close up of M. ERARD's hand, feeling his bread.

> M. ERARD
> This bread isn't properly baked. Baker on holiday?

> MME APOSTOLOS
> Personally I like it like this. With my poor teeth . . .
> (She shifts her denture with her tongue.)
> If you only knew . . .

> M. ERARD
> We haven't that privilege yet.

Enter MARIE. She opens the serving hatch noisily, picks up the soup tureen and puts it down on the table. Exit.

MME COINTET takes off the lid and starts to serve them one after the other. They all begin to drink their soup at once.

There are long silences between their speeches, and the passing time becomes more noticeable, denser.

Clock ticking.

> MME COINTET (to Mme Apostolos)
> May I serve you?

> MME APOSTOLOS (holding out her plate)
> Just a drop . . . What is it?

> MME COINTET
> Celery, I think.
>
> M. ERARD
> You think? It stinks. Couldn't they do
> something else with this celery? It's the same,
> every day.

When M. ERARD starts talking of smells again there is a tap on
the window. FRED looks up: he sees JOHANN, who is shaking his
head.

FRED signs to him to go away.

> MME ERARD (holding out her plate)
> It's amazing how much I like celery. I
> remember, when I was a little girl . . .
>
> M. ERARD
> We know.
>
> MME COINTET (to M. Cointet)
> Give me your plate, what are you waiting for?
>
> M. COINTET (holding out his plate)
> Not too much.
>
> MME COINTET (serving him)
> One . . . two. Very good for your cold.
>
> MME ERARD
> I remember, when I was a little girl . . .
>
> M. ERARD
> Same old story.

MME APOSTOLOS
What?

MME ERARD
My husband is jealous of my childhood. Can
you understand that? I remember, when I was a
little girl . . .

M. COINTET (to M. Erard)
Pass the salt please. Our Marie is certainly not
in love.

M. ERARD (to M. Cointet)
May I?

He helps himself to salt before passing it on.

Silence.

SEQUENCE 3 (i) continuation

EXTERIOR. DAY—GUEST HOUSE GARDEN.

The old man has reached the steps leading down to the cellar. He
goes down a few of them, so as not to be seen by JOHANN, who is
putting his tools away in the shed.

When JOHANN finally goes out of the garden, the old man, whose
face is still not visible, continues his search. The camera follows him,
still from behind, first into the shed, where he rummages around
for a moment. Then he walks along the garden fence, looking in the
bushes, and finally reaches the gate, looks up and inspects the chestnut tree.

MARIE is watching him from the kitchen window. He suddenly
realizes this, and goes back to the house.

SEQUENCE 3 (ii)

INTERIOR. DAY—GUEST HOUSE ENTRANCE HALL.

Just as the old man is about to go upstairs he is intercepted by MARIE, who half opens the kitchen door.

He is M. SONGE, but only MARIE can be seen during this short whispered dialogue.

> MARIE
> What are you doing there?

> M. SONGE (off)
> Nothing.

> MARIE
> What were you doing just now?

He is heard going upstairs.

> M. SONGE (off)
> That bit of paper you "tidied up" . . .

> MARIE
> Pah . . . A trifle . . .

The rest of the speech is lost. She slams the kitchen door shut.

SEQUENCE 3 (ii) (continuation)

INTERIOR. DAY—GUEST HOUSE DINING ROOM.

M. ERARD gets the conversation going again.

M. ERARD (to M. Cointet)
I ask again: Couldn't they do something else
with this celery? Make a celery rémoulade, for
instance?

MME COINTET
A rémoulade! Like they give you in cheap
restaurants, in bistros! (Pause) It's just that it
needs more salt.

MME COINTET (to M. Cointet)
Are you trying to monopolize the salt?

She takes it out of his hand.

M. COINTET
Bistro or not, celery rémoulade is very tasty,
whereas these soups . . .

MME ERARD
I remember, when I was a little girl . . .

MME COINTET
Rémoulade! I never used to make it in my
house.

MME COINTET (to M. Erard)
You probably had it in your transport café.

M. ERARD
Transport café or anywhere else, it's very tasty.

M. COINTET (to Mme Cointet)
Pass the salt.

MME COINTET
No. You'd empty it into your plate. Remember

the doctor. That reminds me—my pill!

She picks up a tube by the side of her husband's glass and holds it away from her eyes to read the label. M. COINTET then picks up a tube in front of her and holds it up to his pince-nez.

> MME COINTET
> That's yours. She's got them wrong again.

> M. COINTET
> She does it on purpose.

They exchange their tubes, and both take a pill out of their own. They hold out their glasses to GASTON, who pours water into them. MME COINTET puts her pill on her tongue and throws her head back to swallow it. As she does so, she casts a penetrating glance up at the ceiling. In the centre of a plaster molding, where a chandelier must once have hung, there is a clearly visible hole.

When she has drunk the water, MME COINTET puts her glass down and turns the same penetrating look on her husband.

SEQUENCE 3A

INTERIOR. DAY—GUEST HOUSE DINING ROOM.

The scene continues, but shot from above, the camera adopting the viewpoint of an observer on the upper floor, just above the dining room.

The characters' behaviour then changes. Their movements become more abrupt, their voices more bitter, their discussions seem on the point of becoming acrimonious, the sounds of mastication become more distinct.

Then, from upstairs, almost drowning out all the other sounds, can be heard sounds of swallowing followed by discreet belches: these are the now obvious manifestations of the presence of the observer who has assumed a kind of power over the guests round the table: M. SONGE.

Outside, intermittently, there are also children's cries, which could be of pleasure or pain.

> GASTON (puts down the water jug and picks up the wine bottle)
> Wine?

M. and MME ERARD turn their heads towards GASTON and hold out their glasses. Then M. ERARD picks up MME APOSTOLOS's glass and GASTON fills it. Their movements are jerky, their outstretched hands shake.

> MME APOSTOLOS (to Gaston)
> This little wine isn't bad, but I preferred the other one. Is there a big difference in price?

> GASTON (sharply)
> Fifty centimes. That's significant. I find this one just as good.

M. and MME COINTET have drunk their water and hold out their glasses to GASTON, who pours wine into them. From upstairs the sound of someone drinking can be distinctly heard.

> FRED
> What do you think of it, M. Cointet?

> MME COINTET
> M. Cointet has no call to have an opinion about wine, he isn't allowed to drink it.

(She snatches his glass away.)

All the same, it's a bit much, at your age, that
I still have to lay down the law. How can I get
you to understand?

MME COINTET (to Gaston)
He only has to dilute it, then it can't do him
any harm.

M. COINTET takes his glass back and GASTON adds a drop of
water to it. In all the following dialogue the acting is still a little distorted, the shots are no longer from above but they are taken from
odd angles.

MME COINTET
I have never seen celery rémoulade at any of
the tables we have been invited to, M. Cointet
and I. Isn't that right Edouard? A . . . a popular
dish, no doubt.

M. ERARD
Popular or not, it's very tasty. Whereas these
soups . . .

MME COINTET (to M. Cointet)
Answer me, for goodness' sake!

M. COINTET
What?

MME COINTET
Have you ever eaten celery rémoulade?

M. COINTET
Er . . .

MME COINTET
At the baroness's? In our Deauville guest house?
On Isola Bella? At Madame Aubier's? Surely
you aren't going to say you have? Drink your
soup. Very good for your cold.

MME APOSTOLOS
It's odd, your colds all year long. Hay fever at
the moment?

M. COINTET
Primrose fever in the spring, hay fever in June,
harvest fever in July, vintage fever . . .

MME COINTET
Are you being witty?

M. ERARD
Doesn't his pill help at all?

MME COINTET
That's for his liver. M. Cointet can't stuff himself
full of pills, what with his stomach. He ought to
go on a diet, that's what he ought to do.

M. COINTET
Let's say on a diet of celery soup.

MME COINTET
Quite so. Celery soup.

M. COINTET sneezes and searches his pockets for his
handkerchief.

M. COINTET
That handkerchief . . .

MME COINTET
Have you come down without a handkerchief
again?

M. COINTET
I can do without one.

He wipes his nose on his napkin.

MME ERARD
I remember, when I was a little girl . . .

MME APOSTOLOS
I always used to get colds too. But I don't any
more, now I'm older. I preferred that to my
rheumatism, though. My poor arms . . .

MME ERARD
You ought to go to the seaside.

MME APOSTOLOS
The seaside? Not likely! A good mud bath,
that's what I need. But it won't be for this year.

M. COINTET
They say it's two-edged. Bad for the heart.

MME COINTET (to M. Cointet)
You don't know anything about it.

MME COINTET (to Mme Apostolos)
They say there are some excellent spas in Italy.

MME APOSTOLOS
Ah, Italy . . .

MME COINTET
Paradise. Our Borromeans, our Borromeans!
Those days will have made me happy all my
life.

M. ERARD
You mean . . .

SEQUENCE 3B

EXTERIOR. DAY—ENTRANCE STEPS, DE BROY MANOR
HOUSE.

M. SONGE is giving rein to his imagination, and we see his fantasies, while below, the dialogue continues, off.

At the entrance to the manor house, we see a delighted M. and MME COINTET, surrounded by running, laughing children.

MME COINTET (off)
Memories, they're all we have left at our age.
Isn't that right Edouard?

M. COINTET (off)
What?

MME COINTET
Isola Bella, you haven't forgotten it I suppose?

SEQUENCE 3 continuation

INTERIOR. DAY—GUEST HOUSE DINING ROOM.

Back to the dining room. M. SONGE continues his observation. (Close-ups.) The intervals between the speeches become longer and longer, time is slowing down, until there is silence.

MME APOSTOLOS
I thought it was the Balearics.

MME COINTET
The Borromeans. Nothing can be confused
with the Borromeans. Those palm trees, those
azaleas! That morning light on the lake!

MME APOSTOLOS
It's odd, I was thinking of the Balearics . . .
or perhaps of the Canaries . . . Pass the salt,
please.

MME COINTET (passing the salt)
With your rheumatism?

MME APOSTOLOS
There's nothing to be done. A good mud bath,
that's what I need. In the Borromeans . . . I
mean in the . . .

MME COINTET
There aren't any spas in the Borromeans.
Luxury hotels, parks, palm trees, azaleas.
Paradise. Isn't that right, Edouard?

M. COINTET
Paradise.

MME APOSTOLOS
I was sure it was the Balearics, your paradise.
Or perhaps the Canaries . . .

MME ERARD
I remember, when I was a little girl . . .

MME APOSTOLOS
I must have been there . . . It's all so long ago.
The sea, that's what I remember. M. Cointet
ought to go to the seaside for his cold.

MME COINTET
The seaside? Not likely! It's two-edged.

M. COINTET
What was I saying?

MME COINTET
Finish your soup.

They all finish their soup with the exception of MME APOSTO-
LOS, who has put more pieces of bread in hers. Close-ups of MME
APOSTOLOS. She is having trouble with the bread, which keeps
falling off her spoon back into her plate.

Long shot: all the guests are immobilized. Only the sounds of MME
APOSTOLOS's soup break the silence. Then a voice from upstairs,
whispering and slightly tipsy, like a prompter in a theatre:

M. SONGE (off)
I remember, when I was a little girl . . .

Then MME ERARD, like a piece of clockwork that has just been
rewound, gets the dialogue going again.

MME ERARD (to Gaston)
I remember, when I was a little girl, celery . . .

MME COINTET
You had it in rémoulade, I imagine?

MME ERARD
Far from it. I couldn't stand it. Even the smell
made me feel sick. Odd, isn't it?

MME COINTET
We change as we get older.

M. COINTET (to M. Erard)
Do you know how to make a rémoulade?

M. ERARD
I . . .

MME ERARD
He doesn't know anything about it.

GASTON
Madame Apostolos, may I ring? You'll have
finished by the time Marie's ready.

He rings a little bell in front of him.

MME COINTET (to M. Erard)
Because you too dream of a rémoulade?

M. ERARD
I don't dream, I . . .

MME ERARD (to Mme Cointet)
I tell you, he doesn't know anything about it.

MME APOSTOLOS has just dropped a piece of bread from her
spoon on to her knees.

MME APOSTOLOS
My beautiful dress! Every time I change my
clothes, I make a mess!

She retrieves the bread and puts it back in her plate.

> MME APOSTOLOS
> Can you explain that? I only have to change . . .

M. SONGE's fantasies: a child eating a piece of celery and then spit-ting it out, are merged with those of MME APOSTOLOS: with each cut there is a change of character (MME APOSTOLOS and the little girl), who, sitting at the same place try to cope with the celery and the soup. MME APOSTOLOS is heard more and more faintly. The images become intermittent. At the same time slight snores are heard: M. SONGE is falling asleep.

> MME APOSTOLOS
> . . . I shan't be able to wear it next year, with its buttons in front, it'll be out of date . . .

> MME APOSTOLOS (to M. Erard)
> Ladies like to follow the fashion . . . They aren't like gentlemen . . . Ladies are clothes-conscious, they like to follow the fashion.

Long silence.

SEQUENCE 3 continuation

INTERIOR. DAY—GUEST HOUSE DINING ROOM.

Return to the beginning of the scene. The characters are themselves again. The exchanges sound natural.

> M. ERARD
> You could put it on back to front, couldn't you?

MME ERARD
Let Madame Apostolos finish her soup.

M. COINTET (to Gaston)
You aren't going on holiday, then?

GASTON
Not this year.

M. ERARD
The washing machine?

GASTON
The machine and everything else.

M. ERARD
What about your niece?

GASTON
She's going to come here for a break.

He squashes a fly on the oilcloth.

M. ERARD
Will you get her to do the washing?

MME COINTET
What's the matter with him today?

M. ERARD
The heat, probably.

M. ERARD (to M. Cointet) Shall I keep it for
you for your fishing?

He puts the fly down by M. COINTET's glass. MME COINTET
flicks it on to the floor with her napkin.

MME COINTET
He's disgusting! Say something, Monsieur
Gaston . . . This table is becoming a pigsty.

Sound of the service hatch. MME APOSTOLOS finishes her soup.
Enter MARIE, who goes to the hatch and puts a dish of meat on the
table. GASTON pulls the dish towards him. Close-up of the meat,
then of the fork inserted into it, then of the knife sawing away at it
ineffectually. Long silence of the guests.

There is a feeling of complicity among them. The sounds are less
intense, but they all seem afraid to touch the meat. The secret that
binds them together seems to be incarnated there, in front of them.
MARIE is the only one who reacts "normally". Although she is also
implicated, she remains rooted in reality.

GASTON
Where did you buy this meat, Marie?

MARIE (changing the plates)
Where did I buy it?

GASTON
Which butcher, for heaven's sake?

MARIE
Which butcher? Is Monsieur making fun of
me? Am I in the habit of changing butchers?

GASTON
It's uneatable. Just look at this.

He can't find the grain of the meat. He turns the joint in every direction. All eyes are riveted on the dish.

GASTON
This muck he palms off on us every time, didn't

I tell you to go to another butcher?

MARIE
That's all we need.

She has finished changing the plates and is about to take the soup tureen.

MARIE
You don't seem to remember what the other one did to us last year at Easter.

Pause.

MME APOSTOLOS
That's just it, he isn't the same . . . He's changed. A lady told me he's much better than ours. It's chalk and cheese. She was amazed that we still go to the same one. He sells her steak that melts in the mouth. You ought to try him, Marie.

MARIE
I tell you, he's just the same. And even if he had changed I wouldn't go to him, d'you hear me? Melts in the mouth, melts in the mouth, don't make me laugh! Unless she treats herself to fillet steak, your lady. Obviously, fillet steak, at the price it is, it can be tender.

MME APOSTOLOS
She told me she bought steak.

MARIE
Steak, steak, there's dozens of different kinds of steak! Don't you realize, that if you're prepared to pay . . .

MME APOSTOLOS
She told me steak, just like us.

Pause.

FRED
What was that joint we had at Easter?

MARIE
An uneatable gigot, that's what it was. I shall
never set foot in that butcher's again. And
if that lady treats herself to fillet, that's her
business.

She puts the soup tureen down in the hatch and goes out, banging
the door. From the kitchen she picks up the soup tureen and shuts
the hatch noisily.

The guests are uneasy, and look at the meat without budging.
GASTON looks as if he is suffering.

Outside, a child's terrified cry rises in a crescendo.

Silence.

Fade out.

SEQUENCE 4

EXTERIOR. DAY—SURROUNDINGS OF THE GUEST
HOUSE.

Exterior view of the house. Rusted shutters, dilapidated walls under
the overgrown Virginia creeper, wisteria. Then, on the other side of
the little stone wall, the dazzling wheatfield, and beyond that the
edge of the dark forest.

The child whose cry has continued since the end of the previous sequence can now be seen running away towards his father, who is calling him from the edge of the forest. A figure seen from behind (who will later be revealed as MORTIN) is watching the child, whom he seems to have terrorized, running away. The child has reached his father, who points at the house and tells him firmly that he must absolutely never go near it again. The child disappears into the forest, while his father, the GIPSY, keeps watch on the guest house. MARIE's voice, off, can then gradually be heard.

> MARIE (off)
> These gippos, these eternal gippos with their baskets. I don't know what to do with their baskets any more. And then they're a thieving lot . . .

SEQUENCE 4 (i)

INTERIOR. DAY—GUEST HOUSE KITCHEN AND STAIRCASE.

MARIE is in the kitchen. She keeps glancing out of the window at the GIPSY, while preparing a tray on which there is a cup of soup, some bread, and a bit of cheese. She continues her monologue while she picks up the tray and goes upstairs.

> MARIE
> . . . hens, rabbits . . . A funny lot. Who knows whether . . .

SEQUENCE 4 (ii)

INTERIOR. DAY—GUEST HOUSE FIRST FLOOR CORRIDOR.

Coming up from the cellar, FRED has followed MARIE, and catches up with her in the first floor corridor. With a finger to his lips he stops her, and puts a bottle of wine on the tray. MARIE speaks to him, but after knocking discreetly on one of the doors, FRED disappears without answering her question.

>   MARIE
>   What did it say in the paper yesterday?

Irritated, she knocks at M. SONGE's door and also disappears.

SEQUENCE 5

INTERIOR. DAY—GASTON'S ROOM.

In the semi-darkness in the room, whose shutters are half-closed, GASTON, whose growing unease has been apparent throughout the discussion with MARIE about the meat, has gone up to lie down on his bed, on the white cotton bedspread. His shirt is stained with perspiration under the arms. He has undone the top of his trousers. On the bedside table, a few boxes of pills. Underneath, the badly-closed door reveals a glimpse of a white china chamber pot. FRED goes up to him. They speak in undertones.

>   FRED
>   What's the matter?
>
>   GASTON
>   A bit of a pain here.
>
>   FRED
>   Where?
>
>   GASTON
>   Here.

FRED
In your stomach?

GASTON
No, higher up.

FRED
What sort of pain is it?

GASTON
I don't know. A sort of contraction.

FRED
Do you want a pain killer?

GASTON
Have you got one?

FRED
An aspirin.

GASTON
I don't know. It'll pass.

Pause.

FRED
Is it better?
GASTON
Yes.

FRED
Here, sit up.

GASTON
Thanks, Pull the pillow up.

Pause.

> You know what I'd like?
>
> FRED
> What?
>
> GASTON
> You to read me a few pages from Don Quixote.
>
> FRED
> Talk about a spoilt child.

Pause.

> If you like.

He goes and finds the volume among a few others on a shelf.

It is obvious that the magnificently bound volume has been much read. FRED goes back to GASTON, turning the pages of the book illustrated by Doré, then sits down on the bed.

> FRED
> What d'you want me to read?
>
> GASTON
> The end.

While FRED is reading, the camera slowly moves backwards until there is a general shot of the room.

> FRED
> "As all human things, especially the lives
> of men, are transitory, being ever on the
> decline from their beginnings till they reach
> their final end, and as Don Quixote had no

privilege from Heaven exempting him from the common fate . . ."

SEQUENCE 6

INTERIOR. DAY—M. SONGE'S ROOM.

Like GASTON's, the room is in semi-darkness.

M. SONGE is sitting in his armchair in front of a little table, his right foot enveloped in a cloth and resting on a stool.

Near him there is an old telescope on its tripod, next to a walking stick. An empty bottle of wine is standing on the floor.

On one wall, a very beautiful portrait of an old man in a Spanish frame. Above the bed, a little crucifix. On another wall, a clock whose frame is similar to that of the portrait. Under the bedside table, can be seen a china chamber pot.

On the other side of the bed, in a corner, M. SONGE's desk, covered in papers (some in his handwriting, newspaper cuttings, pages crumpled up and thrown here and there . . .) A big magnifying glass and a pair of scissors are lying on the desk.

In the middle of the room, it is clear that one of the floorboards has been taken up and put beside the gap it has left.

He starts to eat the frugal meal MARIE has put on the little table. He is trying to finish the celery soup.

Taking great care, MARIE is changing the cloth wrapped round M. SONGE's foot. He complains that she has hurt him.

> M. SONGE
> Ouch! . . . Couldn't you do something else

with this celery, it stinks?

MARIE
A rémoulade for instance? I've heard that one.

M. SONGE
A rémoulade, quite so. Very tasty, celery
rémoulade.

He says this in imitation of M. ERARD in the earlier scene. Pouring
himself a glass of FRED's wine, M. SONGE perks up. He looks at
the label; it isn't the usual plonk served to the other guests.

MARIE
You used to have it with the Baroness of the
Borromeans, I suppose? They've been harping
on that story for the last half hour downstairs.
Old Ma Cointet . . .

M. SONGE
Madame Cointet.

Silence. Close-up of M. SONGE.

SEQUENCE 6A

EXTERIOR. DAY—ENTRANCE STEPS, DE BROY MANOR
HOUSE.

M. SONGE resumes his fantasies. (As in sequence 3B)

MME COINTET is outside the entrance to the manor house with
the children.

MARIE (off)
Madame Cointet and the rest of them. They're

driving me mad with their eternal harping on
the same old stories.

SEQUENCE 6 continued

INTERIOR. DAY—M. SONGE'S ROOM.

Close-up of MARIE.

> MARIE
> Every day, at every meal, the rémoulade, the
> washing machine, the uneatable butcher, the
> Balearics, old Ma Apostolos who's losing her
> marbles . . .

> M. SONGE
> Madame Apostolos. Do you know that she
> used to be a great lady? She's travelled widely,
> she had lots of acquaintances.

SEQUENCE 6A continuation

EXTERIOR. DAY—ENTRANCE STEPS, DE BROY MANOR
HOUSE.

M. SONGE has a brief vision of the same scene as just now, but
MME COINTET is replaced by MME APOSTOLOS.

> M. SONGE
> She is still a friend of Monsieur de Broy, our
> lord of the manor.

On the same steps, seen from the same angle, the children have been
replaced by the DE BROYS, with whom MME APOSTOLOS is
having a discussion. With MARIE's voice, the vision disappears.

SEQUENCE 6 continuation

INTERIOR. DAY—M. SONGE'S ROOM.

Close-up of MARIE.

> MARIE
> You too, you're always harping on the same old
> stories. What do I care about their travels, their
> manor houses, their fine acquaintances? Finish
> your soup, it'll get cold.

> M. SONGE
> It stinks. Couldn't you . . .

> MARIE
> No, no and no. The doctor said you were to
> drink, to drink a lot, to eliminate goodness
> knows what . . .

M. SONGE smiles and pours himself another glass of wine. MARIE
shakes her head in despair, though probably not without some
affection.

> MARIE
> . . . Spite, I suppose. I'll bring you some Evian
> water.

Pause. She has finished changing the cloth. She takes a few steps
towards M. SONGE's desk.

> MARIE
> What does it say in the paper about the
> Ducreux's little boy, his disappearance?

> M. SONGE
> Nothing. The investigation isn't making any

headway.

MARIE
Haven't you any idea?

M. SONGE
None.

MARIE
Your lips are sealed. I know you. Like the
others. They don't say a word about it, they
fall back on the washing machine and all the
rest. In my presence, in my presence. But I've
sometimes overheard conversations under their
breath in the salon which stop the moment I
come in.

M. SONGE
Are you mad? What are you imagining?

Pause. MARIE tries to look at the papers lying about on his desk,
M. SONGE doesn't object, but he's slightly irritated.

MARIE
Me? Nothing. But I have a kind of idea that
they know something.

M. SONGE
Do you actually suspect that some of them are
involved in that horrible business?

MARIE
Oh, I don't suspect anyone, I'm not so stupid.
But they're saying in the village . . .

M. SONGE
What are they saying in the village?

MARIE
Nothing. You can set your mind at rest, like
everyone else.

She goes out, carefully walking round the hole and the floorboard
beside it.

SEQUENCE 7

EXTERIOR. DAY—MARKET.

Seen from the sky, the village market. We gradually descend, and the
market comes closer. MARIE can be recognized.

She goes from one stall to the next, compares their prices, recognizes
several housewives with whom she chats. But we can't hear what they
say, as they are speaking in low voices. Finally we get close enough to
hear a conversation.

MARIE
I tell you they don't, they don't know anything.
What does it say in the paper this morning?

STALLHOLDER
The investigation isn't making any headway.
But your gardener has been questioned by the
investigating judge.

MARIE
Johann? He hasn't breathed a word to me.
What did he say?

STALLHOLDER
I don't know. Mademoiselle Moine mentioned
it to my wife. It seems that on midsummer
night last year . . .

MARIE
What d'you mean, last year?

STALLHOLDER
Johann was at the party at the manor, and he
. . .

MARIE
What are you talking about? Johann wasn't
working at the manor then, he's been with us
for three years.

STALLHOLDER
That didn't stop them interrogating him.

MARIE
Is it in the paper?

STALLHOLDER
No, I tell you. It was Mademoiselle Moine . . .

MARIE
What does that old gossip know about it?
What did she say to your wife?

Resumption of high angle shots, (**medium close ups**). MARIE
makes gestures as if she wants to brush off a fly.

Loud sounds of a bird's wings.

The camera then moves up again.

STALLHOLDER
She said that during midsummer night at the
de Broy manor, the big party they give, Johann
went with some others to look for the Ducreux
boy. That was why the judge . . .

MARIE
Not possible. On midsummer night last year I
was with Johann at Sirancy for the fireworks.
So there!

She points to some fruit and vegetables on the stall. The trader weighs
them and hands her the bags which she stuffs in her shopping basket.
She pays, and nods to the stallholder.
High angle shot, as at the beginning of the scene. MARIE raises her
head, seeming to be looking at something.

SEQUENCE 8

EXTERIOR. DAY—DE BROY ENTRANCE.

At the same time a falcon alights on the gloved wrist of M. DE BROY.
He immediately covers the bird's head with the leather hood.

SEQUENCE 9

EXTERIOR, INTERIOR. NIGHT—GUEST HOUSE GARDEN,
CORRIDOR.

FRED is getting some fresh air, sitting in front of the house. Starry
sky. Owls. Tree frogs. *Don Quixote* abandoned on the grass . . .

After a moment he stands up, takes his keys out of his pocket and
goes and locks the garden gate.

Then he goes into the house and locks the two front doors and the
kitchen door.

He goes upstairs, starts down the corridor, puts his hand on the door
to his room, then changes his mind. He goes to GASTON's door
and opens it very quietly:

GASTON is fast asleep.

FRED shuts GASTON's door. As he is about to go back to his own room M. ERARD is seen coming out of one room like a thief and going into another.

SEQUENCE 9 (i)

FRED sits down at his table and switches on a little lamp in front of him. His room is as barely furnished as the others. Photos pinned on the walls. One, of an old man, is in a black oval frame. A chamber pot at the foot of the bed.

He takes a big bound notebook out of a drawer. He turns its pages. They are all dated and written on except one where only the date remains, all the rest has been carefully scratched out.

FRED soon comes to a blank page. He picks up his pen. He is seen writing, and heard thinking aloud.

> FRED
> What today? Same old story again. The washing machine, the celery rémoulade, the uneatable meat. Old Ma Cointet putting on airs, old man Erard unbearable, Apostolos dropping all her food on her dress.

He thinks back to some of the things he's just said as he writes them.

> FRED (off)
> The celery rémoulade, the uneatable meat, uneatable . . .

> FRED
> Good old Gaston, he does his best to keep

his flock happy. He must be fed up. No more
than I am. What did we let ourselves in for?
Ah, those wonderful days when we met! Me
between two drinking bouts, him between two
bouts of diarrhoea in that Italian health resort
. . . Which one was it, the first . . . Monteculi?
I was going to say the Borromeans . . . What an
absurd idea it was to start this lousy guest house.
All our savings . . . Already a whole life . . .

FRED (off)
. . . Absurd idea to start this lousy guest house
. . . lousy . . .

FRED
With all those poor idioms as Marie calls them.
These poor carcasses dragging themselves
around looking for affection, for kindness . . .

FRED (off)
. . . These poor carcasses . . . carcasses . . .

FRED
Enough to make you die of sadness.

FRED (off)
. . . Die of . . .

FRED
But I keep harping on the same things too. I
must make sure I cross out the unnecessary
repetitions in this notebook.

FRED (off)
. . . unnecessary repetitions . . .

FRED
Marie's probably forgotten the sugar for the
jam. She forgets everything but I understand
her.
Going to get lumbered with stoning the plums.

He makes a note on a different bit of paper.

FRED
Buy sugar. Buy bog paper. (He goes back to
his notebook) What does she do with the
bog paper she stuffs her pockets full of, old
Apostolos? Never managed to find out. Claims
her canary fouls its cage. She told me yesterday
that it doesn't sing any more, that it must be ill.

FRED (continuing)
Diarrhoea too, probably, a nice cure at
Thingummy, what's its name again, it'll come
back to me, for squittery canaries.

FRED (off)
Remember wine . . . Never managed to find
out . . . a nice cure . . .

FRED
Mademoiselle Reber is on holiday. We could
have lumbered her with stoning the plums.
She'll come back from her native Alsace and
regale us with stories of storks, sauerkraut,
nieces who are unmarried mothers and
surreptitious christenings. Her accent that I
haven't been able to stand for the last ten years.
What am I talking about? It's more like fifteen
or twenty. Horrible.

FRED (off)
... Fifteen or twenty years ...

FRED
And old Ma Erard with the dolls she makes
for poor children. They'd prefer electronic
games, poor children would. Will our washing
machine be electronic? I've no idea. Gaston
must know. One more expense. Shit.

FRED (off)
... Dolls ... washing the dolls ... a machine
... shit ...

FRED shuts his diary, puts it back in the drawer, stands up and urinates in the chamber pot.

SEQUENCE 9(ii)

EXTERIOR. NIGHT—GUEST HOUSE GARDEN.

Long shot of the front of the house. The light goes out in FRED's
window. In another room someone puts his on. Then a third goes
out. Owls screech.

SEQUENCE 10

EXTERIOR. DAY—EDGE OF THE FOREST.

Violent contrast in the light. Bright sunshine. At the edge of the forest, the GIPSY is putting his baskets away in his caravan.

His wife is hanging up clothes on a washing line. Their child is playing with several identical, roughly-made dolls: MME ERARD's
dolls. Then the GIPSY takes the child's hand and they go into the
forest. A lot of children's cries can be heard, echoed by adult's calls.

The general effect of the sounds is ambiguous. Bird calls are mixed in with them.

SEQUENCE 11

INTERIOR. DAY—M. SONGE'S ROOM—FLASHBACK.

It's winter. Cold morning light. The bare trees and fields can be seen through the windows. M. SONGE, sitting at his table, is dressed in warm clothes. He has a shawl over his shoulders.

A pile of newspapers is within reach of his hand, he is cutting articles out of them with his scissors. The scene (close-up) begins with one of them: DUPONT CHILD FOUND DROWNED IN POND NEAR CRACHON. POLICE INVESTIGATING.

> M. SONGE
> I must produce something. Finish what
> I began. Where'd I got to? Dupont child
> drowned in a pond after being violated and
> strangled. Quite a programme. The police are
> investigating. Who do they suspect? A villager?
> A stranger? Let's say a gipsy. Change the names
> in the paper.

He starts writing.

He is writing a novel. Hence a mixture of voices: when he's thinking aloud, his voice off when he's writing, and the voice of the character he is conjuring up which sometimes replaces his own.

> M. SONGE (off)
> Questioned by the investigating judge,
> the gipsy categorically denies having been
> in the district at the time. He was in the
> neighbouring department where his wife was

giving birth to a boy. To the judge's question:
"When did you come back to our region to sell
your baskets?" he answers "In the spring, at the
beginning of June, I think. I went straight to
the manor house".

He raises his head, as the ideas come to him he begins to smile.

M. SONGE
Whose manor house? Change the names in
the paper. Monsieur de Broy. What do I risk?
The novel's bound to be a flop, might as well
shove all my friends' names in it. Facilitate the
descriptions.

He starts writing again, concentrating hard, and the voices of the
GIPSY and the JUDGE are heard, off.

GIPSY (off)
The gentleman really likes me, he always tells
Johann the gardener, buy a basket and give him
a drink in the kitchen.

JUDGE (off)
Were you at the midsummer night party that
year?

GIPSY (off)
Oh, I'm there every year, and Monsieur comes
and talks to me and asks me how I'm doing.

JUDGE (off)
Are there a lot of people at that party?

SEQUENCE 11A

EXTERIOR. NIGHT—DE BROY MANOR GARDENS.

From now on, accompanying the dialogue that continues off, the camera returns to the visions that M. SONGE is trying to conjure up: in the first place (**high angle long shot**) M. DE BROY greeting his guests, including the GIPSY. Then, rapid cuts, the guest house characters mixed with less familiar ones.

> GIPSY (off)
> Heaps of people, the whole village is invited for the fireworks at midnight.

> JUDGE (off)
> But before midnight, already a lot of people?

> GIPSY (off)
> Yes, society people.

> JUDGE (off)
> Who, for example?

> GIPSY (off)
> I don't know them, your Honour, but I hear folk talk about them.

> JUDGE (off)
> What names, for example?

SEQUENCE 11B

EXTERIOR. NIGHT—ENTRANCE TO DE BROY MANOR HOUSE.

Corresponding to the names the GIPSY reels off, there are successive shots of the guests, as if conjured up by his voice. M. SONGE himself appears among them, making notes in a little book.

> GIPSY (off)
> Well, M. Mortin, M. Songe, M. de Ballaison, Mlle de Bonne-Mesure, the Duchess of goodness knows what, a beautiful lady, I've often seen her, and another princess, almost all with handles to their names.

> JUDGE (off)
> And the gentlemen from the guest house are there too?

> GIPSY (off)
> Yes, with their maid Marie and their guests . . .

SEQUENCE 11C

EXTERIOR. NIGHTFALL—SURROUNDINGS OF THE GUEST HOUSE.

The GIPSY has just sold two baskets to MARIE who takes them into the house. He watches her as she goes, and stays where he is, observing JOHANN who is moving some earth, and FRED who seems to be on the lookout for something. He pretends to leave, but then hides so as to go on watching without being seen.

> GIPSY (off)
> . . . I know this lot better, I sell Marie my baskets, she laughs when I arrive, she doesn't know what to do with my baskets any more but she still buys them, funny isn't it? The guest house isn't like the manor, they haven't got much money and their garden's neglected, I asked Monsieur Gaston whether he'd like

> me to look after it but he said no, I've got too
> many expenses, but I wouldn't have charged
> him much, every little helps . . .

SEQUENCE 11C (continuation)

INTERIOR. DAY—M. SONGE'S ROOM.

At the moment when the JUDGE's voice interrupts the GIPSY, the
camera returns to a close-up of M. SONGE in his room.

> JUDGE (off)
> Let's come back to the midsummer night party.
> Wasn't there one year . . .

M. SONGE is looking through his magnifying glass at a newspaper
photo of the party. It shows MME APOSTOLOS, PROFESSOR
SAGRIN, some children, including the DUPONT boy, no doubt,
and in a corner, MORTIN . . .

> JUDGE (off)
> . . . . . . About five years ago, a tragic event
> during the party?

> GIPSY (off)
> What d'you mean?

> JUDGE (off)
> The disappearance of the Dupont's child, a
> village boy?

> GIPSY (off)
> Oh, much longer ago than that, maybe ten
> years ago, Professor Sagrin was going to take
> him home to his parents, he couldn't find him,
> the children who were still there were playing

186

in the grounds.

JUDGE (off)
And what happened?

GIPSY (off)
Nothing.

The GIPSY' s word makes M. SONGE smile. He looks up from the photo and puts his magnifying glass down.

SEQUENCE 11D

EXTERIOR. NIGHT—MANOR HOUSE GROUNDS.
The GIPSY is seen dragging a child away, (his son, no doubt). The child struggles.

JUDGE (off)
What do you mean, nothing?

GIPSY (off)
I mean I don't know, I'd gone back to my caravan.

SEQUENCE 11E

EXTERIOR. NIGHT—POND.

The GIPSY can be seen keeping watch by the pond.

JUDGE (off)
But you certainly heard later that the child was found drowned in a pond near Crachon?

GIPSY (off)
Yes, your Honour, but not in Crachon, in the middle of the forest.

SEQUENCE 11F

EXTERIOR. NIGHT—FOREST.

At these words, the GIPSY is seen again, still keeping watch, no longer by the pond but in the middle of the forest.

JUDGE (off)
And no one troubled you, the police didn't question you?

SEQUENCE 11G

EXTERIOR. NIGHTFALL—GIPSY'S CARAVAN AND SURROUNDINGS.

The GIPSY goes back to his caravan, laden with baskets. Then he is seen skinning a rabbit. His son is playing quietly beside him.

Suddenly he hears something: he sends his son into the caravan and goes off towards the forest.

GIPSY (off)
No, your Honour.

JUDGE (off)
You aren't telling me the truth, your caravan was parked at the edge of the forest.

In the darkness of the forest, the GIPSY sees a shadow that seems to be embracing another, smaller shadow. He hesitates, then rapidly makes his way back to his caravan.

> GIPSY (off)
> That's not true, at that time I was camping near
> Chatruse, a nice quiet little place, and then you
> know, we're on our guard against these things,
> us gipsies, we lie low, people are always making
> trouble for us, they blame us for everything,
> we're Christians, we are, even Evangelists, yes,
> you mustn't think . . .

SEQUENCE 11 (continuation)

INTERIOR. NIGHTFALL—M. SONGE'S ROOM.

M. SONGE is fighting against sleep. He pushes his papers away and
rouses himself. He stands up, takes his stick, and goes and urinates
in his chamber pot. Then he adjusts his clothes.

> M. SONGE
> Oof! That's enough for today. We'll wait for
> Marie to bring our tea, and those disgusting
> biscottes she makes me eat. Disgusting
> biscottes. I shall ask my friend Mortin to bring
> me something different.

He goes and sits down in his armchair by the window.

> M. SONGE (shivering)
> It's so cold, it's unbearable. They could at least
> give me a little heater.

He looks at the portrait of the old man.

> M. SONGE
> Well, yes, my dear soldier we're certainly on

our beam ends. When I think of the old days
. . . Our beautiful house, our servants . . . It's
all a long time ago.

SEQUENCE 12

EXTERIOR. DAY—M. SONGE'S FORMER HOUSE.

Summer again. M. SONGE, dressed like a country squire, is on the
terrace of his beautiful house. On a table in front of him, game is
laid out like a shooting bag. Pheasants, partridges, rabbits, with a
few drops of blood dripping from them. He is surrounded by his
NIECE and his NEPHEW, who are listening as eagerly as children
to his account of the shoot, maybe at the DE BROY's place, or of the
poaching activities of JOHANN, who can be seen going by in the
garden with a wheelbarrow full of earth.
From one of the six or seven windows of the facade, a woman
shouts:

> MARIE (off)
> The hors d'oeuvres are ready, will I serve them?

> M. SONGE (off)
> That horrible habit she had of yelling out of
> her window. How many times did I tell her?

SEQUENCE 13

EXTERIOR. DAY—GUEST HOUSE GARDEN.

In front of the house two chairs, and a wicker armchair in which M.
SONGE is sitting. The scene is almost an exact copy of the preceding
one, but it makes a stark contrast. Instead of a beautiful facade, the
dilapidated wall of the guest house. Instead of a well-stocked table,
the little table and the shabby furniture.

M. SONGE is drinking a glass of water. He makes a few notes in his little book. MARIE brings him a cushion and slides it behind his back, and gently replaces the stool under his bad leg.

> MARIE
> You could write here for a bit. It's nice out here before dinner.

He protests a little, sits up as best he can, and tries to look a little more impressive.

JOHANN is working in the garden, his movements are slow, his hands dig up some soil and bring it up to his face, as if he were studying its composition. M. SONGE can't help watching him. MORTIN comes in through the garden gate and walks slowly up to his friend, looking at the dead flowers in the beds. M. SONGE, who had had his back to the gate, looks round abruptly.

> M. SONGE
> Is that you? And about time too!

> MORTIN
> It's me.

He sits down on a chair.

> How's our gout?

> M. SONGE (looking at his foot wrapped in the cloth)
> No better, no worse. And you, your asthma?

> MORTIN
> No better, no worse. That's to say the weather isn't so hot as it was last week . . . (he looks up at the next door house). Still that horrible smell. What on earth can they get up to in that

kitchen?

Pause.

> M. SONGE
> They cook, presumably. But that smell doesn't come from next door. It's ours.

> MORTIN
> Still those uneatable meals?

> M. SONGE
> Alas, yes.

> MORTIN
> What were you dreaming about?

Close-up of M. SONGE. The question has surprised him. He is reluctant to say.

SEQUENCE 13A

INTERIOR. DAY—INVESTIGATING JUDGE'S OFFICE.

We are suddenly transported to an office in the Law Courts.

JOHANN the gardener, sitting down, is answering questions put to him by the investigating JUDGE, whom we never see.

Behind the gardener, a half-open window. The sky is overcast. A few thunder claps are heard in the distance. JOHANN's hands are dirty, with soil under his nails. He can't hear very well, and often cups his hand behind his right ear. The JUDGE then raises his voice.

> JUDGE (off)
> And what were your responsibilities at the

manor house?

JOHANN
What?

JUDGE (off)
What did you do at the manor?

JOHANN
My goodness, a bit of everything.

JUDGE (off)
Meaning?

SEQUENCE 13 (continuation)

EXTERIOR. DAY—GUEST HOUSE GARDEN.

Back to the guest house. JOHANN is still working in a corner of the garden. He is using his spade again.

M. SONGE finally answers MORTIN's question.

M. SONGE
What was I dreaming about?

MORTIN
Yes, what about?

M. SONGE
I've no idea. (Pause) Yes I have though. I haven't written a word of my exercises for I don't know how long.

MORTIN
Because you're still writing them?

M. SONGE
Don't laugh at me. You know very well they
worry me.

MORTIN
I'd no idea. You never talk to me about
anything but your squabbles with Marie,
Cointet and all the rest of them. (Pause) Well
then, so you're going on with them? Still your
novel?

M. SONGE
I'm afraid so.

MORTIN
Why afraid? I think it's very praiseworthy. Me,
I don't do anything now but read the paper and
visit my niece. How's yours, by the way?

M. SONGE
I've no idea.

SEQUENCE 13B

INTERIOR. DAY—M. SONGE'S FORMER HOUSE.

In the kitchen, the NEPHEW and NIECE are smearing chocolate
sauce over each other's faces, and start chasing one another, laughing. While the dialogue continues, off, they meet other nephews
and nieces and go on playing with them like dirty children, running
round the table.

M. SONGE (off)
Have you seen her recently?

> MORTIN (off)
> About a month ago. She was talking of coming
> to see you but I'm not sure when. (Pause) Tell
> me then, that novel? Ah, I remember now . . .
> Still that business of stolen jewellery . . . or
> pictures?

SEQUENCE 13B (continuation)

INTERIOR. DAY—INVESTIGATING JUDGE'S OFFICE.

Close-up of JOHANN.

> JUDGE (off)
> Meaning?

> JOHANN
> Repairs in the house, the electrics, heating,
> plumbing, replacing this or that, errands, and
> especially the gardens, that was hard work.

SEQUENCE 13 (continuation)

EXTERIOR. DAY—GUEST HOUSE GARDEN.

Over a close-up of JOHANN, who goes on working, the JUDGE's
voice is still heard.

> JUDGE (off)
> The de Broy gentlemen are very wealthy. They
> still do a great deal of entertaining at the
> manor, as they did in your time. Actually, how
> long is it since you left there?

JOHANN (off)
Three years. Almost four, now.

JUDGE (off)
Do you still see them sometimes?

The camera pans to MORTIN and M. SONGE, who are still conversing.

M. SONGE
I changed it a long time ago. It wasn't original.
No less original, though, than what I've done
since. Since when? I don't remember.

MORTIN
Since when, since when, all we do is repeat the
same thing.

M. SONGE
We rehash, what d'you expect? What can we
do?

MORTIN
Have a drink. Nothing like it. But what's that I
see? You're drinking water.

M. SONGE
That bitch Marie. She claims she's worried
about my health.

MORTIN (calling)
Marie, I'm here. Bring us something to drink.
Something decent.

MARIE (off, shouting from the house)
Monsieur Songe isn't allowed . . .

The rest of the phrase gets lost.

> MORTIN
> I'll go. We're sure to find something.

> M. SONGE
> That'd surprise me.

As he says this, he looks round at JOHANN, who can still be seen in a corner of the garden.

> JOHANN (off)
> What?

SEQUENCE 13C

INTERIOR. DAY—SALON, DE BROY MANOR HOUSE.

While we hear JOHANN still being interrogated by the JUDGE we see the de Broy manor house.

JOHANN arrives there at night, and is greeted by MARTHE, the cook.

> JUDGE (off)
> Do you still go back to the manor sometimes?

> JOHANN (off)
> It has happened. To see Marthe the cook, but I haven't seen the gentlemen again.

> JUDGE (off)
> Apropos of their guests, who were their close friends?

> JOHANN (off)

What d'you mean?

JUDGE (off)
The people they saw most frequently, who
stayed with them most frequently.

The camera pans. We see the manor house guests at a recent reception. In particular the nephews and nieces. They are a little too elegant, and make seductive gestures to everyone.

JOHANN (off)
My goodness . . . Maybe the Duchess, and
their cousin Mademoiselle Ariane . . . and
also Mademoiselle Lacruseille and her friend
Mademoiselle . . . I can't remember her name.
JUDGE (off)
And among the gentlemen?

JOHANN (off)
Monsieur de Ballaison, Monsieur d'Eterville
. . . Monsieur Mortin, Monsieur Carré,
Monsieur Charbois the antique dealer . . .

JUDGE (off)
Important personages, yes. But among the
young people?

JOHANN (off)
Young people, young people . . . Monsieur de
Broy, that's the nephew, Monsieur de Bonne-
Mesure, that's Mlle. Ariane's nephew, Monsieur
Hotcock the American, Mademoiselle Francine,
Mademoiselle de Hem . . .

JUDGE (off)
But there can't only have been members of the
aristocracy? Monsieur de Broy, even though

he belongs to the nobility, isn't known to be
standoffish, is he?

SEQUENCE 13 (continuation)

EXTERIOR. DAY—GUEST HOUSE GARDEN.

MORTIN comes back with a bottle of Pernod and a glass. He sits
down with M. SONGE again.

> MORTIN
> I've found it. Marie is furious. She probably
> knocks back the Pernod herself.

He serves M. SONGE, and then himself. He raises his glass.

> MORTIN
> Our health!

> M. SONGE (also raising his glass)
> Or what remains of it.

> MORTIN
> Well, go on then. Tell me about your novel.
> What's new in it?

> M. SONGE
> Poof! Not new at all. That old business about
> the Dupont boy, d'you remember? Who
> was found drowned in a pond, violated and
> strangled.

> MORTIN
> That was a good ten or fifteen years ago. Yes, I
> remember . . .

SEQUENCE 13D

INTERIOR. DAY—BISTRO IN THE SQUARE BY THE CHURCH.

M. SONGE at the window, pulls back the curtain.

Dazzling sunshine.

The church doors are wide open, and in front of the porch the undertakers are sliding the little coffin into the hearse. The cortege starts off and passes under the window of the bistro. M. SONGE lets the curtain fall back and joins MORTIN, who is drinking at the bar.

> M. SONGE
> Well, I'm elaborating on it with the help of the newspapers of the time, I've got a whole pile of them on my desk. Though it's not easy to find my way through all the journalists' verbiage. I leave out some details, I add others . . . I imagine, I make my mind a blank.

Pause.

Spadefuls of earth can be heard falling on the child's coffin.

SEQUENCE 13 (continuation)

EXTERIOR. DAY—GUEST HOUSE GARDEN.

Close-up of M. SONGE.

> M. SONGE
> At our age, imagination.., in short, it's a dog-drawn plough. But I intend to continue. (Pause) What might help me is this new

Ducreux business, the kid who disappeared
about two weeks ago I think.

MORTIN
How can that help you?

M. SONGE
With the descriptions, the characters . . . You
know, I've been thinking of sticking the names
of my friends in it, and of their houses, and the
nearby villages . . . Our lords of the manor, the
de Broys, the Ballaisons, old Apostolos . . . and
even the servants and the local hicks . . . yes,
that would be a great help. What d'you think?

MORTIN
What do I think? That you're completely crazy.
Don't you know that they're not making any
headway in the Ducreux business, and . . .

M. SONGE
Precisely. They aren't making any headway. I'm
making it for them. It amuses me . . .

SEQUENCE 13 (continuation)

INTERIOR. DAY—INVESTIGATING JUDGE'S OFFICE.

JOHANN
What do you mean?

JUDGE (off)
That he isn't proud, that he likes simple people,
people who work . . .

JOHANN
Layabouts, yes.

JUDGE (off)
Meaning?

JOHANN
Nothing.

JUDGE (off)
This is between ourselves, Monsieur Johann,
you can speak unreservedly to me, with
complete freedom. What idlers were you
thinking about?

JOHANN
Not specially about layabouts.

JUDGE (off)
Perhaps about young men who are not too
fond of work?

JOHANN
Perhaps, yes.

JUDGE (off)
And that young men like that were frequently
to be found among the guests?

JOHANN
If you like.

JUDGE (off)
It isn't what I like, I'm simply asking.

It has got much darker. The storm, which has been getting closer, finally breaks. Still speaking, the JUDGE stands up and goes and closes the window behind JOHANN. Then he sits down again and switches on his desk lamp. We have not seen his face. The rain trickles down the window.

> JUDGE (off)
> Shall we say that there were usually more young people than elderly people among the guests? You mentioned the Duchess de BoisSuspect, the Princess de Hem, Mlle Ariane, you must agree they are not in their first youth? Nor are the gentlemen you mentioned?

> JOHANN
> My goodness, no.

> JUDGE (off)
> So you see, the de Broy gentlemen are fond of young people, they like to laugh, to enjoy themselves?

> JOHANN
> That's true enough.

> JUDGE (off)
> And the young men, the boys, I mean, were more numerous than the ladies in these invitations?

> JOHANN
> I didn't count them.

> JUDGE (off)
> Did you . . . how can I put it . . . during those evenings . . . or even nights . . . did you come across . . . things . . . that may have shocked you?

JOHANN
What?

SEQUENCE 13 (continuation)

EXTERIOR. DAY—GUEST HOUSE GARDEN.

Close-up of MORTIN. He reacts violently to M. SONGE's project.

> MORTIN
> It amuses you? You're losing your marbles, my dear fellow.

> M. SONGE
> Why am I losing my marbles?

> MORTIN
> Because you ought to know that some of our acquaintances . . . the lords of the de Broy manor, among others, and their gigolos . . . have been more or less suspected since that midsummer night.

> M. SONGE
> Suspected of what? You're talking like Marie.

> MORTIN
> Of having been directly or indirectly involved in this kidnapping which is strangely similar to the other one, quite so. Marie isn't mad. They're talking about it in the village.

> M. SONGE
> I really don't know which of us is losing his marbles. Our de Broy friends, do you realize?

(Pause. He's puzzled.) And anyway, what
does that matter, I ask you, when my novel is
nothing but the simple, inoffensive hobby of
an old failure who doesn't know what to do
with himself?

MORTIN
But your simple hobby will be unsaleable. Do
you realize?

M. SONGE
Did I ever say anything about selling it? Who do
you take me for? Have I ever published any of
my exercises? Have I the slightest illusion about
my talents? Come on, come down to earth.

MORTIN
My dear friend, what if the police, who know
what good neighbours we are with the lords of
the manor, came and questioned you about the
Ducreux affair?

M. SONGE
The police? That would be the day!

MORTIN
The police, quite so . . .

Close-up of M. SONGE. He is considering.

SEQUENCE 13 (continuation)

INTERIOR. DAY—INVESTIGATING JUDGE'S OFFICE.

JUDGE (off)
Did you, during those evenings or nights, ever
come across anything that may have shocked you?

> JOHANN
> I go to bed very early.
>
> JUDGE (off)
> Well, let's say during the day, then, did some
> of those young men or other people behave
> together in a way . . . that you didn't like?

With this last speech, we begin to hear the earth falling on the coffin again (sequence 13D), or JOHANN shovelling it out of his wheelbarrow (sequence 3).

SEQUENCE 13B (continuation)

INTERIOR. DAY—M. SONGE'S FORMER HOUSE.

The NEPHEW and NIECE are smearing chocolate cream over the faces of the children there. This makes them laugh a lot. A little boy struggles, and cries out. Continuation of the dialogue, off, also of the sounds of the earth.

> JOHANN (off)
> I don't like your questions. You began by
> asking me about the Ducreux boy.
>
> JUDGE (off)
> Well, answer me. Who do you think might
> have taken that child off to the forest in the
> middle of the night?
>
> JOHANN (off)
> Professor Sagrin had promised to take him
> home to his parents after the fireworks, he
> couldn't find him in the grounds so two or
> three of us went looking for him as far as the
> forest, it wasn't easy with our torches . . .

JUDGE (off)
So you actually were at the manor that evening,
and not in Sirancy with Marie, the guest house
maid?

JOHANN (off)
Yes.

JUDGE (off)
That's all I wanted to know today.

SEQUENCE 13 (continuation)

EXTERIOR. DAY—GUEST HOUSE GARDEN.

JOHANN finishes digging with his spade, then puts it over his
shoulder and goes off. He passes MORTIN and M. SONGE, who
continue their discussion.

MORTIN
The investigation won't go on hanging fire
for ever. They'll go on questioning just about
everyone, including me, and you, and your
fellow guests, including you, do you hear me?
And what if some inquisitive person takes a
look at what you've written?

M. SONGE
What inquisitive person?

MORTIN
A policeman searching your things, of course.
You'd be in a fine mess. Sent for by the judge and
all the rest of it. And as you stammer and lose the
drift on every possible occasion, that makes you a
suspect as well. And me in the same boat.

MORTIN stands up and makes for the garden gate. M. SONGE also stands up, laboriously, and goes to see him out, leaning on his stick.

> M. SONGE
> My poor old chap, you're making a song and chance about it, as Marie would say.

> MORTIN
> Chance or not, you must immediately stop mixing these people up in your inoffensive hobby. Believe me.

They shake hands, and he goes out.

> M. SONGE (with a slightly ironic smile)
> Good God, what a business! Here I am, high and dry again!

MORTIN is already on the pavement.

> MORTIN
> Come down to earth, then, and wet your whistle with Pernod.

SEQUENCE 14

EXTERIOR. DAY—VILLAGE.

MORTIN passes the bistro, the church, and then the cemetery on the outskirts of the village. He walks along the edge of the forest. The sun is still high in the sky.

> M. SONGE (off)
> Which is strangely similar to the other . . .
> Which is strangely similar to the other . . .

SEQUENCE 15

EXTERIOR. DAY—FOREST.

In the darkness of the forest, where the same laughter and cries can be heard as in sequence 10, the scene with the GIPSY. Midday. Stifling heat. Children are dotted about all over the place, playing hide-and-seek, climbing trees etc . . . THE SCHOOLMISTRESS and the TRAINEE TEACHER, are on their end-of-term outing with their young pupils.

> SCHOOLMISTRESS
> I haven't seen the Ducreux boy for a while.
> He was there with his sister picking bilberries.
> Have you seen him?

The TRAINEE is attending to a child who has hurt his knee. She is dabbing disinfectant on the cut. The child is trying not to cry.

> TRAINEE
> No. But he's always wandering off on his own.
> According to his mother . . .

> SCHOOLMISTRESS
> Do you know her?

> TRAINEE
> Yes, we're neighbours. The boy often leaves the
> house without telling anyone. His mother says
> it's just escapades. But she worries, all the same.
> Hasn't she mentioned it to you?

> SCHOOLMISTRESS
> No. But you ought to have warned me.

> TRAINEE
> I didn't think about it, we were busy collecting

them up outside the school . . .

> SCHOOLMISTRESS
> Keep an eye on all these. I'll go and look over
> by the forest.

The SCHOOLMISTRESS goes over to the edge of the forest where she meets the GIPSY. There are still as many children's shouts. Other, less identifiable sounds are mixed in with them.

The SCHOOLMISTRESS and the GIPSY are very natural. But the spectator must have a very strong feeling of tension.

> SCHOOLMISTRESS
> Good morning, my good man. You haven't by
> any chance seen a little boy wandering off from
> our group? He's wearing a red shirt and a white
> hat.

> GIPSY
> No, I saw you from a distance with all that
> lot of kids and Mademoiselle Cruze. Is it your
> school outing already? Time flies!

> SCHOOLMISTRESS
> If you see him, please bring him back to me.
> We're no more than two hundred metres away,
> under the big oak tree.

> GIPSY
> Oh, I can hear you very well. All the brats
> shouting and laughing. It keeps me company.

> SCHOOLMISTRESS
> I rely on you. After all this time, with your
> baskets . . .

GIPSY
How's your mother, by the way?

SCHOOLMISTRESS
She's well, thank you.

The SCHOOLMISTRESS walks off. The GIPSY goes on standing there while the camera climbs. When the SCHOOLMISTRESS has disappeared, the GIPSY runs into the forest, where the camera follows him.

At the same time, the surrounding noises become fainter and give place to the sound of a butcher chopping up meat. The GIPSY suddenly stops, and strains his ears.

Once again the sounds of the forest return, but they are different: instead of the children's shouts there is the song of more or less bizarre birds, like those in a exotic forest.

The GIPSY turns his head right and left, as if he is looking for something. Then he starts running again: the forest opens out in front of him. Once again there is the sound of cleavers cutting meat.

The GIPSY has stopped again. He again keeps looking round. Then we realize that he has at last found what he was looking for.

As in sequence 11G (with the JUDGE), one shadow is embracing another, as if it was strangling it.

Then this shadow raises a butcher's cleaver and brings it down on its victim. At the same time the sounds of the meal in the guest house begin to make themselves heard (chairs scraping along the floor, knives and forks clinking . . .), but they are dominated by a knife grating on a plate.

The shadow straightens up. It is entirely hidden by an ample garment. All that can be seen is a mouth stained with blood, or perhaps with chocolate cream.

The shadow tucks the knife and hatchet into its belt and moves deeper into the forest, while the camera moves upward, and the guests' dialogue, off, insinuates itself.

> MME APOSTOLOS (off)
> You weren't with me when that lady told me?

> MME COINTET (off)
> I don't remember. But there's no reason not to try the other butcher.

> M. COINTET (off)
> I wonder whether Marie isn't right, about the quality. It must depend on the price.

> MME COINTET (off)
> Don't interfere. Gentlemen don't know anything about such matters but they will insist on giving advice. It's like the rémoulade.

The camera has come to rest at the edge of the forest. The sun is going down. The shadow slowly continues on its way to the guest house.

SEQUENCE 16

INTERIOR. EVENING—GUEST HOUSE DINING ROOM.

The evening meal, seen by M. SONGE from above.

GASTON can't manage to carve the joint and hacks at it, hence the grating sounds of the knife already heard in the preceding sequence.

GASTON helps himself, and then pushes the dish into the middle of the table.

GASTON
You'll have to do the best you can.

The camera descends, but still sees the scene through M. SONGE's eyes. The guests help themselves in turn as if their lives depended on it: each rapaciously cuts and spears a piece from the dish. Then the mastication begins, with more or less discreet manoeuvres of their tongues, and more or less furtive movements of their fingers to remove the fibres from between their teeth.

They are sitting in the same places as before, (still the two unoccupied chairs).

At last the conversation begins again. Each appears first in medium close-up, then in close-up, and the camera doesn't spare any movement of their jaws, teeth or dentures, also lingering over certain looks . . . With one accord, they are all fighting with this "uneatable" meat that doesn't "melt in their mouths".

Through the window, JOHANN can be seen from time to time cutting the hedges with sweeping movements of a gigantic pair of secateurs, whose clicking sounds travel as far as the dining room.

MME APOSTOLOS (to Mme Erard) Or was it you, Madame Erard, who were with me when that lady told me?

MME ERARD
I don't remember. But there's no reason not to try the other one. Is there, Monsieur Gaston?

GASTON
Didn't I already tell her to last week? Don't you remember?

MME ERARD suddenly appears with her face and hands stained with blood.

> MME ERARD
> Perhaps it was Mademoiselle Reber, just before she went on holiday . . . Yes, it must have been Mademoiselle Reber.

> FRED
> I can't understand why Marie is so obstinate. This fellow, palming such muck off on us after all this time. He's got a nerve. Did we have a gigot at Easter last year?

Silence.

> MME COINTET
> Yes, I remember. It was the other butcher.

> MME APOSTOLOS
> But I tell you, he's changed.
> (to Mme Erard)
> I'm sure it was you.

MME ERARD is now perfectly clean.

> MME ERARD
> There may be a solution. Why not try?

We discover M. COINTET who is eating as filthily as possible, his mouth smeared, his sleeves soiled.

> M. COINTET
> You needn't think that so far as quality . . .

> MME COINTET
> Since they tell you that the other, for the same

price . . .

M. COINTET
Fillet, perhaps.

M. COINTET has become clean again.

MME COINTET
What do you know about it, my poor man.
You've never been able to tell a chop from a
steak, or a leg from a wing.

MME APOSTOLOS
Actually it may well have been Mademoiselle
Reber who was with me. Where was it? Let me
think . . .

Pause.

MME APOSTOLOS
At the Magasins-Prix, that was it. At the
Magasins-Prix, quite so. She was amazed that
we still go to the same one. Chalk and cheese,
quite so.
(to Madame Cointet)
Talking of holidays, when are you going away?

MME COINTET
On the second of August.

M. COINTET
That's to say . . .

MME COINTET (to M. Cointet)
The second of August. Have you changed your
mind again?

> M. COINTET
> There was that belote tournament, I told you
> . . .

> MME COINTET
> A belote tournament! Put off our holiday for a
> belote tournament! That would be the limit!
> M. COINTET
> But I told you . . .

> MME COINTET (to Mme Apostolos)
> We're leaving on the second of August. We're
> going to stay with my niece. The poor girl
> needs me after her confinement. Her third girl,
> just imagine.

> MME APOSTOLOS
> What a lovely family! A blessing!

M. SONGE's walking stick can be heard. But we can also hear some-one else's footsteps.

SEQUENCE 16A

INTERIOR. DAY—MME COINTET'S NIECE'S FLAT.

In a small, poorly-furnished room, three little girls are running like mad things round a table, where MME COINTET is trying to cut out some material with a huge pair of scissors. She finally threatens the children with them, to get them to calm down.

> MME COINTET (off)
> Certainly, certainly. I must say, for my part,
> it won't be a real holiday.., or at any rate in
> comparison with the holidays we used to have
> in the old days. Isn't that right, Edouard?

SEQUENCE 16 (continuation)

INTERIOR. DAY—GUEST HOUSE DINING ROOM.

M. SONGE has left his observation post: someone has come to visit him.

The camera, downstairs, is more 'objective'.

Through the window, FRED is watching the GIPSY, who has come to see JOHANN. He has brought a few baskets. They are having an animated discussion.

At first the tone of the guests' conversation drones on like a perfect piece of mechanism. Then the machine gets carried away. The tempo accelerates. No one is really listening, but their accord remains.

And yet the spectator's feeling of anguish is maintained by the difficulty, the real suffering the guests are experiencing as they try to swallow the meat, "to get it down", which is truly the only thing at stake in this meal.

And the tension is such that we should have the impression at every moment that everything can crack, that every character can suddenly breach the rigid social ritual and let the barbaric, sacrilegious feast break out.

> M. COINTET
> The Borromeans!

> MME COINTET
> Isola Bella, the walks among the azaleas, that
> light . . . Our hotel stood in an incomparable
> garden, we could see the lake from our window
> through the magnolias . . .

MME APOSTOLOS stands up and leaves the table as discreetly as possible. She makes her way to the stairs.

> M. COINTET
> The magnolias!

> MME COINTET
> And the cooking!
> (to M. Cointet)
> Do you remember the menu on the twenty-
> fifth of June? That roast beef that melted in the
> mouth? I've never tasted anything like it.

> M. ERARD
> Was it a celebration?

> MME COINTET
> A gala. In aid of the orphans. We left the table
> at four o'clock. I shall always remember the
> scent of the mimosa on the terrace . . . Isn't
> that right, Edouard?

> M. COINTET
> The mimosa!

> M. ERARD
> Mimosa in June?

> MME COINTET
> We always had a fresh vase of mimosa on our
> table. Those lovely evenings by the lake . . .

The sound of the lavatory being flushed upstairs.

> MME COINTET
> The little steam yacht, the full moon . . . There
> were a lot of Englishmen.

M. COINTET
And Englishwomen!

SEQUENCE 16(i)

INTERIOR. DAY—CORRIDOR FIRST FLOOR.

MME APOSTOLOS comes out of the lavatory. She automatically rolls a long piece of pink paper, still lying on the floor, round her hand, and then stuffs it into one of her pockets.

During this time, the dialogue downstairs can still be heard, and even more clearly, since the tone is mounting.

> MME COINTET (off)
> They're such distinguished people. Never a false note. And so thoughtful . . .

> M. ERARD (off)
> Thoughtful? I wouldn't say that. The women are pretty, but the men are boors.

> MME COINTET (off)
> What? Englishmen are boors? You can't have had much to do with them.

> M. ERARD (off)
> This part of the country's lousy with them. I come across practically no one else on my travels. So inconsiderate . . .

> MME COINTET
> That's too much! The most civilized people in the world!

SEQUENCE 16 (continuation)

INTERIOR. DAY—GUEST HOUSE DINING ROOM.

> M. ERARD
> My buttocks, yes!
>
> MME COINTET (to Gaston)
> Monsieur Gaston, say something!
>
> M. ERARD (imitating Mme Cointet)
> This table is becoming a pigsty.
>
> GASTON
> What d'you want me to say?

The attention of both GASTON and FRED is caught by the discussion still going on in the garden between JOHANN and the GIPSY. The GIPSY is pointing to the first floor windows, while JOHANN seems to be refusing him something and trying to make him go away.

At a look from GASTON, FRED stands up and goes over to the window. He tries to attract JOHANN's attention by waving his arms about.

> MME COINTET (to Gaston)
> Didn't you hear?
>
> MME COINTET (to M. Cointet)
> You say something.
>
> M. COINTET
> Very pretty women, yes.
>
> M. ERARD
> They're not a patch on Italian women, though,

when it comes to temperament.

MME COINTET
Monsieur Erard, I demand that you cease your
licentious remarks.

M. ERARD
All right, all right.

He squashes a fly on the oilcloth and puts it down by M. COIN-
TET's glass.

M. ERARD
One more.

MME COINTET makes as if to leave the table, just as MME APOS-
TOLOS is about to take her place again.

FRED is worried, and intervenes from the window.

FRED
Keep calm, Madame Cointet. And Monsieur
Erard must apologize.

M. ERARD (to Mme Cointet)
I apologize.

MME APOSTOLOS (sitting down, to Mme
Cointet)
Do you know England?

M. ERARD
Madame Cointet knows the de luxe English, in
the Borromeans.

MME COINTET
I congratulate myself on that, Monsieur Erard.

It isn't given to everyone to have style.

MME APOSTOLOS
I shan't be seeing my niece this year. My sister
is spending the summer with her. She has
managed to deprive me of that pleasure. She
detests me.

Pause.

FRED goes and sits down again.

MME APOSTOLOS
When I think that I bought this dress for my
holiday . . . It'll be out of date next year.

She drops a piece of meat on her knees. She puts it back on her
plate.

Return to the tempo of the beginning. The characters are like cogs in
a well-oiled machine . . . But the meat still doesn't "go down".

MME APOSTOLOS
Another mark! You see, every time I change
my clothes I make a mess. How do you explain
that? (to Mme Erard) And you Madame?

MME ERARD
What?

MME APOSTOLOS
When are you going away?

MME ERARD
On the eighth. My sister is expecting us on the
eighth. We'll give her a bit of a rest by looking
after the children. They won't be going on

holiday this year.

MME APOSTOLOS
How many has she?

MME ERARD
Four. Two boys and two girls.

MME APOSTOLOS
What a lovely family! A blessing!

MME ERARD
The youngest girl is so adorable! Just imagine,
she's only three years old and she embroiders
little table mats. There's one waiting for me, a
surprise. I remember that I, when I was a little
girl . . .

MME APOSTOLOS (holding her plate out to
the dish, to Mme Cointet)
A spoonful of gravy . . . Is there any left? It's
rather dry for me . . .

MME COINTET (serving Mme Apostolos, to
Gaston)
Perhaps Marie could bring in the aubergines?

Pause. Heavy silence, punctuated by the footsteps upstairs in M.
SONGE's room.

GASTON
To help it go down.

He rings. Pause.

MME APOSTOLOS (to Mme Erard)
Your sister . . . is she younger than you?

Noises coming from kitchen.

SEQUENCE 16 (ii)

INTERIOR. DAY—GUEST HOUSE KITCHEN.

JOHANN, carrying the baskets the GIPSY has sold them, knocks on the windows. He seems very agitated, pointing to the floor above. MARIE lets him in.

Cut back to the dining room.

SEQUENCE 16 (continuation)

INTERIOR. DAY—GUEST HOUSE DINING ROOM.

Sound of voices in the kitchen, but we can't hear what JOHANN is saying to MARIE.

> M. ERARD
> Don't mention the butcher to her again, she's already furious.

> GASTON
> I'm sure I told her last week. Don't you remember, Madame Cointet?

> MME COINTET
> You must have told her in front of Mademoiselle Reber. I don't remember.

> M. COINTET
> Something must be done, though, since Madame Apostolos . . .

MME APOSTOLOS
The lady assured me that the other was better.
No comparison. Chalk and cheese.

M. ERARD
It's surely a question of price. There's no reason
why for the same quality . . .

MME APOSTOLOS
I told you, she buys steak like we do. She was
amazed that we still went to the same one.

MARIE opens the service hatch with a bang and puts the aubergines
down on it.

SEQUENCE 16 (ii) (continuation)

INTERIOR. DAY—GUEST HOUSE ENTRANCE HALL.
BOTTOM OF THE STAIRS.

As MARIE goes from the kitchen to the dining room, a shadow,
dressed in a vast garment (reminiscent of the one seen by the GIPSY
in the forest), comes furtively down the stairs and disappears outside
the house.

MARIE doesn't see it. She goes into the dining room, carrying the
two baskets sold by the GIPSY.

SEQUENCE 16 (continuation)

INTERIOR. DAY—GUEST HOUSE DINING ROOM.

MARIE goes over to one of the sideboards and puts the GIPSY's
baskets away in it among a whole lot of others. She bangs its doors,
then goes to the hatch, picks up the aubergines and puts them on

the table.

MARIE
I won't change the plates, it's my afternoon off.

GASTON
Whatever you do don't change them, it's to
help get it down.

MARIE
Is Monsieur going to start again? I repeat, I
won't change butchers. And the other's the
same. And that lady, I'd like to have a word
with that lady who buys fillet.

MME APOSTOLOS
Steak, she told me steak.

MARIE
There's dozens of sorts of steak. When it's fillet,
obviously it's tenderer. If Monsieur doesn't back
me up, I'm handing in my notice.

FRED
Please don't get worked up, Marie.

MARIE
Don't get worked up, don't get worked up, that's
easy to say, every Sunday they trot it out again,
every Sunday it's uneatable, every Sunday they
pick on me, as if I could do anything about it,
as if we could treat ourselves to fillet steak, as if
Monsieur didn't know that with what he gives
me for the housekeeping . . .

GASTON
Please don't get worked up, Marie, we'll talk
about this later. I . . .

MARIE is perfectly sincere. No comic effect in her monologues. Like them, she "can't get the meat down". Like them, this makes her suffer.

>   MARIE
> We won't talk about it later, we'll talk about it now. As if that lady's tales were going to make me change butchers, as if the other wasn't the same, I tell you it's the same one that palmed that uneatable joint off on us at Easter last year, I tell you he hasn't changed. Does Monsieur imagine that it's pleasant to get cursed every Sunday because the meat's uneatable? Does Monsieur imagine that I enjoy it any more than you people? I repeat, if Monsieur doesn't back me up, I'm handing in my notice.

MARIE is on the verge of tears. She goes out, banging the door. Then, from the kitchen, shuts the hatch noisily.

Pause.

Then FRED gets up and goes out of the room. None of the others moves a muscle.

Long silence.

SEQUENCE 16 (continuation)

INTERIOR. DAY—GUEST HOUSE ENTRANCE HALL.

FRED closes the kitchen door gently. He passes GASTON, who doesn't look well, and is making for the stairs.

>   FRED
>   She's crying.
>
>   GASTON
>   Then she'll piss less.

Fade out.

SEQUENCE 17

EXTERIOR. DAY—GUEST HOUSE GARDEN.

Long shot of the facade of the guest house, seen from the garden. 11 a.m. Bright sunlight.

In their usual place in front of the house (as in sequence 11), M. SONGE and MORTIN are chatting over their aperitifs, while FRED, at the window of M. SONGE's room, is leafing through an exercise book, making sure that M. SONGE doesn't see him.

Then M. SONGE's NIECE and NEPHEW arrive. They are eating ice-cream cornets. They greet MORTIN, and kiss M. SONGE. He surreptitiously wipes his cheek, with an affectionate little smile.

>   M. SONGE
>   Well, children, what a surprise!
>
>   NIECE
>   Oh, a very short visit, Uncle, just for an
>   aperitif. We've come at the right time, I see.

She casts a conspiratorial glance at MORTIN, who smiles at her.

>   NEPHEW
>   I'll go and get a couple of glasses from the
>   kitchen.., and a couple of chairs, if I may.

He goes off.

> M. SONGE
> Won't you stay for lunch? I'm sure Marie . . .

> NIECE
> Some friends not far away are expecting us.
> Just a little detour to say hallo. Can you believe
> this heat! Your Pernod's just the thing for this
> weather. But how's your gout?

> M. SONGE
> No better, no worse. There's nothing to be
> done.., but tell me about yourself, how are
> you? How's your work going?

She sits down on the grass.

> NIECE
> No better, no worse . . . That office gets me
> down. But healthwise, don't worry, I'm very
> well.

> MORTIN
> You look in fine form.

> NIECE (to Mortin)
> And you, how're things? Doesn't this heat wear
> you out?

> MORTIN
> Not really. You get used to everything.

> M. SONGE (to his niece)
> I haven't seen you for such a long time, you
> don't visit me very often these days. Come
> on, tell me, so your office work's getting you

down? Why don't you try and find something
else? I don't know . . . with your education it
shouldn't be difficult.

Pause.

But what's your brother doing? What's he
waiting for to bring us those goblets and
chairs?

NIECE
He's chatting with Marie. They're both dreadful
gossips . . .

She calls out to the kitchen.

The glasses! . . .

SEQUENCE 17A

INTERIOR. NIGHT—SMALL SALON, DE BROY MANOR.
M. DE BROY is leaning against a fireplace. The only light in the
room comes from the fire. The NEPHEW is having a drink with
him. They are chatting in undertones, but the NEPHEW keeps
glancing at his watch.

NIECE (off)
The glasses, 'fewplease!

SEQUENCE 17 (continuation)

EXTERIOR. DAY—GUEST HOUSE GARDEN.

NIECE (off)
Those goblets! One of our good old regional

words! I'm forgetting them. Do you remember,
when we were in Fantoine, how we used to
make each other laugh with our regional
expressions?

M. SONGE
Do I remember! Our perjinketys, our guttlers,
our gimmers, our alkitotles . . . and you were
so sweet! The good old days.

Pause. M. SONGE's reminiscences are interrupted by the return of
the NEPHEW with two folding chairs and two glasses, which he
starts to fill.

NIECE (to her brother)
Just a drop for me.

She sits down on a chair.

NIECE (to M. Songe)
Because I'm not sweet, any more?

M. SONGE
Yes, yes, of course you are. But I hardly ever see
you. As for your brother . . .

NEPHEW
Uncle! Only last week . . .

M. SONGE
I know, yes. But not for the best of reasons.

SEQUENCE 17A (continuation)

INTERIOR. NIGHT—SMALL SALON DE BROY MANOR.

The NEPHEW pours himself another glass, while DE BROY looks at some photos and nods at the NEPHEW with satisfaction.
>   NEPHEW (off)
>   Well, you know, when it comes to the end of
>   the month . . .

SEQUENCE 17 (continuation)

EXTERIOR. DAY—GUEST HOUSE GARDEN

>   NIECE
>   Come on, let's not talk about that.
>   (to M. Songe)
>   How are your de Broy friends?

>   M. SONGE
>   They're getting older, like us.

>   NIECE (to Mortin)
>   Don't you see them as often as you did?

>   MORTIN
>   Not so much, now . . . I mean, what with this
>   Ducreux business . . .

>   NIECE
>   The journalist's old vendetta against the
>   lords of the manor. It's monstrous. The child
>   drowned because of lack of supervision during
>   a school outing. As for the judge, he's an
>   arsehole, a swine. Jealousy there, too.

SEQUENCE 17B

INTERIOR. NIGHT—ANOTHER SALON IN THE DE BROY MANOR.

The NIECE is trying on some jewellery in front of a mirror, while the NEPHEW is playing with some children under the fond eyes of DE BROY.

> NEPHEW (off)
> Can you imagine those gentlemen compromised in that disgusting business? Not surprising that the investigation isn't making any headway. A fine thing, justice these days.

SEQUENCE 17 (continuation)

EXTERIOR. DAY—GUEST HOUSE GARDEN.

Long shot. The NEPHEW and NIECE have gone. M. SONGE, alone is unconsciously caressing his bottle of Pernod. He looks rather sad.

Fade out.

SEQUENCE 18

INTERIOR. NIGHT—THE LARGE SALONS IN THE DE BROY MANOR.

It's the midsummer night party. The salons are brightly lit.

Applause and laughter from the young people, the nephews and nieces, but also from children playing. Firecrackers are heard outside.

We pass GASTON and FRED, who seem to be enjoying themselves hugely, MORTIN with M. SONGE's NIECE, who is showing off the jewels we have just seen.

In a corner by a fireplace, DE BROY is showing some photos to some of the other guests, among them MME APOSTOLOS, who is wearing the same jewels as M. SONGE's NIECE. M. SONGE is watching the scene from a distance.

The start of the firework display is announced. MME APOSTOLOS spills a little champagne on her dress.

SEQUENCE 18 (i)

EXTERIOR NIGHT—DE BROY MANOR GROUNDS

Establishing shot of the grounds and the floodlit manor house

The important guests go out on to the terrace of the manor house, whose facade is floodlit. M. DE BROY has led the way and is waiting for them with a camera with a built-in flash. He arranges them for the photo. MME APOSTOLOS is in the front row.

While this is going on, the GIPSY crosses the grounds and walks past a crowd of villagers gathered in a corner where drinks are being served from trestle tables. He nods to them, then goes up to DE BROY, whose flash has just fired.

DE BROY turns round and holds out his hand to him.

In a corner under the trees, we can just make out JOHANN, a spade over his shoulder.

The firework display suddenly begins. It is superb, and lasts a long time. Ohs and ahs can be heard on all sides.

SEQUENCE 19

INTERIOR. NIGHT—M. SONGE'S ROOM IN THE GUEST HOUSE

A winter evening.

MME APOSTOLOS is paying M. SONGE a visit. She is sitting in the armchair. As they chat, M. SONGE, sitting at his table, is looking at some photos, which he then passes to MME APOSTOLOS.

The first one shows M. SONGE's NIECE sporting the same jewels as MME APOSTOLOS in the preceding scene, beside the DE BROY fireplace.

> MME APOSTOLOS (looking at the photo)
> How young I was then! That hairstyle suited me rather well. My goodness, how time flies!

Pause.

> But who is that gentleman by the fireplace?

> M. SONGE
> Jean de Broy. He's changed too.

> MME APOSTOLOS
> Our friend Jean. What a bon vivant he was! But you weren't short of distractions either, my friend.

He passes her another photo.

> M. SONGE
> And here's Fred with the Duchess and her gigolo. Who was he, do you remember?

She looks at the photo. We recognize GASTON.

> MME APOSTOLOS
> Young Luisot, I rather think. Or was it Vélac?

> M. SONGE
> Vélac, no not Vélac. That fat Margione was
> very involved with him at the time.

He passes her another photo.

> And here we have Gaston and Fred in Italy. I
> don't know what that photo is doing here.

> MME APOSTOLOS
> My goodness, how they made us laugh with
> that story! That cure for their stomachs, wasn't
> it?

> M. SONGE
> Gaston for his intestines, and Fred for
> something else of the same sort, I think. It's
> true they used to make us laugh. That was in
> the good times. When we first came to live
> in this dump. What was it Fred said? "Me
> between two drinking bouts, him between two
> bouts of diarrhea . . ." Or the opposite . . .

> MME APOSTOLOS
> They don't laugh any more these days. This
> guest house is too much of a responsibility.
> Gaston . . .

He interrupts her by passing her another photo.

> M. SONGE
> And here's the midsummer night party at

the manor house. You're in the front row of
the spectators with Mademoiselle de Bonne-
Mesure. That must have been before the
fireworks. Monsieur Jean already had a camera
with a flash for night photos.

MME APOSTOLOS
What year was that taken, do you remember? I
seem to recognize my décolleté . . .

Pause.

But it must have been the Dupont night, the
famous disappearance of that child who didn't
even come from the district, wasn't it?

M. SONGE leans over her, to see the photo better. As if through
his magnifying glass, we can see a detail from it in big close-up: M.
SONGE's NEPHEW whispering in MME APOSTOLOS's ear.

M. SONGE
You may be right. Not because of your
décolleté, but because of the fountain on the
left, can you see it? They moved it somewhere
else a good fifteen or twenty years ago . . .

M. SONGE has picked up his magnifying glass. He leans over the
photo. Big closeup of the fountain surmounted by a little white marble cherub. Behind, in the shadows, JOHANN's silhouette.

M. SONGE
The Dupont affair! I'm going to tell you a
secret . . .

MME APOSTOLOS
Do, do . . .

M. SONGE

Well, with the help of these photos and the
old newspapers you see there, I'm trying to get
to the bottom of the affair, that investigation
never came up with anything. Filed and
disposed of.

MME APOSTOLOS

To get to the bottom of the affair? . . . You
mean . . .

M. SONGE

I mean that I'm inventing the sequel, I rack my
brains, I write pages and pages of suppositions
. . . Which are piling up there.

MME APOSTOLOS

A novel! You're writing a novel! But that's
wonderful, my dear friend! And there I was,
thinking you were unwell, depressed, on the
decline. According to Marie, of course. (She
claps her hands.) A novel!

M. SONGE (delighted by Mme Apostolos's
admiration)

Oh, don't get excited. Some of our friends were
compromised in the Dupont affair.

MME APOSTOLOS

But you don't name them, I hope?

M. SONGE (delighted by Mme Apostolos's
panic)

I'm hesitating, I'm thinking it over . . . It would
help with my descriptions . . . Imagination, at
my age . . .

MME APOSTOLOS
You don't really mean it? That would be
madness! They'd start gossiping about us all
over again, the police, remember . . .

M. SONGE
You talk like my friend Mortin. But you can
set your mind at rest. I have no intention of
publishing anything whatsoever. It'll all remain
among my papers. An inoffensive little hobby . . .

He stands up with difficulty because of his bad leg, takes his stick,
and leads MME APOSTOLOS over to the door.

MME APOSTOLOS
But the police, the police stick their noses
everywhere . . . It would be dreadful . . . Isn't
there another case of violation at the moment
that's more or less the same . . . a Dutrou or
Duchemin child . . . in the papers?

He manages to push her out into the corridor.

MME APOSTOLOS (in an undertone)
They all think me gaga, here, but I overhear
certain conversations . . . Oh, you make me
tremble!

M. SONGE shuts the door behind her. He turns round. He gives
a sardonic little laugh. Still with great difficulty, he goes over to the
window to get the old telescope, which he pulls into the middle of
the room. Then he slides the floorboard out, sits down on a chair,
and fits the front lens of the telescope into the hole in the floor.
While he is preparing with obvious pleasure to continue his observation, we hear him murmuring:

> M. SONGE
> Which is strangely similar to the other . . .
> Which is strangely similar to the other . . .

SEQUENCE 20

INTERIOR. NIGHT—GUEST HOUSE DINING ROOM.

Shot representing M. SONGE's imagination: De Broy, Ariane de Bonne-Mesure, the Duchess de Bois-Suspect, the Princess de Hem, the nephews and nieces, are having dinner in the place of the usual guests. MME APOSTOLOS makes her entry and sits down at the table. She is stained with blood, as the GIPSY was.

> M. SONGE (off)
> . . . strangely . . . the other . . . strangely . . .
> the other . . .

SEQUENCE 21

EXTERIOR, INTERIOR. NIGHT—GARDEN, GUEST HOUSE CORRIDOR.

FRED is getting some fresh air, sitting in M. SONGE's armchair in front of the house. The light in M. SONGE's room goes out. MME APOSTOLOS's light comes on. M. SONGE's comes on again.

Owls, crickets. Full moon.

FRED stands up, takes his keys and goes and locks the garden gate.

Inside the house, he also locks the two front doors and the kitchen door, and then goes upstairs.

In the first floor corridor, just as he is about to go into his room, we hear the lavatory flushing. We catch sight of MME APOSTOLOS, acting like a conspirator, sidling out of the WC and going into her room.

FRED goes into his.

SEQUENCE 21(i)

INTERIOR. NIGHT—FRED'S ROOM.

FRED switches on his little lamp and sits down to write his diary. As before, we hear his voice when he is thinking aloud, and his voice, off, when he is writing.

Outside, still the screech of the owls.

> FRED (off)
> Old Apostolos is definitely losing her marbles.
> Yesterday she was telling me about a police
> enquiry, a Dutrou or Duchemin affair in which
> some of our acquaintances are apparently
> compromised. Assured me that Monsieur
> Songe knows all about it.

He takes an exercise book out of a drawer. We recognize it as the one we saw him taking from M. SONGE's room (beginning of sequence 17). He leafs through it, then puts it back in the drawer, shaking his head.

> FRED
> The poor man, mind's wandering too. And his
> friend Mortin doesn't seem to be in any better
> shape. Their conversations over their Pernods
> must have certain piquancy, I imagine.

> FRED (off)
> Must ask the doctor about the state of the two
> old boys. Gaston and the others chatter about
> the Ducreux affair in the evenings. It passes
> the time. Hm, Ducreux, Dutrou, Duchemin, I
> hadn't made the connection. But they all bore
> me, with their stories from the papers. What
> the hell has it all got to do with us?

He takes another bit of paper.

> FRED
> Ask the doctor.

> FRED (off)
> Buy noodles. Buy sugar. Buy aubergines.
> Forbid Apostolos bog paper. Tell Marie to get
> her to understand.

Sound of lavatory flushing.

> FRED
> She's going to make a song and dance about
> her squittery canary. Couldn't Gaston . . .

He goes back to his exercise book.

> FRED (off)
> Gaston gets too involved in their chatter.
> Irritating. To take his mind off the uneatable
> meals, no doubt. Couldn't we eat out of doors,
> now it's not so hot? Marie would kick up a
> fuss: "What about my service hatch, what
> about my service hatch?"

Sound of the hatch, or of M. SONGE's floorboard.

> FRED (off)
> She can stuff it.

> FRED
> Excellent idea. Our evening meals in the
> garden. There's an old table in the shed, and
> the dining room chairs. Ma Erard could help
> Marie carry things out from the kitchen.

He takes the bit of paper again.

> FRED (off)
> Buy thing to drown wasps. Buy ice bucket. Buy
> . . . buy . . .

We can't hear the ends of his phrases.

Fade out.

SEQUENCE 22

INTERIOR. DAY—GUEST HOUSE CELLAR.

The next morning, in the cellar.

The walls are limewashed, the vault is of blackish stones. On the right, a pile of coal, on the left, empty potato sacks, at the back, bottle racks.

FRED and the PLUMBER are looking at the drainage system. A tangle of pipes of different sizes. The plumber is carrying his leather bag over his shoulder, and takes out a sort of big corkscrew with a strip of pink paper stuck to it.

> PLUMBER
> Well, it's like this. Coming up from the outside

drain to the inside trip, following various twists and turns . . .

FRED
Let's get to the point.

PLUMBER
Well, Monsieur, it's not only the crap. Mixed up in it, like a sort of compact ball, there's a kind of . . . How can I say . . .

FRED
Don't say it, just get on with the job.

PLUMBER
If it was that simple . . .

FRED
What else is there?

PLUMBER
No offence meant, but considering how antiquated and crude the plumbing is here, if you want to avoid any further alarms, I'd advise you, to start by changing the main parts . . .

FRED
A new installation? You don't mean it?

FRED leads the plumber out. They go up the twenty or so steep steps.

SEQUENCE 23

INTERIOR. DAY—GUEST HOUSE KITCHEN.

MARIE, drinking a mouthful of coffee from time to time, is busy in the kitchen, where JOHANN is sitting at the table in front of a glass of red wine. Through the window, we see the rain falling on the garden.

MARIE is more fascinated by her conversation with JOHANN than by her work, which allows her to keep up appearances.

JOHANN is almost all the time off camera, as if we had the reverse shot of the interrogation by the JUDGE.

> MARIE
> And what did you tell him?

> JOHANN
> What about?

> MARIE
> About Madame Apostolos.

> JOHANN
> I must have told him that she knew those
> gentlemen, and Monsieur Gaston and
> Monsieur Fred.

> MARIE
> Is it true, what they say about those gentlemen
> at the manor?

> JOHANN
> What?

MARIE
That they have . . . certain tendencies . . .

JOHANN
True or not, it's none of my business.

MARIE
And the ladies they invite, the same, eh? That must make a fine mixture.

Pause.

Through the window, MARIE and JOHANN watch FRED and the PLUMBER coming out of the cellar and going on talking, under a big hotel umbrella held by FRED.

MARIE
Why don't you answer me?

JOHANN
It doesn't interest me. Those gentlemen can lead whatever sort of life they like, and the ladies too.

MARIE
There's no talking to you any more, you never open your mouth.

JOHANN
I have my reasons.

MARIE
I know what they are, believe me. But I'll know who to go to.

JOHANN
What about?

MARIE
You know perfectly well.

JOHANN
I don't, believe it or not.

MARIE
On midsummer night, why do you make me
tell them in the village that we were together in
Sirancy?

JOHANN
So as not to compromise . . . some
acquaintances.

MARIE
Your pal the gippo. I know.

JOHANN
Then why ask me? Do you think it's bad that
I'm on his side? People are always trying to get
him into trouble, they'd soon be suspecting
him of being involved in that business of the
stolen jewels. I've known the chap for fifteen
years, he's as honest as the day.

MARIE
Doesn't stop him having been at Broy on
midsummer night.

JOHANN
I tell you he wasn't.

Through the window we see the PLUMBER
leaving, and FRED running back to the house.

JOHANN
Here's Monsieur Fred. Put the water on to boil.

SEQUENCE 24

INTERIOR. EARLY MORNING—M. SONGE'S ROOM.
The room is in chaos. The telescope is in its place, but the floor-board has been put back. The floor is littered with papers. We deduce that he's been working all night on his novel. The shutters are still closed.

In spite of his bad leg he's on all fours, trying to sort out the important pages that have accidentally fallen among the others. Muttering, he crumples up the papers he thinks he doesn't need. One of them falls into the chamber pot.

> M. SONGE (between his teeth)
> When you're working, you don't want the drafts getting in your way.

As he picks up and looks at the different pages of his novel, we are given a visualization of what is written there. Each visualization stops when M. Songe puts the sheet of paper down on his desk.

One sheet under the bed catches his attention.

SEQUENCE 24A

EXTERIOR. NIGHTFALL—TERRACE, DE BROY MANOR.

M. SONGE's NEPHEW and NIECE, among other guests are finishing their aperitifs. The NIECE points to her neck, her fingers and her wrists, as if she is talking of jewellery.

SEQUENCE 24 (continuation)

INTERIOR. NIGHTFALL—M. SONGE'S ROOM.

M. SONGE puts the sheet on the table. He continues his search. He finds another, under the telescope.

SEQUENCE 24B

EXTERIOR. DAY—TERRACE, M. SONGE'S FORMER HOUSE.

The NIECE, the NEPHEW and M. SONGE, in exactly the same positions as they were in the guest house garden (sequence 17), are having an aperitif. We can vaguely hear some words of their conversation.

> NEPHEW
> Jewellery that has no value . . . of no importance . . .

> M. SONGE
> Our de Broy friends . . . not of that opinion . . . a certain importance . . .

> NIECE
> I don't understand . . . no safe at the manor house . . . they were saying the other day . . .

SEQUENCE 24C

INTERIOR. EARLY MORNING—M. SONGE'S ROOM.

He puts the sheet on the table, and finds another under the bed.

SEQUENCE 24C (continuation)

INTERIOR. NIGHT—GUEST HOUSE CORRIDOR—MME APOSTOLOS'S ROOM.

M. SONGE accidentally opens the wrong door, and sees MME APOSTOLOS sitting on the bed in her slip. Behind her the flushed face of M. ERARD, who is examining her with a stethoscope. When they see M. SONGE, they smile at him.

M. SONGE shuts the door.

SEQUENCE 24 (continuation)

INTERIOR. EARLY MORNING—M. SONGE'S ROOM.

M. SONGE puts down that sheet of paper, and unscrews another which he had crumpled up by mistake—the one that had fallen in the chamber pot.

SEQUENCE 24 (continuation)

EXTERIOR DAY—TERRACE OF M. SONGE'S FORMER HOUSE

M. SONGE is watching a child of about ten walking by himself along the road in front of his house, while in the interior, in the shadows, the NEPHEW puts the necklace around his sister's neck.

SEQUENCE 24 (continuation)

INTERIOR. EARLY MORNING—M. SONGE'S ROOM.

M. SONGE is tired, and finally stands up with great difficulty. He drags himself over to the window and opens the shutters. Day is dawning. The garden is deserted. Close-up of M. SONGE. His face is haggard.

SEQUENCE 24D

EXTERIOR. EARLY MORNING—GUEST HOUSE GARDEN.

The GIPSY, with a few baskets at his feet, is watching the guest house windows.

SEQUENCE 24 (continuation)

INTERIOR. EARLY MORNING—M. SONGE'S ROOM.

M. SONGE sighs, moves away from the window, picks up a bottle of wine, pours himself a glass, and goes back to the window. The GIPSY is nowhere to be seen.

SEQUENCE 24E

EXTERIOR. EARLY MORNING—GUEST HOUSE GARDEN.

JOHANN throws some big sacks down a hole, gets down on all fours, and with his hands covers them with earth.

SEQUENCE 25

INTERIOR. DAY—GUEST HOUSE KITCHEN.

GASTON and FRED are having breakfast. Boiled eggs and black coffee.

FRED
I've had an idea.

GASTON
A bad sign.

FRED

To change the atmosphere a bit, it's becoming
unbreatheable, and while it's fine, why don't we
at least have dinner in the garden? Yes, that'd
make a change.

GASTON

And the smell of the canteen next door, what're
you going to do about that? And the children's
screams? And Marie serving us all by herself
without her hatch?

The sound, off, of M. SONGE taking up his floorboard, and then
the typical sounds of the previous scene, (papers being handled,
liquid passing from bottle to glass, M. SONGE's stick . . .)

FRED
Madame Erard could help Marie with the a
service, she'd like nothing better, and it isn't far
from the kitchen to the garden.

GASTON
I'd be surprised. As for Ma Cointet, that'll be
the day when she agrees to move from her chair
. . . No, it's impossible. A ridiculous idea.

FRED
I'll take it on myself to ask Marie.

GASTON
Well, take it on yourself then. I already know
what she'll say.

They go on dipping their bits of bread in their eggs.

JOHANN has finished his work and can be seen through the window going by with his spade and wheelbarrow.

SEQUENCE 26

INTERIOR DAY—M. SONGE'S ROOM

M. SONGE, still at his window, holds his nose as if the smell was intolerable. He shuts the window, then pours himself another full glass of wine.

Staggering a little, he goes to the middle of the room where the telescope is still in place. He sits down at it, resting his bad leg on another chair, and puts his eye to the eyepiece.

SEQUENCE 26A

INTERIOR. DAY—M. SONGE'S ROOM.

We are again seeing things through M. SONGE's eyes.

The evening meal. The sun is only just beginning to go down. The guests are in the same places and wearing the same clothes as in the previous scene, as if this was its exact continuation.

But the sounds coming from M. SONGE's room are louder, more present than any other sounds, and they continue throughout this sequence.

We can hear them as if we were in his room, and the guests have to fight to make themselves heard above them. As he is drinking all the time, we have the impression that the meal is becoming contaminated by M. SONGE's drunkenness.

>M. ERARD
>I did say we shouldn't mention the butcher
>again.

>M. COINTET
>Who mentioned it? You're not saying it was
>me, are you?

>MME COINTET
>Don't get involved, Edouard.

>M. ERARD
>Having to keep hearing the same thing,
>obviously that antagonizes her.

MME APOSTOLOS holds out her plate to the dish of aubergines in the middle of the table.

At the same moment the sound of something falling, above, echoes round the room. MME COINTET starts, and knocks a glass of water containing a little red wine over the oilcloth.

The red pool on the oilcloth goes on spreading throughout the meal.

We hear M. SONGE drinking, then cackling.

>MME APOSTOLOS
>Very well, we won't mention it again. But that
>lady did tell me the other one is better, I'm not
>mad you know. At the Magasins-Prix, quite so.

MME APOSTOLOS (to Mme Erard)
Then it wasn't you who were with me?

MME COINTET AND MME ERARD
It was Mademoiselle Reber!

MME COINTET serves them one after the
other, but cautiously casting worried looks at
the ceiling.

Then we hear something else falling, upstairs.

SEQUENCE 26 (continuation)

INTERIOR. DAY—M. SONGE'S ROOM..

The telescope has fallen over.

M. SONGE too has just fallen on to the floor, not far away from the
hole. He tries to get up, but can't. Then he picks up an old newspaper
cutting lying on the floor within his reach. He glances at it.

SEQUENCE 26A (continuation)

INTERIOR. DAY—GUEST HOUSE DINING ROOM.

MME ERARD
She hasn't forgotten the pepper, at any rate.

M. COINTET
In my opinion, it needs more tomato.

MME COINTET
It isn't ratatouille, it's just aubergines, cooked
to a recipe Madame Aubier gave me which I

passed on to Marie.
(to M. Cointet)
Do you remember?

M. SONGE gives a hiccup, which invades the dining room.

M. COINTET
Madame Aubier!

GASTON
She certainly hasn't forgotten the pepper.

MME COINTET
These things must have some taste.
(to Mme Erard)
Do you find them too peppery?

MME ERARD
I remember, when I was a little girl . . .

MME APOSTOLOS
Was Madame Aubier that lady in the
Borromeans?

MME COINTET
Her villa was next to the grounds of our hotel.
Such a distinguished lady! She invited us to
her house. She was French by marriage but of
Italian origin. She was the one who organized
the gala for the orphans . . . She had a niece . . .
What was her name, now?
(to M. Cointet)
Edouard?

SEQUENCE 26 (continuation)

INTERIOR. DAY—M. SONGE'S ROOM

M. SONGE, still on the floor, tries to pull a pillow off his bed.

>   M. COINTET (off)
>   What?

>   MME COINTET (off)
>   What was the name of Madame Aubier's niece?
>   M. COINTET (off)
>   Her niece?

SEQUENCE 26A (continuation)

INTERIOR DAY—GUEST HOUSE DINING ROOM

>   MME COINTET
>   You have no memory. She was sitting on our
>   left on the twenty-fifth of June. Mademoiselle
>   . . . Mademoiselle . . .

>   M. COINTET
>   Can't remember.

MME APOSTOLOS holds out her glass to M. ERARD who holds it out to GASTON.

Very noticeable sounds of swallowing are coming from M. SONGE's room.

>   MME APOSTOLOS
>   Just a drop, please. It's true they're very
>   peppery.

They all hold out their glasses. Some of the glasses chink.

The pool on the table continues to spread. MME COINTET prevents M. COINTET from holding out his glass.

> MME COINTET
> You may have water, nothing else.

She holds out his glass to GASTON, who fills it with water.

> MME COINTET
> It's a good thing we haven't been eating celery
> rémoulade, that would be enough to take the
> roof off your mouth!
> (to M. Cointet)
> Have you still not remembered?

> M. COINTET
> Remembered what?

> MME COINTET
> The name of that young lady.

> M. COINTET
> Mademoiselle Aubier, probably.

> MME COINTET
> No, she was the daughter of her sister, who had
> married . . . It's most frustrating. . . .

> M. COINTET
> Did she live on Isola Bella?

> MME COINTET
> Oh, stop it, Edouard! You went into raptures
> over her orchids.

M. COINTET
Well, you know, after thirty years . . .

MME COINTET
You do it on purpose, you're so insincere.

M. COINTET
Wasn't she English?

MME APOSTOLOS (to M. Cointet)
Do you know England?

A burst of noisy laughter, which seems as if it will never cease, answers her from upstairs.

FRED gets up and goes into the adjoining hall. We hear him dialling a telephone number, then his voice:

FRED
Hallo, hallo . . .

He hangs up, and goes back to his place. Everyone pretends that nothing is happening.

Taking advantage of M. SONGE's silence, M. COINTET decides to answer MME APOSTOLOS.

M. COINTET
We've never visited England. Madame Cointet will regret it all her life.

MME ERARD
It might still be possible . . .

MME COINTET
Alas, the holiday with my niece . . .

> FRED (to Mme Apostolos)
> You aren't going on holiday, then?

> MME APOSTOLOS
> My sister has managed to cut the grass from
> under my feet. She can't stand me. I get on
> much better with my niece than she does. It's
> my niece who'll regret it.

> FRED
> She has three children, hasn't she?

SEQUENCE 26 (continuation)

INTERIOR. DAY—M. SONGE'S ROOM.

Still lying on the floor, M. SONGE has managed to get hold of his
pillow and has put it under his head.
With his ear a few centimetres from the hole, he listens to the conversation absentmindedly, while making little rolls of paper with his
pages and newspaper cuttings.

> MME APOSTOLOS (off)
> Four. The youngest girl is so adorable! Just
> imagine, at her age . . .

> M. ERARD (off)
> She embroiders little table mats?

> MME APOSTOLOS (off)
> What?

> MME ERARD (off, to M. Erard)
> That's enough!

> MME APOSTOLOS (off)
> What did you say?

>M. ERARD (off)
>What does she do at her age?

>MME APOSTOLOS (off)
>She looks like a little fairy. Last year she
>embroidered a bit of material . . .

>M. ERARD (off)
>So there!

SEQUENCE 26A (continuation)

INTERIOR. DAY—GUEST HOUSE DINING ROOM.

>MME APOSTOLOS
>What?

>MME ERARD (to Mme Apostolos)
>My husband is in a bad mood, don't listen to him.

>MME APOSTOLOS
>Hasn't he had his siesta?

>M. ERARD
>The smells from that canteen coming over in
>waves . . .

JOHANN knocks on the open window. He is carrying his spade
over his shoulder. He makes signs to FRED, then goes away.

>GASTON (to Mme Apostolos)
>And you, Madame, do you know the
>Borromeans?

>MME APOSTOLOS
>I visited it very briefly, how long ago now . . . ?

> MME COINTET
> No one could forget Isola Bella. The azaleas,
> the magnolias, and that light. The hotel was the
> best in all Italy at the time, wasn't it, Edouard?

> M. COINTET
> The hotel!

SEQUENCE 26 (continuation)

INTERIOR. DAY—M. SONGE'S ROOM.

M. SONGE, cackling and very drunk, tries to poke one of the paper rolls he has just made through the hole in the floor.

> MME COINTET (off)
> Those sweets, those desserts! I shall remember
> the one we had on the twenty-fifth of June all
> my life. Pears Monseigneur with a blackcurrant
> liqueur sauce.
> (to M. Cointet)
> Do you remember?

SEQUENCE 26A (continuation)

INTERIOR. EVENING—GUEST HOUSE DINING ROOM.

> M. COINTET
> I . . . no . . . the roast beef, yes, but not the
> dessert.

> MME COINTET
> Not possible. No one could confuse the
> Borromeans with anywhere else.

Pause. MARIE comes in with one of the GIPSY's baskets. She puts it in the sideboard with the others. She bangs the doors and goes out, raising the tension a notch.

> MME COINTET
> Mademoiselle Sylvie. That was it.
> Mademoiselle Sylvie.
>
> M. COINTET
> That's just what I said, Sylvie Aubier, just what
> I said . . .

M. SONGE has succeeded. His papers fall from the ceiling, fluttering slowly. They settle everywhere. The pool of wine now covers the whole table.

In spite of everything, the guests do what they can to keep the verbal mechanism going. Once again they do their utmost, as if their lives depended on it, but the silences between the speeches grow longer and longer.

The clock ticking.

Very gradually, night falls.

> MME COINTET
> I tell you, she was her sister's daughter, she
> wasn't called Aubier. You're completely losing
> your memory.

Pause.

> M. COINTET
> Ah, memory.

Pause.

> MME APOSTOLOS
> Pears Monseigneur . . . That reminds me
> of something . . . It must have been in the
> Balearics . . .

> M. ERARD
> With that Mademoiselle Aubier?

Pause.

> MME APOSTOLOS
> Mademoiselle what? . . . Did I mention her to
> you . . . ?

Pause.

> MME APOSTOLOS
> Magnificent grounds overlooking the sea. I
> shall always remember the hibis . . . hibis . . .
> what are they called?

Visibly at the end of his tether, FRED gets up and goes back to the telephone. The camera follows him. He dials the same number.

> MME ERARD (off, to M. Erard)
> Let Mme Apostolos finish her ratatouille.

Close-up of FRED.

> FRED
> Hallo? . . . Monsieur Mortin?

SEQUENCE 27

EXTERIOR. NIGHTFALL—GUEST HOUSE GARDEN.

Long shot of the house. The lights come on on the ground floor and

in M. SONGE's room. We hear M. SONGE's drunken grunts, showing that he is making an enormous effort, and downstairs, snatches
of the continuation of the conversation.

> MME COINTET (off)
> I tell you . . . it isn't ratatouille . . . One of
> Madame Aubier's recipes . . .

> M. COINTET (off)
> . . . more tomato . . .

> MME APOSTOLOS (off)
> It's true they're peppery.

> M. ERARD (off)
> . . . this little wine . . .

> MME APOSTOLOS (off)
> . . . that's significant.

> MME APOSTOLOS (off)
> Hibiscus! . . . a superb flower . . . Hibiscus,
> that's it.

> M. ERARD (off)
> . . . certainly mimosa.

> MME APOSTOLOS (off)
> Unless I'm confusing . . .

SEQUENCE 28

INTERIOR. NIGHT—M. SONGE'S ROOM.

M. SONGE has got rid of all his pages and newspapers. With one
last effort, he has managed to get up. Staggering, without his stick,

which he can't find, he drags himself over to his desk. He sweeps everything that still encumbers it on to the floor with the back of his hand, and only keeps a glass, a bottle of Pernod, his exercise book and his pen.

He writes. Furiously, at times, bursting out laughing at others. But most of the time he stands up, hobbles about his room, mimes the scenes, and ponders.

> M. SONGE
> The gipsy, right, that's good. But what about the others? Jean de Broy in the first place.

(He speaks in a formal voice.)

> Monsieur de Broy, did you see the Dupont family during the midsummer party?

(He speaks in an upper-class voice.)

> Certainly I did, as I do every year.

(Formal voice.)

> You do agree that after the fireworks display, Johann, who was looking after the children, came to tell you that the Dupont boy had disappeared?

(Upper-class voice.)

> Certainly. I immediately ordered a search of the grounds.

(Formal voice.)

> It must have been one in the morning, the

guests from the village had gone.

(Upper-class voice.)

> Which of your intimate friends were still at
> the table?

(Formal voice.)

> My goodness, it's difficult to . . .

He breaks off, realizing he has been using the wrong voices, pours himself a drink, and starts again.

(Formal voice.)

> Which of your intimate friends were still at the
> table?

(Upper-class voice.)

> My goodness, it's difficult to remember . . .
> Probably my friend Louis, Madame de Bois-
> Suspect . . .

SEQUENCE 28A

INTERIOR. NIGHT—DINING ROOM DE BROY MANOR.

At the dining room in the manor, we recognize, among a few other "intimates", the NEPHEW and NIECE, behaving like messy children, MORTIN, looking fondly at them, and DE BROY, who is amused.

M. SONGE (off)

(Upper-class voice)

> Madame de Bois-Suspect, my cousin
> Mademoiselle de Bonne-Mesure, Professor
> Sagrin . . .

(Formal voice)

> Had not the professor agreed to take the
> Dupont child home to his parents, who had
> left earlier?

A character whom we only see from behind, but who can only be JOHANN, comes and whispers in MORTIN's ear. MORTIN looks in the direction of the grounds, and doesn't answer the questions the NEPHEW seems to be asking him. Then he stands up and goes out of the room. We see him, through the window, making his way to the grounds.

M. SONGE (off)

(Upper class voice)

> Yes, when Johann came and told him, he
> immediately went off to search the park with
> him and a few others.

SEQUENCE 28 (continuation)

INTERIOR. NIGHT—M. SONGE'S ROOM.

M. SONGE pours himself another Pernod. He is fighting against drunkenness and sleep. He finally starts again, but with sudden changes in his voice.

> M. SONGE

(Formal voice)

> Did Professor Sagrin join you after the search?

(Upper-class voice)

> I don't remember.

(Formal voice)

> Did you see him the next day, or on the following days?

M. SONGE no longer has the strength to disguise his voice:

> M. SONGE (natural voice)
> Certainly. He was very upset, I remember
> that, he held himself responsible for the child's
> disappearance. He's a nervy, hypersensitive man
> . . . I consoled him as best I could, it wasn't his
> fault, seeing that Johann . . .

M. SONGE, sitting at his desk, drops his head into his hands. He isn't seen to speak any more. The dialogue continues, off, but SONGE's "formal voice" is replaced by the voice of the JUDGE.

JUDGE (off)
Were the owners of the guest house at your
table with their guests?

M. SONGE (natural voice)
I think so, yes.

JUDGE (off)
You aren't sure?

M. SONGE
Difficult to remember.

JUDGE (off)
Madame Apostolos, who has come to spend
her last years in that guest house and whom
you have known for a long time, has stated that
she was with you all at that moment.

M. SONGE
It's possible.

SEQUENCE 28B

INTERIOR. NIGHT—SMALL SALON—DE BROY MANOR

The NIECE, alone in the room, seems to be on her guard. She looks
out of the window. Enter the NEPHEW, who takes the jewellery out
of his pockets and puts it round her wrist and neck, slightly stroking
her neck. Then he snatches it off her, puts it back in his pocket and
goes out.

She resumes her anxious wait, looking out of the window. Then DE
BROY enters. Same business with the jewellery and the NIECE, but
the stroking of the young woman's skin becomes more insistent.

The dialogue continues in voices off. M. SONGE's drunkenness seems to be affecting the JUDGE's voice.

> JUDGE (off)
> She testified that she went to the manor the next day and that you all discussed who might or might not be responsible.

> M. SONGE
> Perfectly normal, in the circumstances.

> JUDGE (off)
> Did you incline towards one suspect rather than another?

> M. SONGE
> How do you expect me to remember? We probably brought up all sorts of names, there were a lot of villagers at the party.

> JUDGE (off)
> Did you mention the gipsy, who every year . . .

SEQUENCE 28C

EXTERIOR. NIGHT—TERRACE AND GARDENS DE BROY MANOR.

The NIECE comes out on to the terrace. The necklace is no longer round her neck. She watches the GIPSY running after MORTIN in the gardens, but he doesn't catch him up. The GIPSY gives up, stops, then goes back to the manor and resumes his usual watchful attitude.

On the terrace, the NIECE is whispering in GASTON's ear while FRED, visibly tense, watches the scene.

The voices off become more and more approximate.

> M. SONGE (off)
> I certainly didn't . . . I know the fellow, he's the
> soul of honesty . . . But it's not impossible that
> some of the others mentioned him . . .

> JUDGE (off)
> Have you yourself . . . any idea who could have
> committed this crime?

> M. SONGE (off)
> I'm convinced that the child.., who, according
> to his parents, was always wandering off on
> his own.., that he left the others after the
> fireworks.., went into the forest . . . where he
> got lost.., and drowned in the pond where the
> police found him.

SEQUENCE 28 (continuation)

INTERIOR. NIGHT—M. SONGE'S ROOM.

M. SONGE is now dozing in his armchair, his head thrown back,
but he can still manage to murmur the lines.

> NIECE (off)
> And the schoolmistress?

> M. SONGE
> What schoolmistress?

SEQUENCE 28D

EXTERIOR. DAY—VILLAGE PRIMARY SCHOOL. THE DAY BEFORE THE MIDSUMMER PARTY—THE EDGE OF THE FOREST.

THE SCHOOLMISTRESS comes out of the school, followed by the children in a crocodile.

> NIECE (off)
> Mademoiselle Lorpailleur, who was taking the primary school children for their outing.

The camera passes them rapidly and discovers JOHANN on the edge of the forest. Hiding behind a bush, he is watching them.

SEQUENCE 28 (continuation)

INTERIOR. NIGHT—M. SONGE'S ROOM.

This vision makes M. SONGE start suddenly in his armchair. He shakes himself, wants to pour himself another Pernod, but can't manage it. He is again overcome by drowsiness.

> M. SONGE (articulating with difficulty)
> I didn't know about that outing . . . What . . . are you trying to establish . . . ?

SEQUENCE 28E

EXTERIOR. DAY—POND.

The SCHOOLMISTRESS pushes a child into the pond and holds his head down under the water.

> JUDGE (off)
> Did you and your friends not suspect her of
> being responsible for the Dupont child's death,
> through lack of supervision?

The SCHOOLMISTRESS stands up, soaked through. The child in the pond has stopped moving.

> JUDGE (off)
> Madame Apostolos claims . . .

It is no longer the SCHOOLMISTRESS, but MME APOSTOLOS, dripping, who is by the pond, watching the child's body still floating for a moment and then sinking.

> DE BROY
> Madame Apostolos talks a lot.., or used to
> talk a lot, at any rate . . . I can't see what the
> schoolmistress . . . could have had to do . . .
> with it all . . .

Now it is MARIE who is by the pond. She pulls a revolting looking piece of meat out of the pond and puts it on a dish.

SEQUENCE 28F

INTERIOR. DAY—GUEST HOUSE DINING ROOM.

Sound of the service hatch.

The guests are sitting in their usual places. MARIE comes in and puts a dish down in front of GASTON. It contains the meat fished out of the pond.

MME ERARD picks up the piece of meat with her hands and throws it out of the open window. She replaces it with one of her dolls, which GASTON begins to carve.

> DE BROY (off)
> My dear judge, do let's have a little common
> sense, a little respect for schoolmistresses and
> schoolmen, for institutions and institutes,
> for substitutes, substitutions, suppositions,
> superstitions, subreptions . . . Come now!

The GIPSY comes slowly towards the dining room from the garden.
He stops, and pushes the window. Close-up of his face: he looks at
the guests as if he were judging them.

Then he steps back and looks up at M. SONGE's window.

SEQUENCE 28 (continuation)

INTERIOR. NIGHT—M. SONGE'S ROOM.

M. SONGE, fast asleep, looks as if he is having nightmares.

Tracking shot up to close-up of his face.

Fade out.

SEQUENCE 29

INTERIOR. DAY—GUEST HOUSE SALON.

A bell rings at the front door. FRED goes and opens it to MORTIN.
They pass in front of the telephone. FRED ushers him into the salon
and carefully closes the door.

Louis-Philippe and Napoleon III furniture. Table mats, cushions in
the armchairs, lace curtains, cashmere shawl over the piano, etc . . .

Everything is very shabby.

> FRED and MORTIN are sitting opposite each
> other, and quite close. They are trying not to
> speak too loudly.
>
> FRED
> I know you well enough to ask you whether
> you think in all conscience . . .
>
> MORTIN
> We aren't in court, my dear fellow. This
> Ducreux affair, it's all you hear about these
> days. Everyone's going on about it. The
> investigation is making no headway, and for
> good reason . . . It's no use talking to me about
> conscience, seeing that according to some of
> your guests I haven't got one. My word is good,
> though.
>
> FRED
> I'll rely on that, then. What do you think
> about this Ducreux business?
>
> MORTIN
> I don't think about it any more than is
> necessary.

He stands up and starts walking round FRED as if he wanted to
make him giddy.

> MORTIN
> There was a serious misunderstanding at the
> outset, a confusion which is spreading among
> the public, between the murder of the Ducreux
> child and the theft of the jewellery from our
> friends the de Broys, because it so happens

276

that the burglar is also called Ducreux, but
he's nothing to do with the sex maniac who
strangled the child. They're both under lock
and key, which gives free rein to the journalists'
imagination.

FRED
I don't understand you very well. I don't read
the papers myself . . .

MORTIN
There's nothing to understand. Just use your
head. Our local rag, like all the newssheets
in the world, gets its information from a lot
of petty crackpots who think they can make
themselves important by pretending to be in
the know. The trouble is that they aren't up to
it and they mislead their readers, our fellow-
countrymen, by their disgusting disregard of
the truth. You've no idea . . .

FRED
Yes, I imagine . . .

Pause.

But what I wanted to know . . . has to do,
excuse me, with Monsieur Songe. Marie thinks
she's discovered in his exercise book . . .

MORTIN
We've no need of Marie. I can tell you myself
that after all these years as a failed writer, our
friend is still trying his hand at writing a novel,
well yes, believe it or not, based on that old
Dupont business which is strangely similar to
the other one . . .

Sound of the service hatch.

>MARIE (off)
>The hors d'oeuvres are ready. Lunch is served.

>MORTIN
>I'll leave you my dear man, it's your lunchtime.
>I'm expected at the manor house.

FRED sees him to the door.

>FRED (to himself, in an undertone)
>Still as much of a snob.

SEQUENCE 30

INTERIOR. DAY—M. SONGE'S ROOM.

M. SONGE is at the window. We only see his back. He watches MORTIN leave.

>M. SONGE (murmuring)
>Which is strangely similar to the other one . . .

Sounds of a chopper, knives, etc., can be heard, off.

SEQUENCE 31

INTERIOR. DAY—GUEST HOUSE KITCHEN.

Continuation of the sounds of knives. MARIE is chopping up a rabbit. Near the window, fluttering in the breeze, are M. SONGE's newspaper cuttings of the Ducreux and Dupont affairs. MARIE is talking to herself.

MARIE

Serve the meals in the garden? Is he taking the
piss? Marie, obviously, she'll do anything, you
only have to tell her, to indulge the gentry, in
the fresh air under the chestnut tree, change
the atmosphere, makes you laugh, what does
it matter if she falls flat on her face with the
dishes, old Ma Erard will come and pick it all
up, 'course she will, she's so kind, so obliging
. . . She's just more bloody stupid than the
rest of them put together, with her simpering
Sunday school airs, "I remember, when I was
a little girl, I remember, when I was a little girl
. . ." They can stuff them, their meals in the
garden, and all the grub too. If they mention
it once again I'll show them what I'm made of,
I'll show them what I'm made of . . .

She opens the hatch.

SEQUENCE 32

INTERIOR. DAY—M. SONGE'S ROOM.

M. SONGE slides his floorboard off. Then he moves his pillows to
the other end of the bed and lies down at the wrong end, his head
not far from the hole.

He opens his exercise book and gets ready to follow the conversation
down below, as if it had already been written down.

The camera descends, passes through the floor and arrives in the dining room, where the guests are coming to the end of another meal.

The atmosphere is more serene. But the machine-like exchanges
occasionally falter. The gaps in the guests' memories are frequent.

(This scene will be treated in a long series of sequence shots, mainly vertical and sideways tracking shots.) M. ERARD wipes his mouth and smells his napkin.

> M. ERARD
> It's intolerable.

He throws his napkin on the floor.

Pause.

> MME ERARD
> Pick up that napkin. Marie will have a fit.

Pause.

> MME ERARD
> Alfred, pick up that napkin, we've had enough of such scenes as it is.
>
> MME APOSTOLOS and MME COINTET
> Monsieur Erard!
>
> M. ERARD
> I'll only pick it up if I'm given a clean one this evening.
>
> MME APOSTOLOS and MME COINTET
> Right, we'll get you a clean one.

M. ERARD picks up his napkin and then thrusts it under his wife's nose. She pushes it away violently.

> MME COINTET
> But what's the matter with him today?

Pause.

MME ERARD
I would adore the Borromeans. Do they have
camels there, and caravans?

MME COINTET
I fear your geography . . .

M. ERARD (to Mme Erard)
The north of Italy, come on, on Lake . . .
Lake . . .

MME ERARD
I'm so sorry, I was mixing it up. All the same,
those flowers, those palm trees, that farniente,
it's tempting.

MME COINTET
The softness of the air in the spring, Madame,
and that light . . . We were staying in the best
hotel. Comfort, luxury, and that cooking . . .

The camera climbs again, passes through the ceiling and discovers M.
SONGE on his bed.

MME ERARD (off)
The menu on the twenty-fifth of June.

MME APOSTOLOS (off)
It was a celebration.

Silence. M. SONGE leans over the hole, like a theatre prompter:

M. SONGE
A gala in aid of the orphans . . .

MME ERARD (off, to Mme Apostolos)
A gala in aid of the orphans . . .

The camera descends to the dining room again.

> MME ERARD
> Weren't Monsieur and Madame Cointet lucky!
> Such a wonderful holiday!
>
> MME APOSTOLOS (drinking)
> Yes, I think I preferred the other one.
>
> M. ERARD (to Fred)
> Actually, with what we're economizing on the
> wine, couldn't we . . . for the quality of the
> steak . . .

Pause.

> GASTON
> You're forgetting the washing machine. We'll be
> buying it on hire purchase.
>
> MME APOSTOLOS
> Is that quite right? Adopting the present day
> standards? A lady told me that young people
> today pay for practically nothing any more,
> with that system . . . whatever you call it . . .
> and one fine day they land up in prison.
>
> GASTON
> You've nothing to worry about on that score, I
> assure you. I've done my arithmetic.

He drinks. Silence. The camera moves up to M. SONGE

> M. SONGE
> I find this one better than the other . . .
>
> GASTON (off)
> Personally I find this one better than the other.

What about you, Monsieur Cointet?

Silence.

> M. SONGE
> Monsieur Cointet has no call to have an opinion
> about wine, he isn't allowed to drink it.

Silence.

> MME COINTET (off)
> Monsieur Cointet has no call to have an
> opinion about wine, he isn't allowed to drink it.

Pause.

The camera comes down again.

> MME COINTET
> It seems to me that that washing machine is
> madness.

> MME APOSTOLOS
> And that.., that system, whatever you call it, I
> don't trust it. That lady was telling me . . .

> MME APOSTOLOS (to Mme Cointet)
> Wasn't it you who were with me?

> M. COINTET and M. ERARD
> It was Mademoiselle Reber!

> MME ERARD
> Actually, is she staying with her niece this year?
> With her sister who can't stand her . . .
> (to Fred)
> Did she tell you where she was going?

Silence.

Then the voice of M. SONGE, still like a prompter.

> M. SONGE (off)
> She was going to stay with her niece, who has
> just had her fifth . . .

> MME COINTET
> She was going to stay with her niece, who has
> just had her fifth baby. She acts as her nurse, her
> cook, and her cleaning woman, no more, no
> less.

Silence.

> M. SONGE (off)
> Poor Mademoiselle Reber!

> M. COINTET & M. ERARD
> Poor Mademoiselle Reber!

> MME ERARD
> She was already very tired before she went, this
> holiday will finish her off.

> MME APOSTOLOS
> It was she who was with me when the lady told
> me, it's coming back to me. She was telling me
> about the butchers' shops in Strasbourg and the
> charcuteries. They eat a lot of sausages in that
> region.
> (to Mme Erard)
> Do you like sausages? They don't agree with me.

> MME ERARD
> I'm not mad about them, either.

GASTON rings.

> GASTON
> Has everyone finished?

> M. ERARD
> Sausages would make a change. With a nice
> celery rémoulade.
> (to Mme Cointet)
> I'll take you to one of my transport cafés
> whenever you like, you'll be surprised.

> M. COINTET
> We could discover the recipe here.

> MME COINTET
> I tell you, you aren't allowed it.
> (to Mme Erard)
> As for your transport cafés, no thank you, they
> aren't the kind of establishment that Monsieur
> Cointet and I frequent. Isn't that right, Edouard?

Silence.

> M. SONGE (off)
> Ah, transport cafés.

> M. COINTET
> Ah, transport cafés!

> MME COINTET (to Fred)
> That washing machine is an unnecessary
> expense. Our laundress satisfies all our
> requirements. What sort of period are the
> payments spread over?

> GASTON
> Two and a half years.

Silence.

> M. SONGE (off)
> Two and a half years.

Silence.

> MME APOSTOLOS and MME ERARD
> Two and a half years!

> GASTON
> You needn't worry, I've done my arithmetic.

Sound of the hatch. A bowl of peaches appears.

> GASTON
> This time, not a word about the butcher.

MARIE comes in, only partly clears the table, and puts the bowl down in the middle of it.

> MARIE
> I won't change the plates, it's my afternoon off.

She goes out, banging the door.

> MME ERARD
> Where is she going this afternoon?

> MME COINTET
> To buy a dress at the Magasins-Prix. For her visit to her niece.

M. COINTET
Is Marie taking her holiday this month?

MME COINTET
No, in August. But she is anxious to buy that
dress.

M. ERARD
Buttons in front?

Silence.

M. SONGE (off)
Big flowers . . .

MME APOSTOLOS
Do you think big flowers will still be
fashionable next year . . . ?

Pause.

M. SONGE (off)
My sister . . .

MME APOSTOLOS
My sister will get her just deserts one day.
Though my niece won't like that.
(to M. Erard)
Ladies are clothes-conscious, they like to follow
the fashion.

M. SONGE (off)
Will get her just deserts . . . her just deserts . . .

They have all carefully wiped their plates with bits of bread. They
take a peach from the bowl and peel it over their plates with the tips
of their fingers. Tracking shot in close-up of all the guests in turn,
while M. SONGE's voice repeats:

> M. SONGE (off)
> Will get her just deserts . . . her just deserts . . .
> will get her just deserts . . .

A feeling of embarrassment comes over them. Bravely, M. ERARD breaks the silence, having first waited for M. SONGE to choose to keep quiet.

> M. ERARD
> These peaches . . . won't the season be over
> soon?

> GASTON
> It's only just begun. Don't you like peaches?

> M. ERARD
> The thing is, after ten days . . .

> MME APOSTOLOS
> The season lasts a good month. My goodness,
> how I love peaches!

She pours sugar over the cut peaches on her plate.

The atmosphere is now very relaxed. The meal has "gone down". The conversation is flowing nicely. The tone is almost jocular. But M. ERARD grumbles enthusiastically. They are like children.

> MME APOSTOLOS
> . . . And next, my little treat.

> M. ERARD
> Isn't there any other fruit to alternate with
> them?

> MME ERARD
> They're very good for you.

MME COINTET
The peaches in the Borromeans, you remember,
Edouard!

M. ERARD (to Mme Erard)
A month? We'll start the season all over again
at your niece's, they're always a month behind.

MME APOSTOLOS
How lucky you are! You'll still be having
peaches when we've gone on to plums. I really
would have liked to go away this year.

M. ERARD
I'll give up my place to you.

MME APOSTOLOS
Monsieur Erard!

MME ERARD
He says that, but he'll be very pleased to be on
holiday.

M. ERARD
To wipe the baby's bottom and play gee-gees,
gee-gees . . .

MME APOSTOLOS (to Mme Erard)
Your sister, is she younger than you?

M. ERARD
Actually, Monsieur Gaston, you'd be able to
buy the meat yourself next time, wouldn't you?

Pause.

I see.

> MME COINTET
> What do you see?

> MME ERARD
> Nothing. He has no experience of running a
> house.

Some of them take another peach, others pick their teeth. MME
APOSTOLOS holds her glass out to GASTON, who pours some
wine into it.

> MME APOSTOLOS
> And now for my little treat. Just a drop.

She pours some of her wine into her plate, and stirs whole spoonfuls
of sugar into it.

She swallows her treat.

> M. SONGE (off)
> Play gee-gees, play gee-gees.

The camera goes up to M. SONGE's room again. He's asleep. He's
having a pleasant dream. We can see his lips murmuring:

> Play gee-gees, play gee-gees . . .

> MME APOSTOLOS (off, echoing him from
> below)
> Play gee-gees, play gee-gees . . .

SEQUENCE 33

INTERIOR. DAY—M. SONGE'S ROOM.

MARIE knocks noisily on the door and goes in. He has had lunch in

bed. The leavings are strewn round him on the bedspread. MARIE
starts collecting them.

> MARIE
> Are you going on much longer refusing to have
> your meals with all the others?

> M. SONGE
> I'm tired. Don't bother me.

> MARIE
> Tired—you've always been tired. It would do
> you good to make a bit of an effort, and it'd
> make things easier for me.

> M. SONGE
> All you think of is making things easier for
> yourself. Do you really think that at my age . . .

> MARIE
> Your age, your age, you never stop harping on
> your age. Good excuse for a loafer like you.

> M. SONGE
> Clear up and clear out.

MARIE clears the leavings and, on her way to the door, catches her
foot in the hole in the floor. She mutters, and then goes out, banging
the door. M. SONGE makes himself comfortable on his pillows and
goes back to sleep.

The camera remains on his face. His brow becomes furrowed: once
again he is a prey to nightmares.

Organ music. Long crescendo up to fortissimo (sequence 33G)

SEQUENCE 33A

The guests are at table. They are chewing the meat in silence The camera shows them to us one by one in a long panoramic shot.

They are all looking towards the camera. All their mouths are covered with blood (or with chocolate cream).

On the table, among the cutlery, are cleavers and big kitchen knives.

INSERT—(CONTINUATION SEQUENCE 33)

M. SONGE turns over.

SEQUENCE 33B

INTERIOR. NIGHT—LIBRARY DE BROY MANOR.

The NEPHEW, in front of the mirror, is caressing the neck of his sister, who is admiring her jewellery. Big close-up of her neck, in which we see the texture of her skin just underneath her ears.

Back to a medium shot: it is now DE BLOY who is caressing the NIECE's neck. Close-up of the face of the excited man.

Back to a medium shot: the NEPHEW is facing DE BROY. Their hands brush against each other and exchange money, and jewellery.

INSERT—(CONTINUATION SEQUENCE 33)

M. SONGE tosses his head in his sleep, as if to shake off something that is hurting him. Then he seems to calm down.

SEQUENCE 33C

EXTERIOR. TWILIGHT—POND.

The SCHOOLMISTRESS is playing with a bloodstained doll. MME APOSTOLOS snatches it out of her hands and then, smiling, moves towards the camera until she is in close-up, looking at the camera as if she were offering us the doll.

SEQUENCE 33D

EXTERIOR TWILIGHT—GUEST HOUSE GARDEN

JOHANN is digging a hole. Then he drops his spade and holds his arms out to the camera, which is advancing towards him as if it were holding the doll out to him. He grabs hold of it and buries it. The GIPSY is observing the scene.

INSERT—(CONTINUATION SEQUENCE 33)

M. SONGE makes a violent gesture, as if to slap someone's face.

SEQUENCE 33E

EXTERIOR. TWILIGHT—POND.

The SCHOOLMISTRESS is scolding DE BROY. He hangs his head, like a child who is ashamed of himself. GASTON and FRED are watching the scene, holding hands like good children.

The SCHOOLMISTRESS points to the pond. The camera follows her gesture: floating near the edge of the pond we discover a doll covered in jewellery.

The SCHOOLMISTRESS and DE BROY suddenly look up at the sky, and then hold their hands over their heads to protect them. Loud sound of wings. DE BROY's falcon swoops down on the doll and carries it off. MORTIN is heard laughing.

SEQUENCE 33F

INTERIOR. NIGHT—LIBRARY DE BROY MANOR

MORTIN, laughing, is being given the jewellery by the NIECE.

Then he points out to her a dark spot in the room where two shadows can be made out. One of them puts a harness round the NIECE's neck. MORTIN's laughter.

INSERT—(CONTINUATION SEQUENCE 33)

M. SONGE is becoming more and more restless in his sleep. He makes one gesture of refusal after another. He mutters:

> M. SONGE
> No ... no ... no ...

SEQUENCE 33F (continuation)

INTERIOR. NIGHT—LIBRARY DE BROY MANOR.

The NIECE, almost completely naked, is still wearing the harness and crosses the room, passing in front of the mirror. MORTIN's laughter.

SEQUENCE 33G

INTERIOR. DAY—ROOM IN DE BROY MANOR.

In a dark, unspecified corner, the NEPHEW is gently stroking M. SONGE's temples.

Organ fortissimo

> M. SONGE (off)
> No!!!

SEQUENCE 33 (continuation)

M. SONGE suddenly sits up in his bed, screaming. He is sweating.

SEQUENCE 34

EXTERIOR DAY—GUEST HOUSE GARDEN

Afternoon. Sunlight.

GASTON and FRED were having a siesta in deck chairs. M. SONGE's scream wakes them up.

> FRED
> What is it?

At the same moment a gendarme carrying an envelope comes in through the garden gate. He goes over to GASTON, who takes the envelope and opens it.

> FRED (terrified)
> What is it?

> GASTON (laughing)
> Don't worry. Just a summons about my car

accident last week. I scratched the wing of a
delivery van that was badly parked. A matter of
a couple of thousand francs at the very most.
We'll have to wait for the washing machine.

SEQUENCE 35

INTERIOR. DAY—M. SONGE'S ROOM.

M. SONGE is back at his desk. He is exultant, jubilant. He is talking silently to himself, nods his agreement, makes gestures with his
hand, moves his lips. He has great difficulty in containing his inner
tumult.

MARIE is heard coming upstairs. M. SONGE watches her approach,
as if he could see through the wall.

The moment she opens the door he launches out frantically:

> M. SONGE
> I've got it, I've found the end of my novel! A
> simple judicial error. All the business of the
> murder, the jewel theft, the drowning, fizzles
> out.

MARIE shrugs her shoulders, turns around, stumbles on the floorboard and goes out, banging the door.

> M. SONGE
> We'll swap it all around with a view to what
> they call a happy ending.

He stands up and puts the floorboard back in its place.

> M. SONGE (tapping himself on the forehead)
> Well, well, there's still something left in this old

head of mine.

He stands up, goes and gets a hammer and some nails from the back of his wardrobe, and sets about nailing the floorboard down.

M. SONGE hammers and hammers . . . His exaltation decreases somewhat, and his smile gradually disappears.

Long fade out.

SEQUENCE 36

EXTERIOR. DAY—CEMETERY.

The sound of M. SONGE's hammer continues for a moment during the fade in, which reveals the two little graves, side by side, of the Dupont and Ducreux children, one cold October morning.

An antimony cross, and another in marble, cracked by the frost, dead flowers, the moldy remains of a religious picture, dead leaves.

Many years have gone by.

Long stationary shot. Then hands bringing fresh flowers come into shot.

The camera pulls back. They are MARIE's hands. As she is tenderly laying some chrysanthemums from the garden on the graves, she can be heard murmuring.

> MARIE
> You don't forget them just like that.., these
> things leave their mark on you . . .

The camera pulls back further

MARIE leaves the cemetery. She goes back to the guest house.

Wide-angle stationary shot of the big house in the fog. MARIE pushes the garden gate open and disappears, while M. SONGE's inner voice is heard, off:

> M. SONGE (off)
> That poor child.., what was his name again? Those little faces give you the shivers . . . The whole thing's a fiasco. Or as good as. Nothing for years . . . At most, a malaise, a certain need to know, perhaps. But it's all so far away . . . Yet I can see him again in the doorway that July morning . . .
> We take tragedy, we chew it over, digest it, absorb it and finally eliminate it.

Long fade out.

Barbara Wright's Principal Translations

1950   in collaboration with Stefan and Franciszka Themerson, *Mr Rouse Builds His House*

1951   Alfred Jarry, *Ubu Roi* (with a preface by Barbara Wright)

1954   Raymond Queneau, *The Trojan Horse; At the Edge of the Forest*

1955   Christian-Dietrich Grabbe, *Comedy, Satire, Irony and Deeper Meaning*
Pol-Dives, *The Song of Bright Misery*

1958   Raymond Queneau, *Exercises in Style*

1960   Raymond Queneau, *Zazie in the Metro*

1961   Monique Lange, "The Catfish" in *New Writers 1*

1962   Fernando Arrabal, *Orison, The Two Executioners, Fando and Lis, The Car Cemetery*, in *Plays* vol 1
Andrée Martinerie, *Second Spring*

1965   Alain Robbe-Grillet, *Snapshots* and *Towards a New Novel*

1966   Marguerite Duras, *The Long Absence*

1967   Raymond Queneau, *Between Blue and Blue*
Raymond Queneau, *A Blue Funk*
Fernando Arrabal, *Guernica, The Labyrinth, The Tricycle, Picnic on the Battlefield, The Condemned Man's Bicycle*, in *Plays* vol 2

1968   Raymond Queneau, *The Bark Tree*
Pierre Lauer, *The Suns of Badarane*
Alain Robbe-Grillet, "The Secret Room" in *The Penguin Book of French Short Stories*
Alain Robbe-Grillet, "In the Corridors of the Underground" in *French Writing Today*
André Couteaux, *Portrait of the Boy as a Young Wolf / My Father's Keeper*
Alfred Jarry, *The Super-Male*

1969   Roland Dubillard, *The Swallows*

1971   Roland Dubillard, *The House of Bones*
Jean Genet, *The Balcony*
Pierre Lauer, *The Suns of Badarane*

1972   Robert Pinget, *The Libera Me Domine*

	Sutherland Sketchbook, translation into French by Marie-Hélène Claret and Barbara Wright
1973	Raymond Queneau, *The Flight of Icarus*
1974	Yves Klein, *Selected Writings* (Tate Gallery) [part of]
1975	Robert Pinget, *Recurrent Melody*
1976	Raymond Queneau, *The Sunday of Life*
	Ludovic Janvier, *The Bathing Girl*, translated by John Matthew and revised by Barbara Wright
1977	Sylvia Bourdon, *Love is a Feast*
	Tristan Tzara, *Seven Dada Manifestos* and *Lampisteries*
1978	Robert Pinget, *Passacaglia*
	Roland Topor, *Leonardo Was Right*
1979	Herbert Le Porrier, *The Doctor from Cordoba*
	Simone Benmussa, *The Singular Life of Albert Nobbs*
1980	Robert Pinget, *Fable*
	Nathalie Sarraute, *It Is There, and other plays*
	Simone Benmussa, "Appearances", in *Gambit* No.35
1981	Muriel Cerf, "Blitz-Fortune" in *Real Life-Writers from Nine Countries Illuminate the Life of the Modern Woman*
	Raymond Queneau, *We Always Treat Women Too Well*
1982	Robert Pinget, *Between Fantoine and Agapa*
	Robert Pinget, *That Voice*
	Nathalie Sarraute, *The Use of Speech*
1983	Michel Tournier, *The Fetishist and Other Stories*
	Nathalie Sarraute, *Childhood*
	Romain Gary, *King Solomon*
1984	Robert Pinget, *Someone*
1985	Henri Guigonnat, *Daemon in Lithuania*
	Eugène Ionesco, *Journeys among the Dead*
	René de Obaldia, *Monsieur Klebs and Rosalie* in *Plays* vol 4
1986	Robert Pinget, *The Apocrypha*
	Michel Tournier, *A Garden at Hammamet*
	Pierre Albert-Birot, *The First Book of Grabinoulor*
1987	Robert Pinget, *Abel and Bela*
	Michel Tournier, *The Golden Droplet*

Raymond Queneau, *Pierrot mon ami*
1988   Robert Pinget, *Monsieur Songe* (with *The Harness, Plough*)
1989   Elisabeth Badinter, *The Unopposite Sex [Man/Woman: The One Is The Other]*
        Robert Pinget, *A Bizarre Will*
1990   Raymond Queneau, *The Last Days*
        Raymond Queneau, "Alfred", *Journal of Literary Translation*, vol XXIII
        Liliane Siegel, *In the Shadow of Sartre*
        Nathalie Sarraute, *You Don't Love Yourself*
1991   Michel Tournier, *Totems*
        Jean Genet, *The Balcony*
        Robert Pinget, *The Enemy*
        Michel Tournier, *The Midnight Love Feast*
        Pascal Quignard, *Georges de la Tour*
1992   Patrick Modiano, *Honeymoon*
        Jean Hamburger, *The Diary of William Harvey*
1994   Robert Pinget, *Be Brave*
        Robert Pinget, *Theo, or the New Era*
1995   Alberto Giacometti, *The Dream, The Sphinx*, and *The Death of T. in Grand Street*, "Space", No. 54
        Coline Serreau, *Lapin, lapin*
1996   Samuel Beckett, *Eleutheria*
        Jean Rouaud, *Of Illustrious Men*
1997   Nathalie Sarraute, *Here*
        Jean Rouaud, *The World, More or Less*
1998   Stefan Themerson, *Fragments from Darkness*
        Ludovic Janvier, *Into the Light*
        Robert Pinget, *Traces of Ink*
2000   Aude Yung-de Prévaux, *Jacques & Lotha*
        Raymond Queneau, *Five stories: Panic, Dino, At the Edge of the Forest, A Blue Funk, The Trojan Horse*
        Simone Benmussa, *Three Plays (The Singular Life of Alfred Nobbs, Appearances* and *The Death of Ivan Illich)* in collaboration with Donald Watson
2003   Pierre Albert-Birot, *31 Pocket Poems*

Introduction and comments with extracts from *Zazie,
Pierrot* and *The Flight of Icarus*, in "Tolling Elves" 5,
February 2003, Raymond Queneau 2003 centenary

2005   *Trio*, new edition of Robert Pinget's *Between Fantoine
and Agapa, That Voice, Passacaglia*

2006   Raymond Queneau, *Exercises in Style*, radio version by
Barbara Wright broadcast by the BBC, transmitted on
25 December 1959 on Radio 3, printed with an introduction by Barbara Wright

*Barbara Wright's output for the theatre, the opera, and
the radio was extensive. She used her skills in music to
translate the libretto of three Mozart operas and translated known or less known playwrights and artists: Guil-
laume Apollinaire, Louis Aragon, Fernando Arrabal,
Simone Benmussa, Paul Claudel, Claude Confortès,
Roland Dubillard, Marguerite Duras, Jean Genet,
Eugène Ionesco, Alfred Jarry, Françoise Mallet-Joris, René
de Obaldia, Picasso, Armand Salacrou, Coline Serreau,
Antoni Tapiès, Roger Vitrac, Monique Wittig, Jeannine
Worms, Françoise Xenakis.*

*In addition to her work as translator Barbara Wright
published numerous prefaces, introductions and reviews
in the fields of literature and the visual arts.*

Barbara Wright
Timeline

1915	October 13, Barbara Winifred Wright was born in Worthing, West Sussex
1930	Her parents die; Barbara is sent to a boarding school, Godolphin School, Salisbury, Wiltshire; she learns the piano
1930s	Between 1930 and 1935 she passes four certificates in Pianoforte, then goes to Paris to study music under Alfred Cortot at the Conservatoire. Gives several recitals as accompanist at the Wigmore Hall in London
1936-37	Teaches at the Beacon Hill school run by Dora Russell
1937	March 18, obtains a diploma in Pianoforte Accompaniment at the Royal Academy of Music
1937-38	Shares a flat with Peggy Ramsay, playwright agent, who re-names Barbara "Bear"
1938	Marries Walter Hubbard
1939	At the Royal College of Music in London, studies music criticism with H.C. Colles and score reading with G. Jacob
1944	March, birth of her daughter Nicola
1945	Writes regular reviews for *Arts Review* from this year onward
1947	Meets the Polish couple of artists and thinkers Franciszka and Stefan Themerson and their niece Jasia Reichardt
1948	Co-founder with the Themersons of Gaberbocchus Press
1949	She helps Stefan Themerson translate his *Pan Tom buduje dom* into English, and Stefan names her as co-author. The book is published by Gaberbocchus in 1950 as *Mr Rouse Builds His House*
1950	Starts work on translating Jarry's *Ubu Roi* for Gaberbocchus Press, and, once ready, writes the text by hand in black ink on the aluminium plates from which the book is eventually printed with Franciszka Themerson's drawings
1950s	Meets Stanley Chapman; it is the beginning of a friendship

which lasted until Barbara's death. Stanley died a few months after she did. They had many friends and interests in common ('Pataphysics, translation, contemporary French literature and art in particular)

1951   Alfred Jarry's *Ubu Roi* is published by Gaberbocchus Press

1950s   Writes and translates art reviews and criticisms. Collaborates with David Sylvester. Travels to America

1953   Promoted Regent of Shakespearean zozology by the College of 'Pataphysics

1954   Travels to India

1957   Separates from Walter, moves to 87 Frognal in Hampstead, London. June 7: awarded a Certificate for a three-year course in Italian at the Regent Street Polytechnic (now University of Westminster, London)

1957   (December)–1958 (February) Travels in India

1957–59 Lends a hand in the Gaberbocchus Common Room, cooking spaghetti and serving coffee and wine, and on April 1, 1958, gives a talk about her work on Queneau's *Exercises in Style*. Records the minutes of the meetings

1958   Travels to France

1959   Translates Brillat-Savarin's *On the erotic virtue of truffles* for Gaberbocchus. It remains unpublished

1961   Meets John Calder and translates Monique Lange's *The Catfish*. It is the beginning of a long collaboration and a friendship which lasted until Barbara's death

1962   Retires as a director of Gaberbocchus Press

1964   Starts reviewing for the *TLS* and meets Pierre Albert-Birot and his wife Arlette in Paris. Passes her GCSE O-Level in Spanish (London University Board)

1966   August, joins Pierre Albert-Birot and friends at Bonaguil for the fiftieth anniversary of *SIC*

1967   Drives Zadkine to Bonaguil for the festival around *SIC*

1975   The Calder Educational Trust is set up; Barbara is a trustee

1976   Travels to Turkey

1978   Travels to India

1980	Meets Nick Wadley
1984	At a conference at the ICA in London meets Madeleine Renouard
1985	Visits Pinget and his mother in Touraine, France
1986	Appointed Officier dans l'Ordre des Arts et des Lettres by the French Government for services to the French language, literature and culture
1980s –1990s	Regularly attends seminars on Queneau in Paris and Verviers, and on Stavelot in Belgium; often meets Robert Pinget and Nathalie Sarraute in France
1987	Wins the Scott Moncrieff Prize for the best translation for Pierre Albert-Birot's *The First Book of Grabinoulor*. Visits Pinget in his farmhouse in Touraine with Madeleine Renouard
1989	October, New York, accompanies Pinget for the performance of *Abel et Bela* and *Architruc* (Ubu Repertory Theatre). Reads *Monsieur Songe* in English/French with Pinget
1990s	until 2008, corresponds with Florence Loeb (the daughter of the famous Parisian art dealer Pierre Loeb and wife of the playwright Romain Weingarten), art collector and traveler. Florence met Antonin Artaud when she was 16; she died in July 2011
1991	February 12, 13, 14 , "A tribute to Robert Pinget", French Institute London. Translates Pinget's *De rien*. The play is performed in London in a bilingual version by Robert Pinget and Peter Gale
1992	Wins the Scott Moncrieff Prize for *Midnight Love Feast* by Michel Tournier. Translates Stefan Themerson's 9-part poem "*Croquis dans les Ténèbres*", published in Stefan Themerson's *Collected Poems*, Gaberbocchus, 1997
1995	September, attends the Cerisy colloquium devoted to Pierre Albert-Birot
1998	February 26, attends the 118th Dîner Grabinoulor organized at the Café Flo in London by Debra Kelly (the first dinner was organized by the poet Jean Follain in 1936), which celebrated the launch of Kelly's *Pierre Albert-Birot: a Poetics in Movement, a Poetics of Movement*. For

the first and only time, the traditional readings from *Les Six Livres de Grabinoulor* were in English, from Barbara's translation of the *The First Book of Grabinoulor*, read by Deborah Manship and Steve Knapper

Spends Christmas in Warsaw with Nick Wadley, Jasia Reichardt and other friends on the occasion of Franciszka Themerson's exhibition at the Kordegarda Gallery

2001   Elected to the eminent group of Satrapes by the College of 'Pataphysics (Arrabal, Baudrillard, Umberto Eco receive this distinction at the same time)

2002   Promoted to Commandeur dans l'Ordre des Arts et des Lettres by the French Government for services to the French language

2003   Introduces Nick Wadley and Jasia Reichardt to her favourite French crime writer, Fred Vargas

2005   Corrects Dariusz Sokołowski's French translation of Themerson's *Pan Tom buduje dom.* Still unpublished

2006   November, leaves Frognal to live closer to her grandchildren Jim and Emma Mackie in Chiswick; her health deteriorates but she keeps reading, writing, doing the *Times* crosswords, going out and seeing friends. She becomes computer literate in a very short time. She donates her archive to the Lilly Library, Indiana University at Bloomington

2007   Attends several evenings at the Calder Bookshop devoted to her work and the memories of the Themersons

2007   February 7, invited by Barry Flanagan to a lunch at the Ivy in London to celebrate the rehabilitation of Franciszka Themerson's Ubu masks

2008   Helps Jasia Reichardt with translating and rhyming of various 1930s texts for children that were illustrated by Franciszka Themerson

2009   Her account of a trip to Nepal with François Caradec and a group of friends is published in *Les Amis de Valentin Brû*, no. 53/53

2009   March 3, Barbara Wright dies in London.

1. Barbara, 1940s

2. Barbara by a window, 1950s

3. Gaberbocchus common room, 1957, Barbara (right)
with Themerson

4. Barbara in a French garden, 1970s

5. Barbara, Stanley Chapman and Juliet Wilson-Bareau

6. Barbara, Robert Pinget and Madeleine Renouard, 1987

7. With Pinget and family at Luzillé, 1987

8. 1995, Pierre Albert-Birot conference, Cerisy, France. From left:
Gaëtane Lechevalier, Arlette Albert-Birot, Madeleine Renouard,
Barbara Wright, and Marie-Louise Lentengre

9. Sketch by Nick Wadley of Barbara in Warsaw, 1998

10. Barbara with Arrabal and Baudrillard, Paris, 2001

11. Nick Wadley, postcard, portrait of Barbara as a lame snail

12. Barbara and Stanley Chapman, London, 2008

13. 2008, Barbara's birthday party. Anti-clockwise from bottom right: Jim Mackie, Juliet Wilson-Bareau, Nicky Hubbard (Barbara's daughter), Barbara Wright, Jill Fell, Stanley Chapman, Sophie Mackie, Nick Wadley.

14. Barbara with Jasia Reichardt, British Library, 2009

15. Nick Wadley and Stanley Chapman,
Putney Vale Cemetery and Crematorium, 2009

16. Sketch by Nick Wadley of John Calder at the Barbara Wright Colloquium, 26 March 2010

Many thanks for Toussaint 2000
cheering card.
     Would it be asking you to
Betray your Art if I asked you to
do a version where the bears were
no longer grumpy, suspicions and
philosophical, but sporting stupid
smiles ? ? ?
     - Well, not STUPID, natch — but
of the order of the merry crew
boys' grins ?
(Are you even aware of the
myriad expressions you give your
sitters ? ?)   L O K 2 Both
                              Barb

17. Barbara Wright's handwriting: Postcard sent by Barbara
to Nick Wadley, November 2000

18. Participants at the 1995 Pierre Albert-Birot conference, Cerisy,
France, including Debra Kelly (back, fourth from left), Barbara
Wright (front, far right), Marie-Louise Lentengre (next to BW),
Madeleine Renouard (front, fourth from left), Arlette Albert-Birot
(front, fifth from left), and Jean-Michel Place (back, far left)

Appraisals, Reviews

"If anyone doubts that pleasure can come from translation, let him look at, for instance, Henri Bué's 1869 version of *Alice in Wonderland* in French, in which even the puns are rendered by equivalent puns, or Barbara Wright's versions of Raymond Queneau, or the Garner-Levine rendering, with the author's help, of Guillermo Cabrera Infante's *Tres Tristes Tigres*—works in which wordplay apparently indigenous to another language is matched in English. For a translator, untranslatability can be as much a lure as a deterrent."

—Alastair Reid
The New Yorker, November 8, 1976

EXERCISES IN STYLE by Raymond Queneau
"Barbara Wright's brilliant translation of Raymond Queneau's *Exercices de style*, originally published in Britain by Gaberbocchus Press in 1958, deserves a new lease of life, and I am delighted that John Calder has seen fit to provide it with just that. This is the famous nonsense in which a trivial everyday incident—a minor brawl on a Paris bus—is told 99 times in 99 different ways by 99 people who witnessed it. Witty, playful, ingenious, it manages to transcend its own sophistication by a sort of verbal slapstick which Miss Wright translates into pure Groucho Marxism."

—Robert Nye
The Guardian, London, February 2, 1980

"This translation is a reissue of an existing version, first published in Great Britain and Canada as long ago as 1958, when Queneau was still alive. He declared himself well pleased with it, as he had every reason to be, since Barbara Wright has exactly caught the spirit of the book, and where direct translation was not possible—as, for instance, in the case of the variations in country dialect or argot—she has transposed creatively into such corresponding forms as West Indian immigrant speech or Cockney jargon. Her rendering deserves the highest praise."

—John Weightman
New York Times Book Review, May 17, 1981

WE ALWAYS TREAT WOMEN TOO WELL by Raymond Queneau
"The English version, as one would expect from such a distinguished translator as Barbara Wright, is a work of art in itself, with appropriate literary allusions poking their heads out through the interstices of a criminal argot that is more cultural than real."

—Fergus Pyle
The Irish Times, February 21, 1981

"Queneau was an alarmingly erudite writer, who thrived on sly humour and buried allusions: he does not translate easily. But Barbara Wright knows all his funny ways, and has translated him beautifully yet again."

—John Sturrock
The Observer, London, February 15, 1981

"The over-formal locution and rotundity of a certain class of Anglo-Irish prose is captured delightfully, interspersed with quick funny dialogue and effective description. It is hard to imagine how the novel reads in French; what is evident is that the translation by Barbara Wright is itself an achievement of the highest quality."

—Stuart Evans
The Times, London, February 5, 1981

THE SUNDAY OF LIFE by Raymond Queneau
"His sprightly redirection of the French language by means of puns, phonetic spelling and a unique blend of argot and formal sentence construction has been rendered imaginatively in Wright's sparkling translation."

Library Journal, U.S.A., April 1977

"*The Sunday of Life*, first published in France in 1951, is now available here in a skillful translation by Barbara Wright. The stylized slang of Queneau and the self-conscious humor of his novel made the labor especially difficult. I can't imagine a more satisfactory translation of this work, one that abounds in colloquial speech, in those devices of rhetoric we tend to associate with Joyce and Faulkner and in mannerisms in bodily behavior reminiscent of Chaplin."

—Wallace Fowlie
New York Times Book Review, July 10, 1977

PIERROT MON AMI by Raymond Queneau
"She has waltzed around the floor with the Master so many times by now that she follows his quirky French as if the steps were in English."

—John Updike
The New Yorker

" . . . Her house was a point of convivial welcome for writers and artists. She was always alert to promoting the creative ventures of others. . . . [Her translation of *Ubu Roi*] fluently conveys Jarry's mingling of Shakespearian parody with schoolboy smut, and is both funny and readily performable. This success was followed by her brilliant translation of the "untranslatable" *Exercices de style* by Queneau (1956). Both were acclaimed as modern classics, as in 1960 was her rendering of Queneau's *Zazie dans le Métro* (1960) . . . Her culture was wide, and she was averse to pretension in any form."

The Times, obituary, 13.3.2009

THE LIBERA ME DOMINE
and
PASSACAGLIA by Robert Pinget
" . . . these two Pinget novels, now supremely well translated by Barbara Wright . . . (Pinget's) language is much more artful, more richly inventive than any genuine spoken language. It is the printed word's tribute to the power of the spoken word. Barbara Wright's translation has matched Mr. Pinget's French with wit and skill; she has kept the sense throughout and found the right equivalent sounds."

—John Sturrock
New York Times Book Review, April 29, 1979

THE ENEMY by Robert Pinget
"In the case of an author such as Pinget, for whom the 'secret ear'—its murmurs, its undercurrents, its interferences—is of prime

importance, the translator must be a sensitive receiver. Moving in the 'space between', the translator is more aware than most of the elusive tones, divergent claims, alternative versions left in parenthesis or in a limbo if not a graveyard of approximations: of recalcitrant language, half-captured with missing dimensions, degrees and relativities of possession, the text as compromise and unsettled negotiation, tension between the original and its derivatives, sameness changing its face or distorted in different contexts. In this, the translator is Pinget's virtual twin: a shadowy double glimpsed in a mirror, at a distance, as through a glass darkly. Barbara Wright is at ease (or perhaps at a finely attuned unease?) with the shifting registers of *The Enemy*. She straddles the gaps, rides the gear-changes, with a natural balance and deftness. She chases the voices with nothing obtrusive to frighten them away. She catches the heterogeneous tones, the flavors of idiom, the threads of colloquialism, the aural touches suddenly injected, with the appropriate dosage of looseness and rigor, drift and direction: two 'secret ears' reverberating to each other's tune."

—Peter Broome
The International Fiction Review 19: 2 (1992)

THE DOCTOR FROM CORDOVA by Herbert Le Porrier
"For anyone who lives here and feels something of the same pull, the book is a treasure. The translation by Barbara Wright deserves special mention: there is hardly a point in the book where I became conscious that I was not reading the original language, and the vocabulary is rich and beautiful. For those who love novels combining intelligence and beauty, I recommend this as a rare gem."

—Bryan Williams
International Daily News, Rome, October 31, 1980

SEVEN DADA MANIFESTOS by Tristan Tzara
" . . . very well translated by Barbara Wright."

—John Willett
The Guardian, January 26, 1978

MONSIEUR KLEBS AND ROZALIE by René de Obaldia
" . . . which in the English version by Barbara Wright is one of the

most interesting productions of the current Pitlochry season . . . To be sure with a writer so fluent in purely verbal as well as theatrical inventiveness there is a more than usually difficult problem of translation, but Barbara Wright showed that this is not insoluble."

—Anthony Curtis
Financial Times, London, June 9, 1980

Index of proper names

Contributors

DAVID BELLOS is Professor of French and Comparative Literature and Director of the Program in Translation at Princeton University. He has translated works by Georges Perec, Ismail Kadare and Fred Vargas into English, and is also the author of biographies of Georges Perec (1993), Jacques Tati (1999) and Romain Gary (2010).

CELIA BRITTON is Emeritus Professor of French at University College London. Research interests include French Caribbean literature and thought, especially Glissant, Fanon, Condé; postcolonial theory; surrealism in the Caribbean; psychoanalysis and colonialism; literature & ideology; images of community; the *Nouveau Roman*.

JOHN CALDER, publisher and bookseller, is celebrated for bringing experimental and controversial world literature—from Samuel Beckett to Eugene Ionesco to Marguerite Duras—to an English-language readership. He also writes on literary and philosophical topics, is a playwright and poet, and, over the years, has organized many arts festivals.

JILL FELL is an Associate Research Fellow of the Department of European Cultures and Languages, Birkbeck University of London and the author of two books on Alfred Jarry. She is currently working on a biography of Sophie Taeuber-Arp.

DEBRA KELLY is Professor of French and Francophone Literary and Cultural Studies at the University of Westminster, London, Director of the Group for War and Culture Studies, and Editor of the *Journal of War and Culture Studies*. She has published widely in textual and visual studies and cultural memory, and on several of the authors translated by Barbara Wright.

MARTIN MÉGEVAND is a Lecturer in the Department of French Literature at the Université Paris-8. His research fields cover the works of Robert Pinget, Samuel Beckett, and drama from 1950 to 1990, particularly the theatre of decolonization and postcolonial theory;

nouveau théâtre; choral drama; and the links between drama, history and politics. He is co-editor of the journal *Littérature* (Armand Colin) and associate manager of the Genèse hub of the works of the *Littérature et Histoires* team at the Université Paris-8.

BREON MITCHELL is Director of the Lilly Library at Indiana University Bloomington. His areas of specialization include literary translation, Anglo-German literary relations, literature and visual arts, Joyce, Kafka and Beckett.

NATHALIE PIÉGAY-GROS is Professor of Literature at the University Paris-7 Diderot, specializing in twentieth-century literature and especially novels. She has edited Aragon's novels for publication by Pléiade (Gallimard), and authored *Aragon et la chanson* (Textuel, 2007) and *Le Futur antérieur de l'archive* (Tangence, 2012). As well as *L'Érudition imaginaire* (Droz, 2009), she has edited (with Martin Mégevand) Robert Pinget's *Mahu reparle* (Editions des cendres, 2009) and *Robert Pinget: matériau, marges, écriture* (Presses Universitaires de Vincennes, 2011). She is currently working on Claude Simon.

MADELEINE RENOUARD is Emeritus Reader in French at Birkbeck, University of London. Her publications are on teaching and learning French as a foreign language, the media, the *nouveau roman* (especially Robert Pinget), contemporary French poetry, the visual arts, semiotics, and writers' correspondence.

CLOTHILDE ROULLIER is an archivist at the Archives Nationales de France. In 2003 at the Université de Tours she defended her doctoral thesis on Robert Pinget, Maurice Roche and Claude Simon. She is the author of *Les Archives de Norodom Sihanouk roi du Cambodge données à l'Ecole française d'Extrême-Orient et déposées aux Archives nationales (1970-2007)* (2010).

RÉGIS SALADO, Lecturer in Comparative Literature at the Université Paris-7-Diderot, researches and publishes on modern literatures in English, French and Portuguese. He co-edited the issues of *L'Esprit créateur* on "Les Etudes de réception en France" (Spring 2009) and *Textuel* on "Modernité/Modernism" (2008).

Nick Wadley taught art history at Chelsea School of Art, London, from 1962 until 1985. Publications include *Noa Noa, Gauguin's Tahiti* and *Impressionist and Post-Impressionist Drawing*. Since 1990, he has published and exhibited his drawings worldwide. With Jasia Reichardt, he cares for the Themerson Estate and Archive. He is a Régent of the Collège de 'Pataphysique.

MICHAL AJVAZ, *The Golden Age.*
The Other City.
PIERRE ALBERT-BIROT, *Grabinoulor.*
YUZ ALESHKOVSKY, *Kangaroo.*
FELIPE ALFAU, *Chromos.*
Locos.
IVAN ÂNGELO, *The Celebration.*
The Tower of Glass.
ANTÓNIO LOBO ANTUNES, *Knowledge of Hell.*
The Splendor of Portugal.
ALAIN ARIAS-MISSON, *Theatre of Incest.*
JOHN ASHBERY AND JAMES SCHUYLER,
A Nest of Ninnies.
ROBERT ASHLEY, *Perfect Lives.*
GABRIELA AVIGUR-ROTEM, *Heatwave*
and Crazy Birds.
DJUNA BARNES, *Ladies Almanack.*
Ryder.
JOHN BARTH, *LETTERS.*
Sabbatical.
DONALD BARTHELME, *The King.*
Paradise.
SVETISLAV BASARA, *Chinese Letter.*
MIQUEL BAUÇÀ, *The Siege in the Room.*
RENÉ BELLETTO, *Dying.*
MAREK BIEŃCZYK, *Transparency.*
ANDREI BITOV, *Pushkin House.*
ANDREJ BLATNIK, *You Do Understand.*
LOUIS PAUL BOON, *Chapel Road.*
My Little War.
Summer in Termuren.
ROGER BOYLAN, *Killoyle.*
IGNÁCIO DE LOYOLA BRANDÃO,
Anonymous Celebrity.
Zero.
BONNIE BREMSER, *Troia: Mexican Memoirs.*
CHRISTINE BROOKE-ROSE, *Amalgamemnon.*
BRIGID BROPHY, *In Transit.*
GERALD L. BRUNS, *Modern Poetry and*
the Idea of Language.
GABRIELLE BURTON, *Heartbreak Hotel.*
MICHEL BUTOR, *Degrees.*
Mobile.
G. CABRERA INFANTE, *Infante's Inferno.*
Three Trapped Tigers.
JULIETA CAMPOS,
The Fear of Losing Eurydice.
ANNE CARSON, *Eros the Bittersweet.*
ORLY CASTEL-BLOOM, *Dolly City.*
LOUIS-FERDINAND CÉLINE, *Castle to Castle.*
Conversations with Professor Y.
London Bridge.
Normance.
North.
Rigadoon.
MARIE CHAIX, *The Laurels of Lake Constance.*
HUGO CHARTERIS, *The Tide Is Right.*
ERIC CHEVILLARD, *Demolishing Nisard.*
MARC CHOLODENKO, *Mordechai Schamz.*
JOSHUA COHEN, *Witz.*
EMILY HOLMES COLEMAN, *The Shutter*
of Snow.
ROBERT COOVER, *A Night at the Movies.*
STANLEY CRAWFORD, *Log of the S.S. The*
Mrs Unguentine.
Some Instructions to My Wife.
RENÉ CREVEL, *Putting My Foot in It.*
RALPH CUSACK, *Cadenza.*
NICHOLAS DELBANCO, *The Count of Concord.*
Sherbrookes.
NIGEL DENNIS, *Cards of Identity.*

PETER DIMOCK, *A Short Rhetoric for*
Leaving the Family.
ARIEL DORFMAN, *Konfidenz.*
COLEMAN DOWELL,
Island People.
Too Much Flesh and Jabez.
ARKADII DRAGOMOSHCHENKO, *Dust.*
RIKKI DUCORNET, *The Complete*
Butcher's Tales.
The Fountains of Neptune.
The Jade Cabinet.
Phosphor in Dreamland.
WILLIAM EASTLAKE, *The Bamboo Bed.*
Castle Keep.
Lyric of the Circle Heart.
JEAN ECHENOZ, *Chopin's Move.*
STANLEY ELKIN, *A Bad Man.*
Criers and Kibitzers, Kibitzers
and Criers.
The Dick Gibson Show.
The Franchiser.
The Living End.
Mrs. Ted Bliss.
FRANÇOIS EMMANUEL, *Invitation to a*
Voyage.
SALVADOR ESPRIU, *Ariadne in the*
Grotesque Labyrinth.
LESLIE A. FIEDLER, *Love and Death in*
the American Novel.
JUAN FILLOY, *Op Oloop.*
ANDY FITCH, *Pop Poetics.*
GUSTAVE FLAUBERT, *Bouvard and Pécuchet.*
KASS FLEISHER, *Talking out of School.*
FORD MADOX FORD,
The March of Literature.
JON FOSSE, *Aliss at the Fire.*
Melancholy.
MAX FRISCH, *I'm Not Stiller.*
Man in the Holocene.
CARLOS FUENTES, *Christopher Unborn.*
Distant Relations.
Terra Nostra.
Where the Air Is Clear.
TAKEHIKO FUKUNAGA, *Flowers of Grass.*
WILLIAM GADDIS, *J R.*
The Recognitions.
JANICE GALLOWAY, *Foreign Parts.*
The Trick Is to Keep Breathing.
WILLIAM H. GASS, *Cartesian Sonata*
and Other Novellas.
Finding a Form.
A Temple of Texts.
The Tunnel.
Willie Masters' Lonesome Wife.
GÉRARD GAVARRY, *Hoppla! 1 2 3.*
ETIENNE GILSON,
The Arts of the Beautiful.
Forms and Substances in the Arts.
C. S. GISCOMBE, *Giscome Road.*
Here.
DOUGLAS GLOVER, *Bad News of the Heart.*
WITOLD GOMBROWICZ,
A Kind of Testament.
PAULO EMÍLIO SALES GOMES, *P's Three*
Women.
GEORGI GOSPODINOV, *Natural Novel.*
JUAN GOYTISOLO, *Count Julian.*
Juan the Landless.
Makbara.
Marks of Identity.

HENRY GREEN, *Back*.
Blindness.
Concluding.
Doting.
Nothing.
JACK GREEN, *Fire the Bastards!*
JIŘÍ GRUŠA, *The Questionnaire*.
MELA HARTWIG, *Am I a Redundant Human Being?*
JOHN HAWKES, *The Passion Artist*.
Whistlejacket.
ELIZABETH HEIGHWAY, ED., *Contemporary Georgian Fiction*.
ALEKSANDAR HEMON, ED., *Best European Fiction*.
AIDAN HIGGINS, *Balcony of Europe*.
Blind Man's Bluff
Bornholm Night-Ferry.
Flotsam and Jetsam.
Langrishe, Go Down.
Scenes from a Receding Past.
KEIZO HINO, *Isle of Dreams*.
KAZUSHI HOSAKA, *Plainsong*.
ALDOUS HUXLEY, *Antic Hay*.
Crome Yellow.
Point Counter Point.
Those Barren Leaves.
Time Must Have a Stop.
NAOYUKI II, *The Shadow of a Blue Cat*.
GERT JONKE, *The Distant Sound*.
Geometric Regional Novel.
Homage to Czerny.
The System of Vienna.
JACQUES JOUET, *Mountain R*.
Savage.
Upstaged.
MIEKO KANAI, *The Word Book*.
YORAM KANIUK, *Life on Sandpaper*.
HUGH KENNER, *Flaubert*.
Joyce and Beckett: The Stoic Comedians.
Joyce's Voices.
DANILO KIŠ, *The Attic*.
Garden, Ashes.
The Lute and the Scars
Psalm 44.
A Tomb for Boris Davidovich.
ANITA KONKKA, *A Fool's Paradise*.
GEORGE KONRÁD, *The City Builder*.
TADEUSZ KONWICKI, *A Minor Apocalypse*.
The Polish Complex.
MENIS KOUMANDAREAS, *Koula*.
ELAINE KRAF, *The Princess of 72nd Street*.
JIM KRUSOE, *Iceland*.
AYŞE KULIN, *Farewell: A Mansion in Occupied Istanbul*.
EMILIO LASCANO TEGUI, *On Elegance While Sleeping*.
ERIC LAURRENT, *Do Not Touch*.
VIOLETTE LEDUC, *La Bâtarde*.
EDOUARD LEVÉ, *Autoportrait*.
Suicide.
MARIO LEVI, *Istanbul Was a Fairy Tale*.
DEBORAH LEVY, *Billy and Girl*.
JOSÉ LEZAMA LIMA, *Paradiso*.
ROSA LIKSOM, *Dark Paradise*.
OSMAN LINS, *Avalovara*.
The Queen of the Prisons of Greece.
ALF MAC LOCHLAINN, *The Corpus in the Library*.
Out of Focus.
RON LOEWINSOHN, *Magnetic Field(s)*.
MINA LOY, *Stories and Essays of Mina Loy*.

D. KEITH MANO, *Take Five*.
MICHELINE AHARONIAN MARCOM, *The Mirror in the Well*.
BEN MARCUS, *The Age of Wire and String*.
WALLACE MARKFIELD, *Teitlebaum's Window*.
To an Early Grave.
DAVID MARKSON, *Reader's Block*.
Wittgenstein's Mistress.
CAROLE MASO, *AVA*.
LADISLAV MATEJKA AND KRYSTYNA POMORSKA, EDS., *Readings in Russian Poetics: Formalist and Structuralist Views*.
HARRY MATHEWS, *Cigarettes*.
The Conversions.
The Human Country: New and Collected Stories.
The Journalist.
My Life in CIA.
Singular Pleasures.
The Sinking of the Odradek Stadium.
Tlooth.
JOSEPH MCELROY, *Night Soul and Other Stories*.
ABDELWAHAB MEDDEB, *Talismano*.
GERHARD MEIER, *Isle of the Dead*.
HERMAN MELVILLE, *The Confidence-Man*.
AMANDA MICHALOPOULOU, *I'd Like*.
STEVEN MILLHAUSER, *The Barnum Museum*.
In the Penny Arcade.
RALPH J. MILLS, JR., *Essays on Poetry*.
MOMUS, *The Book of Jokes*.
CHRISTINE MONTALBETTI, *The Origin of Man*.
Western.
OLIVE MOORE, *Spleen*.
NICHOLAS MOSLEY, *Accident*.
Assassins.
Catastrophe Practice.
Experience and Religion.
A Garden of Trees.
Hopeful Monsters.
Imago Bird.
Impossible Object.
Inventing God.
Judith.
Look at the Dark.
Natalie Natalia.
Serpent.
Time at War.
WARREN MOTTE, *Fables of the Novel: French Fiction since 1990*.
Fiction Now: The French Novel in the 21st Century.
Oulipo: A Primer of Potential Literature.
GERALD MURNANE, *Barley Patch*.
Inland.
YVES NAVARRE, *Our Share of Time*.
Sweet Tooth.
DOROTHY NELSON, *In Night's City*.
Tar and Feathers.
ESHKOL NEVO, *Homesick*.
WILFRIDO D. NOLLEDO, *But for the Lovers*.
FLANN O'BRIEN, *At Swim-Two-Birds*.
The Best of Myles.
The Dalkey Archive.
The Hard Life.
The Poor Mouth.

The Third Policeman.
CLAUDE OLLIER, *The Mise-en-Scène.*
　Wert and the Life Without End.
GIOVANNI ORELLI, *Walaschek's Dream.*
PATRIK OUŘEDNÍK, *Europeana.*
　The Opportune Moment, 1855.
BORIS PAHOR, *Necropolis.*
FERNANDO DEL PASO, *News from the Empire.*
　Palinuro of Mexico.
ROBERT PINGET, *The Inquisitory.*
　Mahu or The Material.
　Trio.
MANUEL PUIG, *Betrayed by Rita Hayworth.*
　The Buenos Aires Affair.
　Heartbreak Tango.
RAYMOND QUENEAU, *The Last Days.*
　Odile.
　Pierrot Mon Ami.
　Saint Glinglin.
ANN QUIN, *Berg.*
　Passages.
　Three.
　Tripticks.
ISHMAEL REED, *The Free-Lance Pallbearers.*
　The Last Days of Louisiana Red.
　Ishmael Reed: The Plays.
　Juice!
　Reckless Eyeballing.
　The Terrible Threes.
　The Terrible Twos.
　Yellow Back Radio Broke-Down.
JASIA REICHARDT, *15 Journeys Warsaw*
　to London.
NOËLLE REVAZ, *With the Animals.*
JOÃO UBALDO RIBEIRO, *House of the*
　Fortunate Buddhas.
JEAN RICARDOU, *Place Names.*
RAINER MARIA RILKE, *The Notebooks of*
　Malte Laurids Brigge.
JULIÁN RÍOS, *The House of Ulysses.*
　Larva: A Midsummer Night's Babel.
　Poundemonium.
　Procession of Shadows.
AUGUSTO ROA BASTOS, *I the Supreme.*
DANIËL ROBBERECHTS, *Arriving in Avignon.*
JEAN ROLIN, *The Explosion of the*
　Radiator Hose.
OLIVIER ROLIN, *Hotel Crystal.*
ALIX CLEO ROUBAUD, *Alix's Journal.*
JACQUES ROUBAUD, *The Form of a*
　City Changes Faster, Alas, Than
　the Human Heart.
　The Great Fire of London.
　Hortense in Exile.
　Hortense Is Abducted.
　The Loop.
　Mathematics:
　The Plurality of Worlds of Lewis.
　The Princess Hoppy.
　Some Thing Black.
RAYMOND ROUSSEL, *Impressions of Africa.*
VEDRANA RUDAN, *Night.*
STIG SÆTERBAKKEN, *Siamese.*
　Self Control.
LYDIE SALVAYRE, *The Company of Ghosts.*
　The Lecture.
　The Power of Flies.
LUIS RAFAEL SÁNCHEZ,
　Macho Camacho's Beat.
SEVERO SARDUY, *Cobra & Maitreya.*

NATHALIE SARRAUTE,
　Do You Hear Them?
　Martereau.
　The Planetarium.
ARNO SCHMIDT, *Collected Novellas.*
　Collected Stories.
　Nobodaddy's Children.
　Two Novels.
ASAF SCHURR, *Motti.*
GAIL SCOTT, *My Paris.*
DAMION SEARLS, *What We Were Doing*
　and Where We Were Going.
JUNE AKERS SEESE,
　Is This What Other Women Feel Too?
　What Waiting Really Means.
BERNARD SHARE, *Inish.*
　Transit.
VIKTOR SHKLOVSKY, *Bowstring.*
　Knight's Move.
　A Sentimental Journey:
　　Memoirs 1917–1922.
　Energy of Delusion: A Book on Plot.
　Literature and Cinematography.
　Theory of Prose.
　Third Factory.
　Zoo, or Letters Not about Love.
PIERRE SINIAC, *The Collaborators.*
KJERSTI A. SKOMSVOLD, *The Faster I Walk,*
　the Smaller I Am.
JOSEF ŠKVORECKÝ, *The Engineer of*
　Human Souls.
GILBERT SORRENTINO,
　Aberration of Starlight.
　Blue Pastoral.
　Crystal Vision.
　Imaginative Qualities of Actual
　　Things.
　Mulligan Stew.
　Pack of Lies.
　Red the Fiend.
　The Sky Changes.
　Something Said.
　Splendide-Hôtel.
　Steelwork.
　Under the Shadow.
W. M. SPACKMAN, *The Complete Fiction.*
ANDRZEJ STASIUK, *Dukla.*
　Fado.
GERTRUDE STEIN, *The Making of Americans.*
　A Novel of Thank You.
LARS SVENDSEN, *A Philosophy of Evil.*
PIOTR SZEWC, *Annihilation.*
GONÇALO M. TAVARES, *Jerusalem.*
　Joseph Walser's Machine.
　Learning to Pray in the Age of
　　Technique.
LUCIAN DAN TEODOROVICI,
　Our Circus Presents . . .
NIKANOR TERATOLOGEN, *Assisted Living.*
STEFAN THEMERSON, *Hobson's Island.*
　The Mystery of the Sardine.
　Tom Harris.
TAEKO TOMIOKA, *Building Waves.*
JOHN TOOMEY, *Sleepwalker.*
JEAN-PHILIPPE TOUSSAINT, *The Bathroom.*
　Camera.
　Monsieur.
　Reticence.
　Running Away.
　Self-Portrait Abroad.
　Television.
　The Truth about Marie.

SELECTED DALKEY ARCHIVE TITLES